THE GOD OF WAR

FRANK KENNY

Copyright © 2024 Frank Kenny

All rights reserved. No part of this publication may be reproduced, distributed, or transmitted in any form or by any means, including photocopying, recording, or other electronic or mechanical methods, without the prior written permission of the publisher, except in the case of brief quotations embodied in critical reviews and certain other noncommercial uses permitted by copyright law. For permission requests, write to the publisher, addressed "Attention: Permissions Coordinator," at the address below.

Jin Hua Publishers
jinhua@earthlink.net

ISBN: 978-1-7392704-0-7 (paperback)
ISBN: 978-1-7392704-1-4 (ebook)
ISBN: 978-1-7392704-2-1 (audiobook)

Ordering Information:
Special discounts are available on quantity purchases by corporations, associations, and others. For details, contact jinhua@earthlink.net

Cover design by Michael Kenny
Maps by Martin Lubikowski, ML Design, 2024

To Margaret and our children, Bláthnaid, Olga, and Michael.

CONTENTS

INTRODUCTION 1
1 ABRAHAM: PROPHET OF A DEMON OR A GOD? 7
    FAITH OR MADNESS 8
    A VOICE COMMANDS 8
    A SON SCORNED; A SON CHOSEN 11
    A TERRIBLE SACRIFICE 13
    LEGACY 15

PART ONE: HEBREWS

2 GOD'S MURDEROUS TRIBE 21
    SON OF THE SON OF GOD 22
    ENTER THE HEBREWS 22
    DESTROY OR BE DESTROYED 25
    THE FIRST KING 27
    A KINGDOM DIVIDED 29
    INVADERS ON THE HORIZON 31
3 A SACRED SECT OF THE PURE 37
    A MESSIAH TO THE RESCUE 39
    ONLY THE SELECT NEED APPLY 40
    THE HOLY BOOKS 43

LITERAL OR ALLEGORICAL?	45
LAWS AND RITUALS	48
NEW CONQUERORS	52
ANOTHER MESSIAH	55
THE SEEDS OF REBELLION	59
4 IS THIS THE ONE?	**63**
A VOICE CRYING IN THE WILDERNESS	64
JESUS GOES IT ALONE	66
TENSION IN JERUSALEM	68
ARREST AND INTERROGATION	70
A STRANGE TALE UNFOLDS	71
5 THE ONE WHO IS REMEMBERED	**75**
A SUBVERSIVE CULT	75
DIVISION	77
A REBELLIOUS ATMOSPHERE	78
A FINAL PROVOCATION	80
CONFLICTING REPORTS	82
MORE CLARITY OR MORE DOUBT	84
ANOTHER VERSION	86
ALTERNATIVE ACCOUNTS	88
A PARTING OF WAYS	90

PART TWO: CHRISTIANS

6 GAMEKEEPER TURNED POACHER	**95**
CONFLICT WITH THE DISCIPLES OF JESUS	97
PAUL CHASTISED	99
CHANGING THE MESSAGE	101
PAUL PREVAILS	103
7 THE MESSIAH BECOMES GOD	**107**
THE MESSAGE IS CHANGED AGAIN	109
GOD'S KINGDOM, ON EARTH OR IN HEAVEN?	111
8 SUICIDE MARTYRS	**113**
REVELATION	115
A DEGENERATIVE CULT	116

THE ROMAN PERSPECTIVE 117
"THE SILLY, THE MEAN, AND THE STUPID" 119
"THE BLOOD OF CHRISTIANS IS THE SEED OF
    THE CHURCH" 121
MARTYRS REMAIN FEW IN NUMBER 124

9 RIVAL FAITHS 127
AN ASSERTIVE CHURCH 127
A TIME OF UNCERTAINTY 129
VYING WITH THE COMPETITION 131

10 THE GREAT PERSECUTION 135
STABILITY RESTORED 135
TOLERATION TURNS TO HOSTILITY 137
EXTERMINATE THE SECT 138
INCONSTANT CAMPAIGN 140
PERSECUTION ENDS, DIVISION INTENSIFIES 142

11 CHRISTIAN VS. CHRISTIAN 145
TROUBLE IN AFRICA 145
THE FAITH ENDURES 148

12 AN UNEXPECTED TRIUMPH 149
POWER STRUGGLE 149
THE EDICT OF TOLERATION 151
CONSTANTINE'S VISIONS 152
A CHRISTIAN EMPEROR 154
TRUE FAITH OR TYRANNY 156

PART THREE: HERETICS

13 CHRISTIANS DIVIDED 161
VENOMOUS ERRORS 161
THE COUNCIL OF NICAEA 164
"SUPERSTITIOUS AND SENSELESS MEETINGS" 166

14 ONE EMPIRE UNDER GOD 171
DEMONS IN THE DESERT 172
MAGIC RELICS AND MYTHIC MARTYRS 174
CONSTANTINE SECURES HIS LEGACY 176

15 AN ELUSIVE PEACE 181
- BROKEN FAMILY, BROKEN EMPIRE 181
- CONSTANTIUS GETS A BREAK 184
- BATTLE OF THE POPES 185
- CONSENSUS IS FUTILE 186
- ATHANASIUS THE OBSTINATE 188
- EGYPT'S NEW BOSS 189
- THE ONE THAT GOT AWAY 190

16 EMPEROR STRIKES BACK 193
- JULIAN BEGINS HIS REFORMS 194
- SETTLING SCORES IN EGYPT 195
- SETTLING SCORES IN PERSIA 197

17 AN UNFORESEEN DISASTER 199
- DIVIDED AGAIN 200
- BARBARIANS AT THE GATE 202
- A CALAMITY UNFOLDS 203
- A TENUOUS ALLIANCE 204

18 FREE WILL BITES THE DUST 207
- A RELUCTANT BISHOP 208
- A POWERFUL BISHOP 210
- PERSECUTION INTENSIFIES 212
- HOLY MOBS 213
- "DRINKING POISON WITH HONEY" 216
- TEMPORAL JUSTICE SIDELINED 218
- A SOMBRE LEGACY 220

19 GOD'S PHILOSOPHER 221
- CHASTE AND CELIBATE 222
- TRAMPLING EVIL UNDERFOOT 223
- HARSH COUNCILS 225

20 JEALOUSY AND MISTRUST 229
- GOTHS RETURN TO THE WARPATH 229
- AND STILL THEY COME 231
- THE PURSUIT OF HERETICS 231
- ROME THREATENED 234
- DIVIDED CITY 235

THE SIEGE BEGINS	236
21 A TRAGEDY UNFOLDS	**239**
RESPONSE OF THE EMPEROR	241
AFRICA DEVASTATED	241
ITALY THREATENED	243
AUTHORITATIVE CHURCH, DIMINISHING STATE	244
THE FATAL BLOW	245

PART FOUR: CITY OF GOD

22 THE BISHOP WITH THE GOLDEN MOUTH	**251**
THE EAST STANDS ALONE	252
CARNAGE IN CONSTANTINOPLE	253
TENSION WITH THE EMPRESS	255
DISCORD IN EGYPT	256
SYNOD OF THE OAK	257
EXILE AND RETURN	258
FINAL EXILE	259
23 ELIMINATE THE HERETICS	**261**
THE EMPEROR, HIS HOLY FAMILY, AND HIS FAITH	261
EGYPT'S MILITANT PATRIARCH	263
CYRIL'S REVENGE	265
CONSTANTINOPLE'S UNWELCOME PATRIARCH	266
CLASH OF THE PATRIARCHS	267
THE COUNCIL OF EPHESUS	268
HERETIC PERSECUTOR BECOMES PERSECUTED HERETIC	270
A NEW CREED EMERGES	271
24 DIVIDE WITH THE SWORD THOSE WHO WOULD DIVIDE CHRIST	**273**
A SIMPLE MONK	273
THE ROBBER COUNCIL	275
PULCHERIA TAKES CONTROL	277
A TENUOUS COMPROMISE	278
THE FALLOUT FROM CHALCEDON	279

    SCHISM WITH ROME..282
25 FAITH BY FORCE OF ARMS..**285**
    BLUES, GREENS, AND A FUTURE EMPRESS 286
    RUTHLESS PERSECUTOR..288
    WAR, PEACE, AND PESTILENCE...291
    THE NIKA RIOTS..291
    HOLY WISDOM 293
26 WAR IN GOD'S NAME..**295**
    AFRICAN EXPEDITION...295
    NEXT STOP, ITALY 297
    THE PRICE OF VICTORY...299
    APPEASING THE MIAPHYSITES, CONFRONTING
        THE POPE...300
    CHRISTIAN DISHARMONY..302
    JUSTINIAN CODE 303
    NO LONGER NECESSARY TO THINK 304
    LAST OF THE SCHOLARS...306
    END OF ENDLESS PEACE 307
    LEGACY..308
27 MUTUAL DESTRUCTION **309**
CONCLUSION..313
ACKNOWLEDGEMENTS 315
ENDNOTES 317

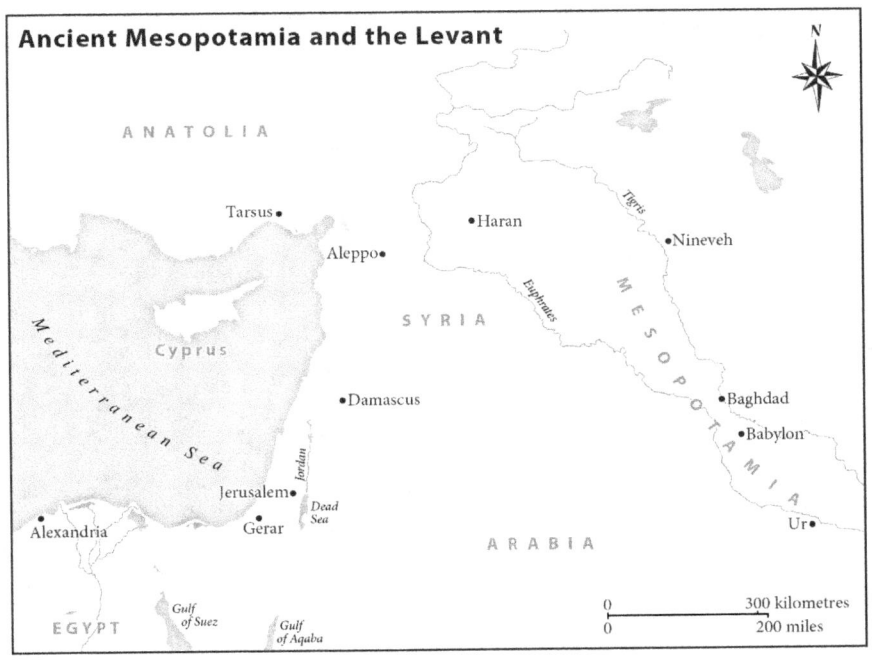

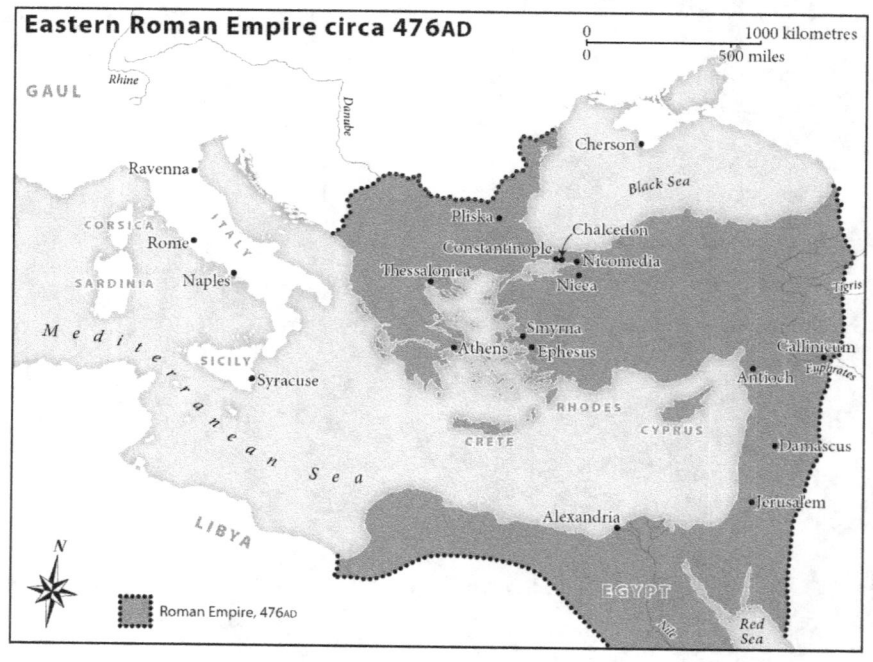

INTRODUCTION

WHAT IF THE god of peace is really a god of war? What if the god of love is really a god of hatred? What if, instead of hope and harmony, He is a master of despair and division?

We speak here of the god of Jews, Christians, and Muslims, who appears in their Scriptures as creator, lawmaker, and judge.

Exploring these questions may help us understand the contradictions and complexities surrounding the nature of God. This book aims to provide the reader with a deeper understanding of this issue. It focuses on the God depicted in ancient texts and aims to shed light on the multifaceted nature of this divine figure. Through a thought-provoking exploration of faith and theology, it encourages readers to find their own answers.

So much has been written on these faiths that one may enquire, "Why add yet another volume to the vast pile of literature on the subject?"

Several compelling reasons immediately present themselves. First, a rebellion by religious fundamentalists against secular modernity. This is evident in the United States, where Christian literalists are battling with secularists in state legislatures and courts. A more virulent process has been underway elsewhere. In the Middle East, North Africa, and south Asia, radical Islamists have been enforcing their agenda through intimidation and terror. Tension in Europe is rising over issues of free speech and the religious sensitivity of a traditionalist immigrant population. And, of course, one cannot ignore the endless conflict between Palestinians and Jews in the Middle East.

These geopolitical issues are a mere public manifestation of a basic human quandary: the quest for meaning and purpose in our lives. For a significant portion of the world's population, that meaning is found in the Scriptures. These sacred texts guide their morals, affirm their hopes, and comfort their despair. However, many perceive these values to be under threat by secular forces bent on destroying their religion.

For others, the idea that laws written by ancient men should regulate our lives or explain our existence is either absurd or repulsive. They see religion as a source of intolerance and discord.

This book will take a journey through history to uncover a fresh perspective on this subject. It will explore the roots of monotheism to its far-reaching impact on the modern world. This voyage will furnish the reader with the tools to shape their own convictions and navigate the complexities of a faith that has transformed the world in a profound way.

For me, this journey began in rural Ireland, where I grew up immersed in the traditional Catholic values of the time. Life centred around the church and the parish priest. No one tangoed with the parish priest. Significant passages of our lives were marked by holy rituals: baptism, communion, confirmation, and marriage, until the finality of the last rites.

Before I became an altar boy, my aunt, a nun (no one tangoed with nuns either), taught me the essential prayers in a language I didn't understand, Latin. At school, as we prepared for our First Holy Communion, we learned the Catechism, a brief summary of Catholic dogma written in a thin book with big words. This was in English, but I still didn't understand.

Then I went on to a boarding school run by priests. Here, for five years, I received a fine education from good men who hoped that I and my fellow pupils would follow their vocation. Some of my classmates did, but I had

INTRODUCTION

doubts. Later, in a monastic retreat, I shared my concerns about scriptural inconsistency and doctrinal flaws with learned clerics. They listened patiently. They understood; they had been there too. Their explanations were carefully crafted—whether to convince me or reassure themselves, I was not sure. The believer needs the comfort of belief. Non-belief is a cold place. I understood that.

Instead of the seminary, I pursued a career in engineering. Yet religion was ever-present.

Nearby, in Northern Ireland, Catholics and Protestants were locked in a struggle that had defied the efforts of countless generations to resolve. Ostensibly, the issue centred around political identity. Yet it was impossible to ignore that religious boundaries defined the political divide.

In the Republic, I actively participated in two successive referenda to alter the Irish Constitution—one relating to divorce and the other to abortion. A prominent Catholic pressure group ensured that the church's position on both issues was upheld. Several decades later, these results were reversed in a dramatic shift in Irish values.

In 1989, Ayatollah Khomeini, supreme leader of the Islamic Republic of Iran, issued a fatwa that brought religion to the international spotlight. This called for the assassination of the British writer Salman Rushdie for "insulting" Islam in his book *The Satanic Verses*. In England, where I was living at the time, my local newsagent, a mild-mannered Muslim of moderate persuasion (or so I had thought), presented me with a pamphlet supporting the fatwa. He angrily ranted against the "obscene book," although he had never read it himself.

Remarkably, Rushdie managed to survive the fatwa unmolested until August 2022, when he was attacked while lecturing in New York. Although seriously injured, he survived. The would-be assassin had not read the book either. The word of an Iranian cleric was enough to motivate both my shopkeeper and the attacker.

My career took me to far-flung corners of the world, where I worked on projects in Europe, Asia, Africa, and the Americas. Everywhere, religion permeated peoples' perspectives and actions.

In Memphis, Tennessee, I was frequently asked which church I attended. This polite question did not assume a "none of the above" tick box. Curiosity took me to a nearby Baptist church, the second-largest church in the United States, I was assured. In an impressive performance, complete with choir, orchestra, TV cameras, and public baptism, the preacher told his flock that no rain had fallen on Earth before the biblical flood. I glanced enquiringly at those sitting nearest me. Did they really believe that? It seemed they did. Perhaps they had not read other books, or perhaps they had but chose to believe the preacher.

In Witbank, South Africa, most of the local bookshops exclusively stocked Christian literature. (One had a small section devoted to non-religious works.) God's reign prevails on that continent. Further north in Nigeria, the name of the local Muslim terror group, Boko Haram (roughly translated as "books are sinful"), challenged secular scholarship. Library construction did not feature in their manifesto.

In Saudi Arabia, where Sunni Islam reigns supreme, the authorities prevented me from promoting a local engineer despite his obvious talent. He belonged to the minority Shia branch of Islam. Right religion, wrong sect. A common theme in the Middle East. In neighbouring Bahrain, street barricades were erected to prevent members of that sect from rioting. While navigating these obstacles, a friendly taxi driver tried to convert me to Islam.

In Malaysia, social and economic policies in favour of the Bumiputra ("sons of the soil") effectively discriminate against non-Muslim minorities on a range of issues, from housing to government jobs.

In Iraq, those of my staff who lived in Mosul, close by our site, were fearful of answering my phone calls in public lest they were overheard speaking English. They warned me of an extremist faction that was steadily gaining control of the city. Later, these fanatics revealed themselves to the world under the name ISIS.

INTRODUCTION

Extending their franchise beyond its place of origin, they made random strikes in the most unexpected quarters. They were not the only ones initiating religiously motivated attacks. In January 2015, at the headquarters of the satirical magazine *Charlie Hebdo* in Paris, gunmen belonging to al Qaeda massacred staff members for "insulting" their prophet. Their action invoked memories of the fatwa against Salman Rushdie. It underscored the rising tensions in Europe as communities grappled with an immigrant population that did not share its secular values.

The United States is not immune to this phenomenon. Here, we observe the rising influence of assertive Christian fundamentalists, more aptly described as literalists due to their literal interpretation of the Scriptures. Ranged against them are "progressive" reformers, many of them equally intolerant. Moderate Christians and secularists hold the middle ground. Historical evidence and the premise of my book demonstrate that if the divide is not resolved, then tension becomes conflict, ultimately compelling moderates to take sides.

Why do the Abrahamic religions hold so much power over their believers? There must be a compelling reason. From embryonic origins more than 3,000 years ago, these faiths have endured endless setbacks, persecution, and conflict while competing ideologies have faded and slipped into obscurity. The Abrahamic religions have not only survived but sustained a continuous trajectory of growth that displays remarkable resilience.

Despite a bloody history of war and conflict, their adherents refer to God in terms of love and deliverance: "Jesus the Saviour" or "Allah the Merciful." This reveals something very special and intimate in those who believe. Why so? Why so much trust? What fuels the conviction?

And you, the patient reader who has come this far, if you expect a simple answer to these questions, stop now. I have no simple answers. Belief is a personal journey, and each will choose what they want to believe in the end.

This book is primarily a story of our inheritance, for we have all inherited a world formed by the believers. It is part of the human quest to comprehend the universe and find inner peace. For the faithful, this is a struggle to preserve God and His laws against hostile adversaries and to impose their interpretation of His message by peace or by war on the rest of humanity.

It explores the unique complexity that exists between the theology, ideas, and politics that shape religion today. It examines the clash of ideologies that these religions have generated and the tools people can use to understand them. It offers an impartial examination of the historical path that led to present-day Judaism, Christianity, and Islam.

If this sounds like a journey you want to take, then I invite you to continue reading as we explore the story of *The God of War*.

1

ABRAHAM: PROPHET OF A DEMON OR A GOD?

ISAAC LOOKED AT the tall figure above him with a knife raised, ready to strike. Beneath him, the rough wood set on a makeshift altar of stones supported his thin frame. On the ground nearby, a clay pot held the flickering fire to light the sacrifice.

As Isaac lay there bound in silent terror, he tried to discern the look in his father's eyes. Was it anger, despair, or insanity? He was not sure.

For three days, they had been travelling through the hills of Moriah. On the third day, after ordering the slaves to wait, father and son had continued the journey alone. Isaac carried the wood on his back, while his father held the knife and fire.

"Where is the lamb to be sacrificed?" Isaac had asked.[1]

His father answered only that God would provide, but now Isaac understood: *he* would be the sacrifice.

He thought of crying out, but the slaves were too far away to hear. Anyway, he had always obeyed; he had always submitted. This is how it was.

Closing his eyes, he waited for the blow to strike and prayed it would be quick.

FAITH OR MADNESS

This is the story of Abraham, father of Isaac. Abraham's life, assuming he existed, is shrouded in mystery and conjecture. Yet his beliefs have shaped the religious views of most of humanity.

Was he driven by faith or madness? Did he kill his son, or was there a last-minute reprieve? Were later scriptures altered to hide a terrible offence? Should we even care?

To the last question, the answer is unequivocal. Yes, we should care. Today nearly 57% of the global population identifies as Jewish, Christian, or Muslim.[2] All three religions recognise Abraham as their father. To understand the contemporary world, we must understand their faith. To understand their faith, we must first understand him.

A VOICE COMMANDS

The story began in the ancient city of Ur, where the river Euphrates flowed into the Persian Gulf. The dusty remains of that city, now landlocked by a retreating coastline, can still be found in present-day Iraq.

The inhabitants of this Mesopotamian city adopted a cuneiform writing system and educated their children in arithmetic and languages. Their religion involved the worship of several divinities, the chief of whom was the moon god, Nanna. In addition, each inhabitant had their own personal god, a guardian angel of sorts, who watched over and protected them.

Into this town, according to the book of Genesis, was born Abram.[3] The time was somewhere between 2000 BC and 1200 BC. He and his wife, Sarai, were childless when his father led them out of Ur to a place called Haran. It was a 1,000-kilometre journey upstream along the valley of the Euphrates and one of its tributaries to what is today south-eastern Turkey.

Abram was rather old—75 years old, in fact—when he decided to leave his parents' house. He had been hearing voices in his head.

Like his compatriots, he had his own personal god. But the relationship was unique and significant for Abram. He conversed with it, sometimes debated with it, and always followed its instructions. Hebrew Scripture would give it many names: Yahweh, El Shaddai, and Elohim. Later, it became El Gibbor, God Almighty.

By command of God, Abram departed Haran and headed south with his nephew, Lot, and other clan members. They journeyed to Canaan, a land that would later be called Palestine or Israel. When they reached Shechem, west of the Jordan River, God made a promise to him. "To your offspring I will give this land."[4] But after moving further southward, near Bethel and later the Negev, he was forced to abandon the Promised Land due to severe drought. The clan headed for Egypt.

As they entered the new country, Abram became possessed by the notion that his life might be in danger. He judged that men would be so enamoured by the charms of his 70-year-old wife that they would kill him and kidnap her for themselves. At least, this was the fear he confided to Sarai. At his suggestion, she consented to pose as his sister.

There was some truth in the pretence. She was his half-sister, the same father, different mother.[5] In any event, it had the effect, probably intended, of freeing her to the attention of Egyptian men.

When news of her charms reached the pharaoh, he requested her presence at his palace and later his bedchamber. He seemed pleased with the new addition to his harem and richly rewarded the couple with sheep, oxen, he-asses, she-asses, and slaves—both male and female.

However, when the pharaoh eventually discovered the deception, he returned Sarai to her husband, admonished Abram for his behaviour, and expelled him and his clan from the country. It had been a highly profitable deceit, though. Abram departed Egypt a wealthy man, "heavily laden with cattle, with silver and gold."[6]

In Canaan, the clan split after a dispute over pasturing rights for their large herds. Lot and his family headed towards the Jordan River and pitched their tent near the towns of Sodom and Gomorrah. Abram went to Hebron after first travelling for a time throughout the region. At Hebron, he received news that Lot had been captured following tribal conflicts in the region. Mustering 318 of his followers, the geriatric Abram advanced to the town and retrieved his nephew.[7]

Lot returned to Sodom, but his problems were not over. While he was entertaining two male guests in his house, some local men gathered outside, demanding the right to rape them. The bizarre request, which would forever link the city with wanton homosexuality, giving rise to the word "sodomy," was rebuffed by Lot. Adamant that he would not permit such behaviour, Lot offered the mob his two virgin daughters instead to "do whatever you like with them."[8] The offer did not interest the ruffians, who threatened to do even worse to Lot if he did not relent.

Frustrated by his refusal, they attempted to break down the door, but Lot was saved when his guests intervened and struck the intruders blind. Then, revealing that they were angels, the visitors advised Lot to escape with his family before the city's imminent destruction and to not look back.

Forewarned, the family departed as fire and brimstone rained down on Sodom and the neighbouring town of Gomorrah. During the escape, Lot's wife turned to watch the destruction and was immediately turned into a pillar of salt.

Lot had similar misfortune in his next home, the city of Zoar, where conflict with his neighbours again forced him to flee to the nearby mountains.

The reasons for these disagreements are not clear. However, offering his young daughters to the baying mob in Sodom and later committing incest with them in a drunken state while in exile[9] hardly flatters the man. Genesis blames his victims for the latter offence.

A SON SCORNED; A SON CHOSEN

Abram and Sarai were childless during this time and longed for an heir. Sarai hit upon a solution. She suggested that her husband take one of her slave women to his bed. Since the woman was her property, the offspring would be as well. Hagar, an Egyptian, was chosen as the surrogate.

As might be expected, the resulting pregnancy caused friction between slave and wife. Although Sarai had suggested the liaison, she found it difficult to tolerate Hagar's new status and haughty demeanour. She complained bitterly to Abram, who merely responded, "She is your servant, so deal with her as you see fit."[10] Given a free hand, Sarai did as she wished, and the slave, tiring of the abuse, fled the camp.

Alone and pregnant, Hagar had time to reflect. Her prospects were dim. The timely intervention of an angel persuaded her to return and endure the harsh treatment on the promise that she would bear a son who would "be a wild ass of a man."[11]

When Hagar finally gave birth, the tension between her and Sarai continued. A final showdown was yet to come. As for Abram, he now had what he most desired in life and named the boy Ishmael ("God has heard").

Thirteen years later, when Abram was 99 and his wife over 90, the voice again spoke. It proposed a covenant by which he and his descendants would inherit all the lands of Canaan as an everlasting possession. Henceforth he would call himself Abraham, "father of many nations." His wife would be called Sarah and would give birth to a son. Sarah was less than enthusiastic at the news, considering herself well past the age for pregnancy.

Their ongoing migrations took them next to the Philistine district of Gerar, where the couple repeated the ploy that had worked so well in Egypt. On this occasion, it was Abimelech, king of Gerar, who took Sarah into his house. As with the pharaoh, the king returned the woman when he discovered the deception. Once again, Abraham was richly rewarded with sheep, oxen, male and female slaves, silver, and additionally, grazing rights in the territory.

Genesis is at pains to point out that the king made these generous gifts for fear of punishment from God and that no sexual relationship took place between Abimelech and Sarah. Thus, the Scriptures firmly quash any suspicion that a Philistine king might be the true father of her future child.

In due course, Sarah gave birth to Isaac. This restored the privilege she had unwillingly relinquished to Hagar. The tables were turned. Sarah would have her revenge. To safeguard her son's inheritance and her position as first lady of the household, she demanded that Abraham banish the former slave and her child to the desert. The pretext was that Ishmael had mocked them. Abraham consented.

Once again, Hagar found herself alone in the wilderness, but, on this occasion, she was with a child and had only one day's supply of water. In desperation, she searched the barren sands of Beersheba for a well but to no avail. When the last drop of water had run out, Hagar left the boy under a bush so as not to see him die. Then, in her final moments of despair, God revealed a water supply, so they survived.

Mother and child remained in the wilderness, where Ishmael became a seasoned bowman and confrontational man: "his hand against everyone and everyone's hand against him," as prophesied in Genesis 16:12. Eventually, he married a woman from his mother's homeland of Egypt. The Qur'an credits him with constructing the Ka'ba at Mecca,[12] and Arabs claim descent from him.

Abraham's rapport with God continued to dominate his behaviour. He would hear the voice of his master and respond accordingly. Sometimes the voice spoke directly, sometimes through a messenger, and on occasion, it adopted human form.[13] God made promises, issued commands, engaged in debate (e.g., on the fate of Sodom and Gomorrah), and made contracts with him.

The voice promised Abraham that the lands of Canaan would be given to him and his seed. These assurances were repeated on many occasions. Sometimes the offer was specific to Abraham himself. For example, "I am the

Lord, who brought you out of Ur of the Chaldeans to give you this land to take possession of it."[14] Other times it referred to his descendants: "To your offspring I will give this land."[15] And at Salem on his return from the campaign at Sodom, it said: "To your seed I have given this land, from the River of Egypt to the great river, the Euphrates River."[16] The extent of this territory varies with the telling in Genesis and in later scriptural accounts. In response, Abraham gave submission and loyalty, built altars, offered sacrifices, and was obliged to perform one additional duty.

The promise that Abraham's seed, through his son Isaac, would inherit Canaan came with a caveat: Abraham must remove a part of his flesh now deemed superfluous. Ever obedient, Abraham performed this act of self-mutilation, circumcision. Then, bringing together all the male members of his clan, including slaves and his son Ishmael, he circumcised them all.

Henceforth in accordance with the pact, all males and their slaves for future generations had to undergo circumcision eight days after birth. The covenant applied to the lineage of Isaac only.[17] Those of his descendants who failed to uphold the ritual would suffer expulsion from the tribe.

A TERRIBLE SACRIFICE

The force that guided Abraham was not a benevolent one. It was amoral. It did not set out an ethical code of behaviour,[18] nor did it expound a philosophy based on virtue or goodness. It did not demand of Abraham that he practise kindness, honesty, or any mode of conduct that could be considered upright or just. All it demanded was blind obedience manifested by reverential rituals. In return, it protected Abraham unequivocally: "I will bless them that bless thee, and curse them that curse thee."[19]

This philosophy divides humans into holy and impure camps, one set against the other. It punished both the pharaoh[20] and later Abimelech[21] for taking Sarah into their harems even though, in each case, the deception was Abraham's. It did not admonish him for his brutal treatment of Hagar and his firstborn when he left them to die in the desert. It spared his disreputable nephew, Lot, in preference to the inhabitants of Sodom and Gomorrah.

The voice promised Abraham that his seed would multiply as the stars of heaven and the sand on the seashore, and they would possess the gate of his enemies.[22] In return for this, Abraham surrendered his free will in absolute submission to his master. An ominous and final test of that total surrender was soon to come.

Unlike the "wild ass" Ishmael, a skilled archer and desert survivor, Isaac was a rather timid being. He was teased by his brother[23] and coddled by his mother. Later, he was deceived by his wife and outwitted by his second son, Jacob.[24] This simple individual, born of an incestuous union between Sarah and her half-brother (assuming the king of Gerar had no hand in the matter) and easily manipulated, was perhaps a disappointment to his father.

In any event, Abraham heard the voice of God once more. This time, the command was to take his son to a nearby mountain and sacrifice him on an altar. The immensity of the request was explicit: he must destroy the very thing he had waited for all his life, his son by Sarah.

There was no debate on this occasion. Abraham immediately obeyed and prepared for the deadly task. The next day, he set out with Isaac and two slaves for the land of Moriah.

Genesis does not say what age Isaac was at the time. Traditionally, he is portrayed as a child, but he was at least old enough to carry the wood for the sacrifice. Some scholars have speculated[25] that since Sarah was 90 when she gave birth to him and her death at 127 is reported at the start of the following chapter,[26] Isaac was already in his thirties. Whatever his age, he didn't resist. There was no fight. Either from a weakness of mind or body or an attachment to his father's blind faith, he allowed himself to be bound and placed on the altar.

Only at the last moment, with his knife raised to strike the deadly blow, did Abraham hear a voice. Not within his head this time but in a vision, an angel ordered him to stop. "Now I know that you fear God."[27] The test was over; faith had won.

A ram conveniently entangled in a nearby bush became the replacement sacrifice. But in the account of Abraham's return to the waiting slaves, his son is not mentioned. Abraham appears to be alone.

Did Isaac, awakened to his father's madness, simply flee? Or was the script altered to hide a terrible crime? Was the death of his mother, recounted in the following chapter, due to grief? If he did die, then we must assume it was the adult Isaac who was sacrificed, since the lives of his offspring are recounted later.

After the death of Sarah, Abraham bought a plot of land for her burial. He married again and continued to sire children by wife and concubine, finally dying at the age of 175.

LEGACY

There is no historical evidence other than accounts in Genesis and, much later, in the Qur'an that Abraham existed. The story is set during a time of mass immigration from Mesopotamia to Canaan that began around 1800 BC. The journey of the Abraham clan follows this pattern. Told and retold over the ages, it was finally put in writing by various scribes many centuries later when the first drafts of the Scriptures were written. Subsequently, as with other biblical scripts, the narrative underwent changes and reinterpretations as the prevailing policies of the time dictated, as we shall see in later chapters.

But whether Abraham is a genuine or a fictitious person is not important. Real or fabricated, the story has shaped the character of three great religions. For 15 million Jews, 2.4 billion Christians, and 1.9 billion Muslims,[28] Abraham is their spiritual father. These religions have dominated the history of humankind for the past two millennia and have affected the lives, directly or indirectly, of every living person today.

The legacy of Abraham is unquestioning loyalty to an all-powerful deity. It involves exchanging free will for submission to God and believing that those who oppose God or his people are cursed and deserve punishment.

Monotheism is the religion of Abraham, but his legacy was not a single monotheistic faith. Instead, it became a pluralism of monotheistic beliefs including Judaism, Christianity, and Islam, as well as subsects within these religions. Each has its unique perception of the true path, and each is incompatible and often at war with another. Obedience to a single deity is the common ground they share.

The will of this deity has been interpreted in different ways by succeeding generations. Some, like Isaac, were prepared to die for their beliefs, while others, like Abraham, were prepared to kill for them.

Yet, for all the promises made to Abraham, the only land he owned in Canaan was the cave of Machpelah in the field he bought from Ephron, son of Zohar the Hittite, to bury his wife. Here, he and other members of his family were later interred.

The site of the tomb is in present-day Hebron in the West Bank. Above it stands a large structure built at the time of Herod I, within which a synagogue was later constructed. Over its ruins, the Christianised Romans built a church, which was later converted to a mosque by conquering Muslims, and then converted back to a church by Crusaders, only to become a mosque again under Saladin. Each sect that controlled the edifice placed restrictions on entry and worship. Jews were not permitted beyond the seventh step of the stone entrance stairway until it was reconquered in the Six-Day War of 1967. The victors promptly blew up the stairway to obliterate the memory of the seventh step and the centuries of humiliation it represented.

Today the tomb remains a symbol of acrimony and division, with a separate entrance to a new Jewish synagogue and the Muslim mosque. Armed soldiers guard each entrance.

It has been the site of riots, grenade attacks, drive-by shootings, and two massacres (of Jews in 1960 and of Muslims in 1994). In neighbouring districts, the self-styled descendants of Ishmael and Isaac, Arabs and Jews respectively, continue the ancient feud of Hagar and Sarah.

Initially, the chosen ones were of the line of Isaac. With this tribe, God made his covenant. Or so they would claim.

ABRAHAM: PROPHET OF A DEMON OR A GOD?

Whether Abraham was guided by a divine force or malevolent entity, we may speculate. After all, he had sold his wife to royal harems, abandoned one son to die in the desert, and possibly killed another. What beliefs drove such a man, and how do they inspire those who today follow in his footsteps?

Whether he even existed is of no consequence. To believers, he is real, and his faith is their inheritance. The first inheritors were the self-proclaimed line of Isaac. Through their Scripture, his legacy would justify their journey of conquest. That journey would begin in the land promised to him and his seed.

PART ONE

HEBREWS

"For the Lord thy God is a consuming fire, a jealous God."

—Deuteronomy 4:24 (BST)

2

GOD'S MURDEROUS TRIBE

WHEN THEY ARRIVED in the Promised Land, the descendants of Isaac faced an awkward problem: Other people were already living there. However, this was a minor obstacle to a determined band of armed and violent tribesmen. It helped that Egypt's grip on the land in question, Canaan, was temporarily loosened. The moral justification for their actions would present a more difficult dilemma for future scribes.

To confront this challenge, they invoked the memory of Abraham—or, a cynic might argue, invented him. A divine power had pledged this land to his seed, and his seed had arrived to claim it. Anyone who stood in their way was defying divine will and would be treated accordingly. The natives could expect no mercy.

But how to explain their absence? Why did they, the descendants of Abraham, not already reside in the land of their great forefather?

That, too, the prophets would later explain. A sad tale of enslavement in Egypt, complete with dramatic escape and desert wanderings, would reinforce their righteous entitlement. A god of war aligned with the spirit that spoke to Abraham had directed their campaign. They esteemed this deity above the gods of their enemies. In this regard, they may have drawn inspiration from a mighty king.

SON OF THE SON OF GOD

In 1352 BC, Amenhotep IV became pharaoh of Egypt. The new monarch revered the divine Aten, depicted in hieroglyphs as the sun disc discharging its rays on a grateful Earth. To the 1,400 various gods and goddesses worshipped by Amenhotep IV's subjects, he merely allowed a perfunctory tolerance.[29] In the fifth year of his reign, he discarded even this concession. Removing the mask of tolerance, he uncovered the face of a tyrant.

Changing his name to Akhenaten ("servant of Aten"), he precipitated a major religious revolution where he closed the temples of the ancient gods and forbade their worship. As his police prowled the streets of the capital, the fearful citizens chiselled away the stone carvings of rival gods or hid their images. Reverence to Aten, the source of all creation, became obligatory. This supreme being ruled the earth through the divine children, the pharaoh and his wife, Nefertiti.

The reformation, humankind's first known venture into monotheism, did not survive long. After Akhenaten's death, the Egyptians returned to polytheism, restored the ancient temples, and tried to obliterate the memory of the radical pharaoh. A relieved priesthood resumed its former prominence.

ENTER THE HEBREWS

At this time, the lands of Canaan and Syria were within the Egyptian sphere of influence. Ancient Egyptian and Sumerian texts mention the peoples of the region, among whom were the Habiru and Shasu, variously described as brigands, thieves, merchants, mercenaries, or slaves. Often in conflict with the pharaoh, these nomadic peoples lived on the periphery of Egyptian society or migrated within its borders. The sedentary population viewed them with some degree of hostility and disdain.

From these obscure references, one tribe emerged to make its mark on the world. [30] They lived in the highlands and were called Hebrews, meaning "to traverse or to pass over." This suggests their origin lay elsewhere, perhaps east of the river Jordan. There dwelt the Midianites, a confederacy of desert tribes that worshipped many deities, including Yahweh, the god of Abraham.

The Hebrews also adopted Yahweh as one of their own. Whether influenced by the doctrine of Akhenaten or not, Yahweh became their chief god and, much later, their only god. Thus, they revived the creed of monotheism.

By their own account, written centuries later, the Hebrews formed themselves into a violent sect with complex rituals designed to set them apart from their fellow tribesmen. These rituals involved circumcision, purification rites with fire, water, and burnt animal offerings. Each of these customs followed precise patterns of observance. Failure to adhere was considered a sin. They were strictly forbidden to intermarry with other tribes: "Do not intermarry with them. Do not give your daughters to their sons or take their daughters for your sons."[31] The arbitrary murder of anyone who transgressed that rule was sanctioned.[32]

They saw themselves as an elite community, an idea reinforced repeatedly in their doctrine: "For you are a people holy to the Lord your God. The Lord your God has chosen you out of all the peoples on the face of the earth to be his people, his treasured possession."[33] This bred a pattern of confrontation in their relations with others: "Do not be afraid of them; the Lord your God himself will fight for you."[34]

Yahweh was the god of war. The scriptures are explicit: "The Lord is a man of War"[35] who "[dwelt] among them"[36] in the Ark of the Covenant, a gold-plated wooden box they carried into battle. From these modest quarters, "the Lord your God is the one who goes ahead of you like a devouring fire. He will destroy them."[37]

The Ark symbolised the agreement between God and Abraham, whom the Hebrews called their ancestor. Adoration of this being was absolute and unconditional. Deviation or respect towards any other deity was forbidden and punishable by death; "For I, the Lord your God, am a jealous God."[38] So, also, was any act or word deemed insulting to the divine being (blasphemy).

The Hebrews were urged to attack and destroy those who did not share their beliefs: "Break down their altars, smash their sacred stones and burn their [sacred groves] in the fire; cut down the idols of their gods and wipe out their names from those places."[39] "You will pursue your enemies, and they will fall by the sword before you."[40] The order applied equally to those who did not worship Yahweh and those who did worship him but also worshipped other gods.

The Hebrews made war first on their neighbouring Midianite tribes, treating them with extraordinary viciousness: "They fought against Midian, as the Lord commanded Moses, and killed every man. ... The Israelites captured the Midianite women and children and took all the Midianite herds, flocks and goods as plunder. They burned all the towns where the Midianites had settled."[41]

Under the leadership of Moses, the creed of Hebrew exclusiveness was brutally applied. When his victorious warriors took captive Midianite women and children back to the camp, Moses was furious. He rebuked the warriors, saying, "Have you allowed all the women to live?"[42] Then he commanded, "Kill all the boys. And kill every woman who has slept with a man," and he sanctioned the abuse of those who remained: "But save for yourselves every girl who has never slept with a man."[43]

They continued to harass and slaughter the inhabitants east of the Jordan River: "The Lord our God delivered him [King of Heshbon] over to us and we struck him down, together with his sons and his whole army. At that time we took all his towns and completely destroyed them—men, women and children. We left no survivors."[44]

Arriving as invaders "to a people quiet and unsuspecting, [they] put them to the sword, and burned down the city."[45] This was the land promised by God to Abraham. The goal was to destroy the entire population and replace them with the chosen race: "Do not look on them with pity."[46] Thus, the killing increased, and they "totally destroyed all who breathed, just as the Lord, the God of Israel, had commanded."[47]

One by one, the cities and towns were razed, together with their inhabitants: "They devoted the city [Jericho] to the Lord and destroyed with the sword every living thing in it—men and women, young and old, cattle, sheep and donkeys."[48]

They hanged the rulers, sometimes after torture or dismemberment. The ferocity of the destruction bears the barbarian's malice towards civilisation and its trappings: "The Lord said to Moses ... drive out all the inhabitants ... destroy all their carved images and their cast idols, and demolish all their high places."[49]

DESTROY OR BE DESTROYED

The decision to exterminate the population of the Promised Land was part of a deliberate policy. Outside that territory, the Hebrews could enslave the inhabitants of any city that surrendered peacefully and massacre the men if they resisted. But in Canaan, the slaughter was mandatory, whether the inhabitants submitted or not. The possibility of another culture subsisting with their own, worshipping another god, or even intermarrying and diluting their obsessive creed could not be contemplated. The Holy Land was reserved exclusively for the "holy people."

Yahweh gave the Hebrews a sinister warning. If they faltered in their duty and left anyone alive, they would suffer a similar fate themselves; for "when the Lord your God has delivered them over to you and you have defeated them, then you must destroy them totally. Make no treaty with them, and show them no mercy."[50] "But if you do not drive out the inhabitants ... then I will do to you what I plan to do to them."[51]

Continuing to infiltrate Canaan under the command of Joshua, the Hebrews gradually took possession of the central highlands, killing "everyone in it [the city of Makkedah]. He left no survivors."[52] The success of their relentless aggression can be summed up in the following passage: "So I gave you a land on which you did not toil and cities you did not build; and you live in them and eat from vineyards and olive groves that you did not plant."[53] Heady times indeed.

Settling in their new homes, the Hebrews maintained the ritualistic practices and laws that set them apart. These laws pronounced the death sentence for various misdemeanours, including witchcraft, worshipping other gods, and making molten images.[54] Even a woman who failed to demonstrate her virginity on the marriage bed could be put to death. The laws permitted the enslavement of all non-Hebrews and justified the slaughter of their victims because the Canaanites were "wicked people."[55]

It is unclear how a narrative that prescribed stoning wives and burning witches could assign wickedness to another race and demand its destruction.

However, the Hebrews did not have the fighting all their own way. They encountered more formidable opponents when they moved into the coastal plain adjoining the Mediterranean coast. The Philistines, with whom Abraham and Sarah had sojourned during their visit to Gerar, were migrant sea peoples. Their chariots gave them a tactical advantage in the plains but were ineffective in the wooded highlands where the Hebrews maintained control. The conflict reached a stalemate as the two sides engaged in perpetual war, each unable to score a decisive victory over the other.

In one encounter, the Philistines captured the Ark, which they gleefully paraded throughout their domain. The Hebrews were mightily indignant. After all, losing God, or at least His sanctuary, was rather embarrassing. The Philistines paid a heavy price. Misfortune visited every location where they displayed the trophy. People were afflicted with hemorrhoids or tumours, plagues of mice appeared, and images of gods lay prostrate. Suitably chastened, the Philistines returned the Ark, together with gifts of gold, to the rightful owners. They would not mess with Yahweh again!

THE FIRST KING

Up to that time, the Hebrews were a loose confederacy of 12 tribes led by commanders called judges: "In those days Israel had no king; everyone did as they saw fit."[56] We may assume the number 12, with its ancient cosmic references,[57] to be symbolic. Regardless of the number, a loose confederation existed, and soon this presented problems.

An internal dispute ended in the slaughter of the tribe of Benjamin, leaving only 600 male survivors. When peace was restored, the question of finding wives for these 600 who remained had to be resolved. It was essential to maintain the numerical strength of the race. They solved the problem by attacking the city of Jabesh with the usual ferocity: "Kill every male and every woman who is not a virgin."[58] Then they embarked on gang rape: "They found 400 young virgins ... and they brought them to the camp."[59] These were given to the Benjamites. That, of course, still left 200 without wives. The Benjamites themselves resolved this problem. During an annual festival in Shiloh, north of Bethel, the young women would dance near the local vineyards, away from the rest of the community. The tribesmen hid, awaited their chance, and then each man captured one woman for himself.[60]

The injunction against intermarriage having been temporarily suspended, they resolved to avoid a recurrence of further infighting. For this reason and to halt the continued successes of the Philistines, the Hebrews decided to appoint a single chief to rule over them. Thus, their first king, Saul, was anointed. Uniting the tribes, he embarked on a new campaign: "This is what the Lord Almighty says: '... Now go, and attack the Amalekites [a tribe hostile to the Hebrews] and totally destroy all that belongs to them. Do not spare them; put to death men and women, children and infants, cattle and sheep, camels and donkeys.' "[61]

At least, this is what a prophet called Samuel says the Almighty commanded. Saul duly complied. Well, almost. He decided to spare the life of the Amalekite king, and he allowed his own troops to keep the choicest livestock rather than destroy them as ordered. It was an act of mercy to his captive and a pragmatic concession to the troops.

Unfortunately, that's not how Samuel saw it. He was greatly upset by this dilution of God's writ and warned Saul that the Lord had now rejected him. To appease the prophet, Saul had the captive king brought before Samuel, hoping perhaps God's bloodlust might have subsided. No such luck. The prophet ordered the prisoner to be cut to pieces.

It was too late, declared Samuel. God regretted that he had made Saul king over Israel.[62] The prophet anointed a shepherd boy called David, whom he had furtively groomed for the role as successor. Soon, David would undermine Saul and eventually succeed to the throne.

Once he had taken power, David (1010–970 BC) began to reverse the triumphs of the Philistines. A worthy candidate for a bloodthirsty god, David pushed them back to their coastal cities, attacked tribes to the north, enslaved the defeated people for use in construction projects, and slaughtered all he did not enslave. David's victims included Saul's sons and, indirectly, his own son Absalom.

David captured Jerusalem and made it his capital. Within its walls, he planted the Ark of the Covenant on Mount Moriah where Abraham had built the sacrificial altar for Isaac. The city and its temple became the symbol and spiritual centre for the Hebrews.

David's son and successor Solomon consolidated his conquests, forced the defeated territories to pay tribute, and maintained a lavish court complete with a coterie of wives and concubines. He launched a massive building programme fortifying Jerusalem and commissioning various projects. The foremost was a temple on Mount Moriah, with an inner sanctuary, the holy of holies, containing the Ark.

However, the cost of Solomon's opulence was borne with some resentment by his subjects. The main beneficiary of this spending, Jerusalem, was in the south. This did not sit well with the tribes of the north. The more righteous among them were offended that Solomon had married foreign wives, contrary to a prohibition in Deuteronomy 7:3. Worse still, he allowed them to worship their deities, giving rise to the charge that he himself might also be guilty of idolatry.

A KINGDOM DIVIDED

After Solomon's death, this discontent surfaced when the northern Hebrews of Samaria and Galilee broke away from their southern brethren. Some saw it as a belated punishment for the sins of Solomon. Two new states came into being within the region of Canaan: Judah, with its capital at Jerusalem, and to its north Israel, comprising the breakaway provinces. Ideological differences on matters of ceremony and worship deepened the partition. Archaeological evidence suggests the northerners even consumed pork, challenging later scriptural narratives.[63] Violence erupted between the two. The new situation weakened the Hebrews, making each state more vulnerable to attack from powerful neighbours.

To secure their position, the northern leaders allied with the Phoenicians, coastal dwellers of what is today Lebanon. The union was underpinned by a marriage between Ahab of Israel and Jezebel, daughter to the king of Sidon. As part of the alliance, Ahab built a temple in Samaria dedicated to Baal, enabling his wife and her associates to worship while they resided there. Unlike the warlike Yahweh, Baal had skills in the rain and fertility departments. These were useful in a region heavily dependent on agriculture.

This pragmatism cut no ice with the guardians of the true creed. Elijah, a moralist and prophet, railed against the concession and complained bitterly that the altars of Yahweh were being destroyed and their priests persecuted. He provoked discontent in Israel and instigated a massacre of the rival priests after luring them to a ceremony on Mount Carmel.[64] Fearful of royal retribution, he fled for his life into the desert wilderness—but not for long.

Elijah soon returned and continued to profess his dogma, proclaiming death and destruction on the followers of Baal. This time he had a new disciple called Elisha, who persisted in following the older man despite repeated requests by Elijah to be left alone.

The humourless Elisha, whose absence of hair was matched by an excess of self-righteousness, was not a man to be trifled with. On a journey to Bethel, some children started catcalling him because of his baldness, saying, " 'Get out of here, baldy!' He turned around, looked at them and called down a curse on them in the name of the Lord. Then two bears came out of the woods and mauled forty-two of the boys."[65] An overreaction, one might say, and we only have Elisha's word that the bears did it.

Earlier, while the two prophets were journeying near the banks of the Jordan River, Elijah was suddenly taken to heaven in a fiery chariot, leaving nothing behind except his cloak. Lest any suspicion fall on the head of Elisha, Scripture provides him with an alibi. Fifty men of Jericho happened to witness the event from the opposite bank. These men insisted on searching the area for a body but found nothing, proving that, indeed, there was no trace of Elijah's remains, at least not on the ground. Whether they checked the fast-flowing river is not mentioned.

Tellingly, Elisha had earlier requested to inherit a "double portion" of Elijah's spirit.[66] He insisted on following the older man on the final leg of his fateful journey, although Elijah had again requested to be left alone. It is tempting to postulate some indiscretion by Elijah as the two men travelled together. Perhaps a reference to receding hairlines might have provoked a violent reaction in his sensitive companion!

Or perhaps Elisha needed no provocation. He had now inherited the mantle of his former teacher and become the foremost prophet of Israel, a position of considerable influence and power. While he appeared to have the trust of the reigning monarch, he secretly plotted subversion.

An army commander called Jehu led the revolt and quickly killed King Jehoram, son and successor to Ahab, with an arrow in his back. Knowing she could expect little mercy from the usurper, the Queen Mother, Jezebel, put on her makeup, donned the royal regalia, and awaited her fate. The rebels threw the unfortunate woman from an upstairs window. Her blood-spattered corpse was trampled underfoot by horses and left for the dogs to devour. For challenging the prophets of Yahweh, her name became synonymous with tarnished womanhood.

Jehu was not done. He massacred the children and supporters of the former rulers. Then, declaring his intention to offer sacrifice to Baal, he enticed those who worshipped the deity to a ceremony before slaughtering the lot, much as Elijah had done years earlier. God rewarded him for his efforts. Jehu had restored the status quo and gained the kingship of Israel. But devotion did not save the Hebrews.

Another casualty of Jehu's revolt was the king of Judah, a relative of the royal family of Israel. His death ended the rapprochement between the two kingdoms initiated by Ahab. Israel was again isolated from its southern neighbour.

INVADERS ON THE HORIZON

After his triumphal revolution, Jehu was forced to bow before a more potent force, Assyria. This emerging power was on the warpath, aggressively expanding its borders and crushing all opposition. Realising their god of war was no match against Assyrian power, Jehu and his successors paid homage and offered tribute.

Amos, the new prophet in town, offered an explanation: Yahweh had changed sides and was supporting the Assyrians. How else was one to account for their numerous victories? Amos scorned the noisy and futile rituals of the priests of Israel and warned of dire consequences: thunder, drought, fire—you name it.

Prophet and fellow doomsayer Hosea criticised the ongoing devotion to Baal, which seemed to have continued despite the revolt of Jehu. He accused the Israelites of spiritual adultery, a phrase that might have been inspired by his own marriage problems. His wife had absconded with another man, forcing him to repurchase her for 15 shekels and a quantity of barley. Clearly, he still loved her. Yahweh, too, he surmised, had a soft heart and would continue to love the Israelites despite their infidelity. But first, there would be a price to pay. According to the Scriptures, both Amos and Hosea prophesied the destruction of Israel.

The destruction began in 732 BC. Following an unsuccessful Israelite revolt, the Assyrians invaded, annexed part of the territory, and exacted retribution on the population. Ten years later, after further insubordination, they returned and took the remaining territory. They deported thousands of inhabitants and replanted the land with loyal tribes from various corners of their empire, which was standard Assyrian policy for dealing with troublesome nations. The Scriptures record that the king of Assyria brought "people from Babylon, Kuthah, Avva, Hamath and Sepharvaim and settled them in the towns of Samaria to replace the Israelites."[67]

Israel was destroyed. Its people were leaderless, and much of the land was occupied by strange people whose customs and beliefs did not correspond with their own.

The deportees became known as the Ten Lost Tribes of Israel[68]—although they were not quite lost. For all the savagery of the invaders, they incorporated defeated tribes into Assyrian society once they had been subdued and deported. They then allowed them considerable freedom, provided they remained loyal. Many who had not been deported fled to Judah, taking the writings of Hosea and Amos with them. As we shall see, these writings are later referred to as the E version of Scripture.

The defeat of the northern kingdom left Judah at the mercy of the Assyrians. The Judean king, on the advice of the prophet Isaiah, had not assisted Israel. The king was now forced to submit to the new power, and his kingdom was obliged to pay the exacting tribute they demanded. Judah became a vassal state, forced to allow the worship of Assyrian deities within the walls of Jerusalem.

A later king, Hezekiah, outlawed the "strange gods" and confined worship to Yahweh. For this, he earned favour with the prophets but provoked the ire of the Assyrians. They saw it as subversion and promptly attacked Judah and besieged Jerusalem.

According to the Hebrew Scriptures, Yahweh intervened to destroy the besiegers.[69] Egyptian chronicles claim that pharaoh drove away the attackers.[70] Assyrian accounts brag that their army laid waste in the countryside and forced Hezekiah to retreat to his citadel but did not take Jerusalem.[71] In any event, Judah was devastated, its towns ruined, and Jerusalem was spared in return for a humiliating surrender that proved to be a temporary respite.

Manasseh, son and successor of Hezekiah, was a pragmatist who reversed his father's policies, allowed toleration of worship, and oversaw a period of peace and stability during a long reign. Naturally, the prophets deplored his actions and chastised him for abandoning the true God.

After Manasseh's death, his grandson Josiah reverted to the true path. Restoration work was carried out on the temple, during which the high priest Hilkiah "discovered" scrolls that Yahweh had given to Moses. The opportune find included a new scripture later called Deuteronomy, or the Second Law, and additions to the exodus story. The priests claimed these were lost texts. More likely, they were a clever way of introducing new ideas or giving authenticity to policies that were already planned. Failure to counter the Assyrians had diminished the prestige of the Davidic monarch. So, they shifted focus to the older stories of Abraham and Moses, the good old days. Several accounts, including Joshua, Judges, Samuel, and Kings, were recorded, instigating a process of revision that would continue.

This fuelled a period of radicalisation. Pagan temples were torn down, their priests were slaughtered, and idols ground to dust. Devotion was concentrated in the temple of Jerusalem. The temple was cleared of all references, implicit or otherwise, to other beings or spirits, as recounted in 2 Kings 23. Atonement through fundamentalism was the chosen path. The oral tradition of the Hebrews was transformed into a written series of laws. But not everyone bought into this innovation. The prophet Jeremiah bewailed the "lying pen of the scribes."[72]

As the power of Assyria began to wane, a resurgent Egypt vied with the emerging Babylon for control of the region. Caught in the infighting between these powers, Josiah was killed in a skirmish, and Judah oscillated between allegiance to Egypt and Babylon. In the following struggle, the Babylonians emerged as the stronger of the two. By 612 BC, they had overrun the Assyrian capital, Nineveh, and destroyed it. But Egypt still provided a potent challenge.

At a crucial point in the conflict, Judah, having first sided with Babylon, cancelled their tribute to its king, Nebuchadnezzar II, and cut a deal with Egypt instead. It seemed to be the right policy. The Egyptians had just repulsed an attempted invasion by the new power. According to the Scriptures, the prophet Jeremiah knew better and advised against the alliance. Whether he did or not, Judah had backed the wrong horse.

Nebuchadnezzar attacked and captured the city of Jerusalem, first in 597 BC and again after a rebellion in 589 BC. He burned the temple of Solomon and deported the population en masse to far-flung corners of the new empire. Only the rural population, the poorest of the poor, remained. Judah entered a period of decline.

As with the capture of Israel, many Judeans escaped deportation and settled in Egypt, where earlier Hebrew settlements were already established. Here, they would "not see war or hear the trumpet or be hungry for bread."[73] They practised their faith in a loose fashion, far from the overbearing dogma of the Jerusalem zealots. Or at least, they would have, if one of those dogmatists had not followed them.

The prophet Jeremiah disapproved of the migration to Egypt, fearing it would undermine ritual orthodoxy—or his version of it. He implored the flock to return; otherwise, they would "die by the sword, famine and plague."[74]

His warnings fell on deaf ears. No doubt the migrants observed that Josiah's reforms—compliance with strict rituals, temple sacrifices, and demolition of pagan shrines—had not served them well. In Egypt, they did not die by sword, famine, or plague, and they did not return. Neither, strangely enough, did Jeremiah.

The prophet Ezekiel was equally hostile to the migrants. From his confinement in Babylon, he railed against them, comparing their status to that of their enslaved forebears before the exodus: "Will you defile yourselves the way your ancestors did and lust after their vile images?"[75] His rantings had as little effect as Jeremiah's.

The Hebrews had brutally conquered the lands promised them by God, exterminated or enslaved the weaker inhabitants, and lived off the fat of the land. They had tasted the sweet fruits of victory and built a great temple to the god who made it all possible. But for all that, theirs was a minor kingdom caught amid the aspirations of great empires. Yahweh had proved impotent against these earthly powers, and division hindered their capacity to resist.

The party was over, the Hebrews were broken, and the Promised Land was snatched from their grasp. Yahweh, it appeared, had absconded to join forces with the enemy. No longer the chosen people in the Promised Land, they seemed destined to fade into obscurity, assimilated into the populations of Egypt and Assyria. Whose fault was it—theirs or God's?

Yet salvation awaited them in an unlikely form. The blind devotion of Abraham and the adopted god of his seed might yet endure.

3

A SACRED SECT OF THE PURE

"**THE PROBLEM WE** have with Moses," quipped Golda Meir, former Israeli prime minister, "is that he took us 40 years through the desert to the one place in the Middle East that has no oil."[76]

No matter. The Hebrews, in their desperation, found something more precious than oil: fiction! They simply reinvented their past and, by that means, shaped their destiny.[77] Unintentionally, they would also shape the destiny of others.

They reinvented something else too: religion. Up to this point, humankind had worshipped deities whose abodes were identifiable. They lived in streams, springs, mountains, the moon, or images crafted by human hands. The Hebrews' god had resided in the Ark of the Covenant before upgrading to the temple of Jerusalem. The now homeless Yahweh henceforth would dwell "among them." Whether in Israel, Judah, or exile, he lived in the hearts and minds of those who believed.

This was a radical departure in human perception of the divine. Just as Abraham's spirit had accompanied his wanderings, so Yahweh would accompany the Hebrews.

Having formulated this doctrine, the scholars faced the task of rescuing themselves and their god from obscurity. They would have to return to Israel and sell the message. To accomplish this, they created a more distinctive version of the faith with unique rules and character.

The Babylonian exile lasted for 50 to 70 years. Some captives settled in the city of Babylon itself. Others lived in the various towns ruined in the Assyrian–Babylonian war. They maintained their identity and religion, preserving ancient customs and absorbing some traditions of their hosts. The most influential of these was Zoroastrianism. The followers of this faith believed in one universal, all-good, uncreated supreme deity. These convictions, which their descendants retain to the present day, included immortality of the soul, last judgement, hell, and heaven.

It was not a brutal captivity, although later accounts claimed some persecution.[78] Captives had religious freedom and enough latitude to accumulate considerable wealth. Ezekiel, for example, had his own house. This was a level of tolerance Hebrew prophets did not extend to others.

But exile, however mild, is still exile. A famous psalm bemoaned their condition and rejoiced in the ultimate fate of their captors: "By the rivers of Babylon we sat and wept when we remembered Zion."[79] The sad lamentation turns bitter in the last verse: "Daughter Babylon, doomed to destruction ... happy is the one who seizes your infants and dashes them against the rocks."[80]

While in captivity, most of the Hebrews remained separate and preserved their traditions. They sought solace in the Scriptures. In the absence of a temple, the written word became the focus for their reverence.

They believed their fate was a punishment for disobedience to God. They might have reflected that disobedience to a stronger earthly power was a more plausible explanation. At any rate, their remedy was to intensify their devotion to Yahweh.

Ezekiel, who inspired this line of thought, made it known that Yahweh had left his sanctuary in Jerusalem and was with them in exile in Babylon. In their misery, his presence bestowed blessings upon them.

A MESSIAH TO THE RESCUE

In 539 BC, Cyrus II of Persia conquered the Babylonian Empire. This king, referred to as a messiah, or "anointed one,"[81] by the grateful Hebrews, allowed them to return home. This was part of a general concession by the new ruler towards all displaced minorities. It was a wise policy that guaranteed their allegiance.

Not all returned; many had settled and would remain in the region for centuries to come. But for the most devout, the lure of Jerusalem, the desire to be reunited with the old centre of worship, was strong. Gradually, a trickle of exiles made its way back to Judah.

Their behaviour on returning suggested a new sense of purpose and a conviction that they were a special people. No longer would their god be one among rivals—He was the one and only: "I am Yahweh, and there is no other; there is no God but me."[82] Among the returnees tasked with implementing royal policy were two functionaries of the Persian crown: Nehemiah and Ezra would determine the character of the evolving religion.

Nehemiah was a satrap, a kind of regional governor. By the king's authority, he set out for Judah with a small armed detachment. On arrival, he described a desolate land of abandoned villages and farms. Jerusalem was no longer a city. Instead, it had become a shabby town of impoverished inhabitants and derelict buildings. One of his first acts was to make a clandestine tour of its ruins by night, taking stock of the shattered walls and burned-out gates. There was a need for caution: not everyone welcomed the returning exiles, or *golah*, as they were called.

ONLY THE SELECT NEED APPLY

The next day, Nehemiah called together the priests and leaders of the Hebrews, some of whom were *golah*. He told them of his mission from the king and God. They must first rebuild the walls. Otherwise, they could neither defend themselves nor become strong. Under his stewardship, volunteers began the work with a singular intensity. Each group was assigned to a specific section of the fortifications. Only those of pure Hebrew blood were permitted to partake in the labour. Ever fearful of attack, the workers carried weapons at their sides. While some laboured, others stood guard, ready to counter any action by hostile locals.

Neighbouring satraps were alarmed at the construction and feared a new power to challenge their own. Three of them—Tobiah, an Ammonite, Geshem, an Arab, and Sanballat, a Horonite—openly confronted Nehemiah with threats. When that failed, they tried to discredit him by circulating rumours that he was committing treason against the crown. Nehemiah responded that he and his people were the servants of God, and they (the three antagonists) and their people had no claim to Jerusalem or any historic right to it.[83]

Despite the opposition and intimidation, Nehemiah completed the wall with gates and citadels in 52 days.[84] He then began a strict procedure to "purify" their race, using genealogy to segregate the chosen people from Judah's other inhabitants. Those who could not authenticate their lineage were not permitted to partake in the religious ceremonies.

Local Hebrews and *golah* who had taken foreign wives faced a choice: abandon their spouses and children or be excluded. This fear of foreign women and their pagan influence was nothing new. Jezebel, Delilah, and the alien wives of Solomon all received bad press. Moses was criticised for marrying a Cushite.[85] Ammonites and Moabites were barred from the congregation.[86] Warnings against marriage to "daughter[s] of a foreign god" were revived.[87]

Nehemiah was foremost in opposition to mixed couples: "[I] cursed them and beat some of them and pulled out their hair,"[88] and "I purified the priests ... of everything foreign."[89] When not cursing, pulling hair, and purifying, he ensured the people brought their taxes and offerings to the temple, satisfying both God and king. He made them keep the Sabbath, and he defended the poor against exploitative lenders.

In his work as a reformer and rebuilder, another famous returnee aided Nehemiah. Ezra was a scribe and priest, a teacher of the law, who sanctified the strategy of Nehemiah. He, too, was shocked at the state of the city, the apathy of its inhabitants, and their lack of piety. In despair, he tore his garments, cried aloud, and adopted the posture of a mourner.

Like Nehemiah, he supported the policy of purifying the "holy seed"[90] from the malignant influence of foreigners and their women. Pursuing that policy was his primary task. While the wall was a physical barrier between God's people and outsiders, the law and rituals marked the boundary between true believers and the Gentiles (non-believers). That barrier had been maintained in Babylon against "foreigners," to some degree, preserving the Hebrews as a separate people. Now Jerusalem imposed the same barrier.

The *golah* had brought with them the scriptural scrolls compiled during the exile. These chronicles outlined their version of Hebrew history from creation to the deportation. This included sacred rituals and purification rites. Gathering the people together, Ezra recited these obligations to the astonished listeners. It seemed that much of what he read was new to them. They were clearly overwhelmed, for Ezra had to implore them not to weep.

A royal decree permitting construction and maintenance of the temple dedicated to "the law of your God and the law of the King"[91] was enacted. But, as with the building of the walls, only those of pure blood, the "holy seed," could participate.

The exclusionary system favoured Babylonian captives, who now began to rebuild the temple. All others were excluded. Even some *golah* failed the ethnicity test, as did the Samaritans. The latter were survivors of the former northern kingdom who also worshipped Yahweh. Their offer of help was rejected due to their assimilation with Assyrian immigrants. The term "Jew" originated at this time to distinguish those of pure Judean ancestry from other Hebrews.

The second temple, as it became known, secured two objectives of Persian policy: a grateful, compliant subject people and a centre for collecting taxes.

During the temple's construction, Ezra had been busy producing a list of those who "mingled the holy race with the peoples around them"[92] by taking foreign wives, and he recorded this list for posterity. The process of determining the origin of every woman took three months. At the dedication of the temple, Ezra called another assembly of the Hebrews. As they huddled together in the teeming rain, he exposed the "sinners," instructing them to abandon their non-Hebrew spouses or face the consequences. Men had to choose between love for their families or love for God. Failure to comply meant confiscation of property and expulsion from the community. Many took the divine option. Families were torn apart as tearful wives, with children in tow, were forced to leave compliant husbands.[93] This rather pitiless act can be understood only in the context of a minority culture trying to preserve itself, a process that had served it well during exile.

Ezra was not finished with lists—there were more. In addition to recording those engaged in mixed marriages, he made a list of *golah* and those who accompanied him. For posterity, Ezra also included transcripts from decrees of the Persian kings and relevant correspondence to lend official authenticity to their mission.

But the work of a reformer is never done. After Nehemiah left Jerusalem to attend to his king at Susa (modern Shush, Iran), the Jews fell into sin once more. That is, they allowed Gentiles to trade inside the city and lease storerooms in the temple. They began fraternising with those awful foreign women again. We must assume Ezra, a stickler for protocol, was also absent. When Nehemiah returned, he immediately ejected the infidels and, for good measure, ritually purified the sullied rooms of the temple.

While in exile, the Hebrews had reflected on their plight, sought answers in their Scriptures, and, where no answers existed, invented them. They added passages to Deuteronomy and Exodus attributing disasters to predecessors who strayed from Yahweh's path instead of to the kings whose policies led directly to defeat. The true path required purification, separation, and distinctive rituals. It also demanded the rejection of foreign gods and foreign women.

For Ezra, restoration to the Promised Land fulfilled God's covenant with his chosen people. But the land was no longer theirs. They dwelt as slaves on its soil and submitted its riches to Persia. This was because they had sinned, explained Ezra. But there was a solution!

Inspired by the earlier writings of Ezekiel, their religion had transformed itself. It was now a movable creed, dependent not on a temple but on the Scriptures themselves. After all, Yahweh had been in exile with them in Babylon and had managed quite well without a temple.

THE HOLY BOOKS

While in Babylon, the exiles had begun a revision of the old faith and traditions. From this period, the compilation of the books that formed the Tanakh, and later the Bible, started to take shape. Some, such as Deuteronomy, had already been accumulated during the reign of Josiah with the "discovery" of the "lost" scrolls. Others were revisions of older texts. Together, they comprised three versions of the Scriptures. Scholars today refer to these as the J, E, and P texts (classifications derived by various French and German scholars working in the 18th and 19th centuries).

The E, or Elohist, source originally came to Jerusalem with the refugees fleeing from the northern kingdom after its destruction by the Assyrians. Called "Elohist" because it uses "Elohim," the name of the god of Israel, its central hero is Moses. Elohim is an abstract God who remains aloof, only sending the odd angel or messenger when he needs to intervene in temporal matters.

In contrast to Elohim is the hands-on God of the J version (J for "Jahwe," the German spelling of "Yahweh"). This deity walks through the Garden of Eden, calling out to Adam, "Where are you?"[94] apparently unable to find him. This God is prone to temper tantrums and sometimes changes his mind. The J version focuses on Abraham, Joshua, and Jacob. There are other differences. In the J source, the name given to Moses's father-in-law is Reuel, the mountain is called Sinai, and the natives who live west of the river Jordan are referred to as Canaanites. In the E source, the name for Moses's father-in-law is Jethro, the mountain is called Horeb, and the natives are Amorites.

The P, or Priestly, text originated during the exile and is what Ezra read when he preached the law to the citizens of Jerusalem. It focused on ritual, ceremony, the role of the priests, and genealogy. After Ezra and Nehemiah had returned, it was still a work in progress among the priests remaining in Babylon. Putting these together into one Scripture resulted in separate and contradictory versions of events, such as the two creation narratives in Genesis.

Yet to cite three separate sources is an oversimplification. The texts had many origins and were revised, altered, and edited as prevailing politics determined. One example is when Hilkiah produced the scrolls that Yahweh had given to Moses. The revision process continued long after the returning exiles put these editions together.

Later modifications contained codes of laws, customs, and punishments. The book of Psalms and the teachings of the prophets were edited. Among the former was Psalm 104, derived from the Egyptian "Great Hymn to the Aten." With these revisions, the first five books of the Pentateuch, or Torah, began to take their final shape.

The key elements are the books of Genesis and Exodus, which tell the story of the creation. The covenant with Yahweh was backdated to the time of Abraham. The flight of the Hebrews from Egypt conceives the triumph of an oppressed people against the forces of tyranny. It promoted the fiction that Yahweh alone was worshipped and that the adoration of other deities was a lapse that had to be corrected occasionally. In reality, it was the norm.[95]

The revisionists even deprived God of his spouse. An eighth-century BC inscription on pottery found in the Sinai desert at Kuntillet Ajrud suggests that he had a wife called Asherah—and not just a wife, but an entire family.[96] There remains a brief reference to her being worshipped in the temple of Yahweh in Jerusalem.[97] In some other places, her name is translated as "sacred tree" or "grove."[98] Otherwise, she is banished to obscurity like the foreign wives of Jerusalem. We do not know how Yahweh felt about this. He seems to have had no say in the matter.

LITERAL OR ALLEGORICAL?

Not an original work, Genesis reflects various legends about creation that abounded at the time. It includes elements of ancient writings, such as the *Epic of Ziusudra*, *Epic of Gilgamesh*, *Epic of Atra-Hasis*, and *Theogony of Dunnu*.

An example is the story of Noah and the flood. This is a retelling of an earlier epic from Gilgamesh originating in Sumer (in today's Iraq) around 2900 BC, probably inspired by flooding in the Tigris and Euphrates. In the original story, the ark was a round vessel made of stretched skin similar in shape to those used by local fishermen down to recent times, called a kuphar, or coracle.[99]

The Hebrews added their unique interpretation of these ancient myths, giving them the form of a historical narrative. But as an accurate record of history, they fail any serious examination. Many anachronisms abound. For example, Genesis 26 identifies the king of Gerar as a Philistine ruler, although the Philistines did not occupy the coast of Canaan until the 12th century. Camels appear in the story of Abraham,[100] although they were not domesticated until centuries later.[101] Egyptian place names, including those on the Israelite escape route such as Ezion-Geber, did not exist when the exodus was purported to have happened.[102]

Other tales challenge both history and logic. Take the flood, for example. The Tanakh sets the event around 2300 BC (i.e., after the original Sumerian account was written).

The devastation left only eight people on Earth. These were Noah, his wife, three sons, and their wives. However, historical records before and after that date indicate flourishing civilisations in China, India, and Egypt.

To achieve this feat, Noah's sons and their wives would have had to reproduce at an alarming rate following the flood, more than a million children per couple. These children would have had to take on the physical appearance, DNA, language, religions, customs, infrastructure, technology, and geographical location of the civilisations wiped out in the flood. They would have had to discover and settle in western Europe, Egypt and the Mediterranean, China, India, sub-Saharan Africa, North and South America, and their various peripheries. Some of them would have had to reinvent bricks, glass, and candles, while others had to forget the invention of the wheel and writing, all within a mere decade or so. According to Genesis, however, Noah had only 14 grandchildren.

To fit all the world's creatures in their boat, they would have needed room for an estimated 30,000 species of animals (at present count), not including insects. If they were in pairs,[103] that would be 60,000, or seven pairs of each clean animal and one pair of unclean,[104] which would be more than 400,000, again excluding insects. They would have had to be fed for 40 days,[105] 150 days,[106] or one year,[107] and would have needed measures to prevent them eating each other or being eaten. Presumably, no spider swallowed a fly, no owl ate a mouse, and no lion a sheep, either in the ark or for several decades after the flood to allow their prey to procreate and multiply. We must assume carnivores went on a prolonged diet. We do not know what Noah and his family did for food.

It would have been easier for Yahweh to dispense with the flood and use his great powers simply to terminate the sinners. But he chose a more challenging route, even closing the ark door himself.[108] Why the opera, one might ask?

The flight from Egypt is another case in point. "The Israelites journeyed from Rameses to Sukkoth, about 600,000 men on foot, besides children. A mixed crowd also went up with them, and livestock in great number."[109]

Assuming the female population equalled the male, and allowing two-plus children per couple (a conservative estimate for the time), the numbers fleeing would amount to 2.5 million souls, almost equal to the entire population of Egypt of the day:

> Such a number, particularly when combined with "livestock in great number," would have constituted a logistical nightmare and is impossible. If all 2.5 million people marched ten abreast, the resulting line of more than 150 miles would need 8 or 9 days to march past any single fixed point. Taken

at face value, such a host could not have crossed any ordinary stretch of water by any ordinary road or path in one night; nor could these numbers or anything remotely approaching them have been sustained in the inhospitable Sinai desert.[110]

Outside of Scriptures, there is no record of the enslavement of the Hebrews in Egypt. The legend might have arisen from a collective memory of enslavement during the Egyptian occupation of Canaan in the 19th or 20th dynasties.

That the Hebrews attacked Canaan, massacred the inhabitants, and destroyed the cities, as recounted earlier (see Chapter 2), is not supported by historical records or extensive archaeological investigations. That the Hebrews were inspired by Abraham, held in Egyptian captivity, and led by Moses and Joshua can only be surmised from their own narrative.

Fundamentalist scholars, Jewish, Christian, and Muslim alike, insist that these early Scriptures are a literal record of events from the creation to the invasion of Canaan dictated by God and transcribed by Moses (making Moses the only historian to have recorded his own death). Neither science nor logic can penetrate such conviction.

Other interpreters of the Pentateuch see it as a set of allegorical stories intended to convey a symbolic rather than literal narrative. For them, the Scriptures bear a message revealing the nature of the Creator, His (yes, the Jewish creator is a male, unlike Aten, who appears to have been androgynous) purpose for humankind, and a set of moral codes.

However, this interpretation must confront the scriptural narrative outlined above: the brutal invasion of Canaan and the attempt to exterminate its population. The story has no historical basis, but it signifies intent. The message is one of exclusivity and hostility, recounted with brutal triumphalism, whether it occurred or not, by the command of a vengeful ogre intent on genocide.

These violent stories appear to have been invented by the later kings of Judah to legitimise specific policies. In contrast, the archaeological evidence shows a gradual transition from an agricultural society to city kingdoms by peoples who had already lived there or migrated from east of the Jordan River. The Hebrew and Canaan dialects have a common origin,[111] indicating a possible civil conflict leading to a fratricidal struggle for power rather than invasion.

LAWS AND RITUALS

The Scriptures also give much attention to the forms of ritual sacrifice. For example, which animals are permitted for various sacrifices, and which are not. Where the animal must be slaughtered ("at the north side of the altar")[112] and how the innards must be dispensed. Where to sprinkle the blood, where to place the head, what to do with the kidneys and liver, and how to dispose of the hide and dung ("burn [them] outside the camp").[113] Enter Yahweh the micromanager.

There are laws covering the treatment of leprosy and the plague. Curiously, Yahweh does not have a cure for either. Additional laws include the sacrifices to make in the event of sickness, the buying and selling of property, the treatment of slaves, and a protocol for menstruation. The laws even dictate which animals may and may not be eaten. Forbidden animals include camels, pigs, hares, and sea fish without fins or scales. Locusts and grasshoppers are permitted.

The laws determined who could and could not worship within the assembly: "No one who has been emasculated ... may enter the assembly of the Lord. No one born of a forbidden marriage (a "bastard") nor any of their descendants may enter the assembly of the Lord, not even in the tenth generation."[114] Some laws, such as the rituals of purification influenced by the Persian religion Zoroastrianism and designed to prevent pollution by corpses or bodily emissions, are sensible precautions against infection. As we will see later, other aspects of Zoroastrianism influenced offshoots of the Jewish religion, such as Christianity and Islam.

These books also set out codes for basic ethical behaviour that tried to address every contingency. This included bestiality, "Cursed is anyone who has sexual relations with any animal,"[115] and incest, "Cursed is anyone who sleeps with his mother-in-law."[116]

It covered relationships with slaves "if a man has sexual relations with a female slave who has been acquired by another man but has not yet been redeemed or given her freedom, an investigation shall be made. They shall not be put to death, because she has not been freed."[117] and responsibility to one's family "If you see your fellow Israelite's ox or sheep straying … take it back to its owner."[118]

The manuscripts gave advice on animal husbandry—"Do not muzzle an ox while it is treading out the grain,"[119] and "Do not plow with an ox and a donkey together"[120]—and even the wearing of clothes—"Do not wear clothes made of both wool and linen."[121]

Punishments were set out for those who failed to keep these laws. For example, "The Lord will cause you to be defeated before your enemies. … [He] will afflict you with the boils … and with tumors, festering sores and the itch. … Another [man] will take her [your wife] and rape her." And, as if all that was not bad enough, "Your ass will be forcibly taken from you."[122]

Central to these were a set of laws known later as the Ten Commandments (although the actual number was more than 10[123]) in Exodus and Deuteronomy. They proclaimed principles common to all societies and religions throughout the ages:

> Honour your father and your mother.
>
> You shall not murder.
>
> You shall not commit adultery.
>
> You shall not steal.
>
> You shall not give false testimony.
>
> You shall not covet your neighbour's goods [which includes his house, his wife, male and female slaves, ox, ass, or any other possessions].

Nothing is really new here. However, the ethical commandments were prefaced by a set of divine commandments unique to the Hebrew tradition. The first of these, "I am the Lord your God. ... You shall have no other gods before me,"[124] is a statement of stark exclusivity!

Statues and murals were proscribed lest they distract from any reverence due to the Almighty: "You shall not make for yourself an image in the form of anything in heaven above or on the earth beneath or in the waters below."[125] Also included was a tyrannical decree forbidding any act, word, or deed likely to be interpreted as offensive: "You shall not misuse the name of the Lord your God."[126]

Finally, a special day was set aside each week for veneration: "The seventh day is a Sabbath to the Lord your God."[127]

These divine commandments, each of which carried the death penalty if breached, underpin the dogmatic nature of the faith. They also place a provision on the ethical commandments. Killing, stealing, and forced adultery (rape) are permitted against those perceived to have violated the divine laws. Thus, punishment by death is prescribed for anyone who worships another god[128] or abuses Yahweh: "Anyone who blasphemes the name of the Lord is to be put to death. The entire assembly must stone them."[129] The guilty may be robbed of their possessions and enslaved along with their families and descendants.

The Jews used these divine commandments to torture, imprison, and slaughter their neighbours. In later centuries, the new followers of the "true God," Christians and Muslims, would condemn the Jews and each other by the same laws. Within these religions, various sects and divisions would arise, and each would persecute the other based on this shared intolerance. The "heathen," of course, would suffer at the hands of all three. Entire cultures and nations would be exterminated in the name of Yahweh, Allah, and various other aliases.

After the first five books, Scripture takes on a pseudo-historical narrative. For example, Joshua, Judges, Samuel, and Kings tell of events from the invasion of Canaan to the return from Babylon in an idealised manner.

Reigns are rounded off to multiples of 10, miracles proliferate, and there is much prophesying after the fact. From the reign of David onward, these accounts roughly follow the actual history of the region. Inaccuracies and inconsistencies abound, as the scribes were less concerned with historical precision or chronological integrity. Their primary purpose was to recite a moral tale. Non-sequential events were often grouped together to deliver an ethical message.

For priests, it was not the historical occurrences that interested them. They were concerned with how events sat in the context of a narrative that foreshadowed their present condition. Where necessary, they revised the texts to better serve this purpose. Theology trumped historical truth when the need arose.

The final books of what was later called the Old Testament (broadly similar to the Jewish Tanakh) are prophetic. Isaiah, Jeremiah, Ezekiel, Micah, and many others lament the present state of the Jews and ponder the sins that brought about this condition. They prophesy in vengeful terms the coming of a leader, a messiah, who would exact bloody revenge on the enemies of the chosen people and force the world into submission.

Apologists have argued that these scriptures were a simple set of laws for a simple people—a guideline for society in its immaturity. The implication is that humankind was not yet ready for a more sublime doctrine. However, this idea fails serious scrutiny when placed in the context of fifth-century BC philosophy. The ideas of Confucius in China, Buddha in India, and nearer to home, the Greek philosophers demonstrate a level of enlightened thinking independent of the scriptures.

Early writers of the Bible seemed unaware of these philosophies. Their horizon encompassed the Euphrates and the Nile, beyond which they knew little. Phrases such as "King Solomon was greater in riches and wisdom than all the other kings of the earth"[130] betray an ignorance of technologies and wealth exceeding their own. Far from being divinely inspired, the Tanakh reflects the preoccupations and superstitions of an insular tribe that saw the world in terms of their destiny in it. They revelled in a mythical past where violence brought them a measure of power at a provincial level and gave them a feeling of invincibility for a time.

NEW CONQUERORS

Yahweh's pledge to the chosen people that their borders would extend "from the Red Sea to the Mediterranean Sea, and from the desert to the Euphrates River"[131] and that He "will grant peace in the land ... and no one will make [them] afraid"[132] remained unfulfilled despite their reverence. The Jews retained control over a small part of the Promised Land, subject to payment of tribute to their Persian overlords. When Alexander the Great defeated the Persians in the fourth century BC, they paid tribute to their Greek masters.

The god they worshipped had no power to keep His promise. Belief in the covenant has both sustained and blighted them to the present day. Yet away from the Jerusalem elite and its inflexible prophets, a different kind of Judaism survived and prospered.

The Jewish diaspora in Egypt, who had ignored Jeremiah's rantings, went about their lives independent of the interfering priests in Jerusalem. They observed the obligatory rituals, after a fashion, rubbed shoulders with the Gentile unbelievers, intermarried with them, and prospered. When it suited, they appealed to the local courts rather than the Jewish court. Egyptian law was more liberal on many matters. For example, women had rights of inheritance that Mosaic law prohibited. To the chagrin of the holy men in Jerusalem, Jews even built their own temples, sometimes close to those of the heathen. This was in defiance the fundamentalists, who would not tolerate temples outside the Holy City.

Jews had primarily entered Egypt as mercenaries in the service of the pharaoh. Later, they served the Persian invaders during a brief period when the latter empire held sway. This caused resentment among the native Egyptians, provoking retribution when the Persians were forced to withdraw. But they endured, and the antipathy subsided.

Jewish merchants established commercial networks across the eastern Mediterranean, trading with the emerging Greek city-states. When Alexander the Great eventually conquered the Persian Empire, they and their fellow Jews in the Levant came under the control of the various Greek successor regimes. This included the Ptolemaic dynasty based in Alexandria, Egypt, and the Seleucid dynasty of Mesopotamia and Syria.

Whether Ptolemaic or Seleucid, the Jews were now firmly within the Greek Hellenistic sphere of influence. In Alexandria and elsewhere, they followed Greek fashion in clothing and children's names. Houses of prayer imitated a Greek architectural style that was later reflected in synagogue design. They noted that the numerous gods of the westerners were as jealous and haughty as Yahweh, though not quite to the level of denying each other's existence. In times of friendship and in the interests of diplomacy, Greeks and Jews assured each other that Yahweh and Zeus were the same, though the Jews might secretly whisper that if that were so, then Zeus surely preferred the chosen people.

The pretence did not extend to philosophical matters. Here lay a chasm. Where Greek texts explored the human condition, the Jewish writings invoked fearful submission. Some learned Jews immersed themselves in the philosophy of their overlords and attempted to rationalise the Scriptures. Among these was Aristobulus of Alexandria and his successor Philo, the latter seeking allegorical rather than literal interpretations in the Scriptures. They got short shrift from the literalists, to whom the word of God meant precisely what it said on the script. Yet Greek thought ultimately found its way into later writings and subsequently played a part in Yahweh's theology, adding more confusion than clarity, as will be seen. The Greek baby had entered holy bathwater and would not be removed.

The inspiration was not one way only. Ptolemy II invited Jewish scholars to Alexandria to translate the Hebrew Scriptures into Greek. Known hereafter as the Septuagint, this later formed the basis of the Christian Greek Old Testament.

Things were not so good back in Palestine (from "Philistia," the Greek name for the lands west of the river Jordan), where the Seleucids held sway, despite many Jews sharing the Hellenistic outlook of their overlords. An uneasy relationship existed between rulers and ruled, sometimes friendly, sometimes hostile. The Seleucids were impatient with the traditionalists and the singular exclusiveness of their worship, precluding Gentiles from entering the temple, for example. They would have preferred a more Hellenistic approach, where temples were open to all and the gods were not taken too seriously, except by the superstitious. Wisely, the Seleucids refrained from imposing their views, at least for a while.

Any resentment felt by traditionalist Jews was kept beneath the surface for the most part. Yet they fumed as their Hellenist brethren supported Seleucid reforms and "repudiated the holy covenant." That all changed in the reign of Antiochus IV.

It started with a bidding war between two ambitious rivals, Jason and Menelaus, for the position of high priest. The beneficiary of their largesse was the king. For a while, Jason had the upper hand. He sought to make Jerusalem a polis, essentially a Greek city where the inhabitants, or at least those with land and means, could call themselves citizens and have a say in the administration. Naturally, this was popular with those who had land and means.

Menelaus was having none of this—and not for any religious or ideological motive. He was not opposed to the new policies. He just wanted power and was willing to pay a higher price than Jason to get it. The grateful king accepted the bribe. Jason was deposed and fled across the Jordan River for safety.

Once in power, Menelaus proved a trifle heavy handed. He set about building a citadel for the Seleucid troops and, in the process, demolished some dwellings, not a popular move in a very crowded city. A riot ensued, and word of the unrest reached the ears of Jason, who made preparations and bided his time.

Meanwhile, a rumour spread that Antiochus IV, who was engaged in a military campaign in Egypt, had suffered defeat and was dead. Seizing the moment, Jason crossed the Jordan River with a small force.

Ever the opportunist, the one-time Hellenist now revealed himself as the champion of the Jewish faith and defender of the common people. His troops took the city and, with help from the mob, massacred the Greek garrison and any Jewish collaborators they found. It was a severe miscalculation. Though defeated in Egypt, Antiochus IV was very much alive and in a raging fury.

He marched on the city and exacted brutal revenge on the inhabitants. Thousands perished or were sold into slavery. Proclamations were issued against the reading of the Torah, observance of the Sabbath, circumcision, and other rituals of the Jewish faith. An "abomination of desolation,"[133] probably just a Greek altar, was installed in the temple. Jason, the instigator of the disaster, fled once again and died alone in exile.

ANOTHER MESSIAH

At that crucial moment, the long-awaited Messiah appeared in the form of Judas Maccabeus. The timing was opportune, as the Seleucids, overstretched and fighting enemies on all sides, were in decline. Jewish rebels reconquered their old territories and new ones to boot, pushing the boundaries of an independent kingdom beyond the borders of ancient Judah and Israel. The sacred Scriptures, including the writings of the long-dead prophets Jeremiah and Daniel, were reinterpreted and re-edited to foretell such events. Those Hellenistic Jews who survived the rebel onslaught kept a low profile.

The first two books of the Maccabees, which describe this period, are counted among the Septuagint and the Catholic and Orthodox Old Testaments. Written in the epic style of Homer and Euripides, they highlight the defeat of the Greeks on the battlefield while betraying the mark of their influence.

The Hasmonean dynasty, as it became known, did not work out. Maccabean kings proved to be no friends to orthodoxy. They assumed the title of high priest, mixing secular and priestly power. This challenge to Mosaic tradition did not endear them to the priestly class nor to purists who reserved kingship for the family of David. The Maccabean kings might have gotten away with it if not for their corruption and greed, which offended the common people. Yet the dynasty endured more than a century until the arrival of the new kids on the block.

Having conquered the remaining Seleucid province of Syria and dispatched Cleopatra, the last Ptolemaic regent in Egypt, the Romans were ready to take Palestine, as indeed they did. In 63 BC, after a successful siege, General Pompey entered the city and the temple. The Jews were once again under the yoke of a foreign power. They were allowed their own ruler, Herod Agrippa, but real power rested on the banks of the Tiber.

Roman lordship offered peace, stability, and even prosperity for some. During this period, the second temple was renovated as a magnificent structure under the patronage of King Herod. The Romans generally adopted a tolerant approach to religion, permitting the conquered peoples to practise whatever faith they followed. In return, they expected similar respect towards their gods, observance of the law, payment of taxes, and service in the armed forces. For many throughout the empire, that was an acceptable trade-off.

For die-hard Jews, this involved compromise with non-believers—not an option for the righteous: "Do not make a covenant with them or with their gods."[134] They would neither tolerate any other religion, for Yahweh was "a jealous god,"[135] nor allow non-Jews, "with their detestable practices,"[136] to partake in theirs.

Like the Seleucids before them, the Romans regarded the Jews as an awkward subject race. Despite their refusal to serve in the army, intolerance in matters of religion, and reluctance to pay taxes (a reluctance hardly unique to the Jews), they were nevertheless given some latitude. Julius Caesar exempted them from armed service and designated Judaism a *religio licita* ("permitted religion"). Up to the reign of Caligula, no attempt was made to force Roman religious observance on them.

But simmering resentment mounted in Palestine. Dogma did not allow the most devout Jews the latitude to explore new ideas or embrace the varied cultures of the empire. Instead, it bred anxiety and greater introspection. Had not the Scriptures warned them about this? If they strayed once again, what would be the consequences? Yet they were the chosen people—why had God abandoned them to the heathen?

This latter question had troubled the Jews for several hundred years, since the destruction of Israel and Judah and the early days of their vassal state. Later books of the Bible reflect this concern. From Isaiah onward, prophets lamented the condition of the chosen people, admonishing them for the sins that reduced them to this state and foretelling a day when they would be victorious again as in the days of Joshua and David.

Prophets foretold that the lands of their enemies would be laid waste and the Jews would rule over them: "They will make captives of their captors and rule over their oppressors."[137] A bloody conflict would herald this new age: "The Lord is coming with fire";[138] "for with fire and with his sword the Lord will execute judgment on all people, and many will be those slain by the Lord."[139] The enemies in this conflict would be the non-believers, the Gentiles: "Those who consecrate and purify themselves to go into the gardens [i.e., pagans], following one who is among those who eat the flesh of pigs, rats and other unclean things—they will meet their end together with the one they follow."[140]

The slaughter would be great: "The mountains will be soaked with their blood."[141]

Following this great victory, a reign of peace would last forever on Earth, during which time the "wolf will live with the lamb."[142] The Gentiles would be pillaged by the faithful: "You will feed on the wealth of nations."[143] "You will drink the milk of nations and be nursed at royal breasts."[144] And Gentiles would be forced to submit to their new Jewish masters: "They will bow down before you with their faces to the ground; they will lick the dust at your feet."[145] They also would be reduced to slavery: "Strangers will shepherd your flocks; foreigners will work your fields and vineyards."[146]

To lead this great war, a new king would be born of the house of David: "The virgin [young woman] will conceive and give birth to a son, and will call him Immanuel."[147] This king would sit on the throne of David and reign on an earthly kingdom that would last forever.

As it was during the Seleucid era, thoughts of a messiah resurfaced. Holy men reminded themselves of Jeremiah's prediction that a king would arise from the house of David and "reign wisely and do what is just and right,"[148] and that "Jerusalem will be holy; never again will foreigners invade her."[149] As for the Gentiles, they would reap the consequences! "The remnant of Jacob [i.e., Jews] will be among the nations, in the midst of many peoples ... like a young lion among flocks of sheep, which mauls and mangles as it goes."[150] "I will take vengeance in anger and wrath on the nations that have not obeyed me."[151] "They will lick dust like a snake. ... They will come trembling out of their dens; they will turn in fear to the Lord our God and will be afraid of you."[152]

Prophet after prophet repeated the message. Nahum, Habakkuk, Zephaniah, Haggai, and Obadiah all foretold the Lord's vengeance against the nations of the earth, the rise of Israel, and a period of peace when the Jews would lord it over the Gentiles. The Messiah would live in Jerusalem, and those nations that did not come to pay homage to him would "have no rain."[153]

Malachi foretold that Elijah would appear to herald this momentous event: "I will send the prophet Elijah to you before that great and dreadful day of the Lord comes."[154]

Christians later interpreted these messages not as a conquest of the Gentiles but rather as their inclusion into the family of Yahweh. Yet it is difficult to reconcile this analysis with prophecies that speak of a violent conflict in which the Gentiles are beaten into submission by the Jews: "You will break to pieces many nations."[155]

These beliefs sustained the devout in a fantasy world for centuries. Waiting for the Redeemer to lead them in a war of domination, they remained culturally aloof from the rest of humankind. But the dream created a dilemma. The contrast between prophecy and reality was stark. The ideal future, when "I will place over them one shepherd, my servant David [i.e., the house of David] and he will tend them,"[156] so that "they will live safely, and no one will make them afraid,"[157] seemed a long way off. After hundreds of years, domination by the heathen continued with no end in sight. The Jews had been promised so much and had so little. The little they had was not even under their control.

THE SEEDS OF REBELLION

The northern province of Galilee became a hotbed for lawlessness and insurrection. Two uprisings, the first led by Ezekias "the Brigand" and a later one by Judas the Galilean, rumoured to be his son,[158] were suppressed violently. Other smaller revolts were crushed as simmering discontent prevailed in the region.

In Jerusalem, a power struggle for control of the temple and different views on the nature and protocol of religious observance that emerged following its reconstruction continued into the first century BC.

Different interpretations of the Scriptures spawned several opposing factions within Judaism. Among these factions were the Sadducees, a social elite who played a significant role in the priestly functions at the temple. Many were descended from the Babylonian exiles and formed a kind of governing aristocracy within Jerusalem. They rejected oral traditions and any beliefs not explicitly mentioned in the Scriptures. Like all privileged peoples, they accepted the political status quo, fearing that opposition to Roman rule would put their religious freedom at risk.

The second, smaller group was the Pharisees, who demanded strict adherence to the rituals set down in the Torah. Although some Pharisees served in the temple, their worship was primarily community based. They frequently clashed with the Sadducees due to their scholarly interpretation of the Scriptures. The high priests restricted themselves to a literal reading of the written word. Unlike the Sadducees, the Pharisees believed in an afterlife. On matters of ritual, they were meticulous to an absurd degree. Working within communities brought the Pharisees closer to the ordinary Jews, and consequently, they became more popular than the lofty priests.

The temple became the focus of discontent for the poor provincials. Reduced to grinding poverty by heavy Roman taxes, they resented the wealthy priests who supported the status quo. These priests helped maintain the oppressive imperial system and profited greatly from it. Zealots, who wished to overthrow Roman rule, and religious purists, who felt that the Sadducees had defiled the Holy City by their compromises with Rome, all contributed to the discord. Others thought the temple had been tainted and should no longer be a centre of worship.

This latter view was shared by the third religious group, the Essenes. Most lived in smaller communal groups in Judah's towns and cities, relinquishing private property and preparing for the end of days.

An extreme faction left Jerusalem and set up a secluded community in Qumran near the Dead Sea. Despising both Sadducees and Pharisees, they led a strict life of ritual and learning. Placing great ceremony in the cleansing power of water, they regularly immersed themselves for purification.

The parchments they used were discovered in 1942 in local caves. These Dead Sea Scrolls, as they became known, were multiple versions of the Scriptures, some of which were edited and changed. One document, the War Scroll, included detailed preparations for a military campaign. The Essenes believed that a messiah would lead them in battle against the forces of darkness. After crushing their enemies underfoot, they would set up the kingdom of God on Earth.

The religion fashioned by Nehemiah, Ezra, and later prophets, complete with mythical origins and borrowed ideas, had given the Jews a unique identity. The temple had been replaced by Scripture written on parchment made holy by His words. It set them apart from the other peoples of the Roman Empire. At the same time, it set them at loggerheads with each other over scriptural interpretation and policy towards their various conquerors. Their religion united and divided them all at once. Oh, how difficult it was to discern the will of God!

Cosmopolitan Jews scattered throughout the empire and loyal to, if not entirely enamoured with, the prevailing powers saw their influence decline in the face of growing militancy.

Even the most inept prophet could see the dark clouds gathering on the horizon. By the end of the first century AD, the battle anticipated by the Essenes of Qumran came to pass as they perished in bloody insurrection against Rome. The obsessive faith that fuelled their passion, confined as it was to a distant province of the empire, might have died with them, consigned to oblivion by Roman arms. But a series of events caused their faith, or a version of it, to emerge from this backwater and engulf the empire that conquered it.

They had fashioned a myth to sustain their identity and, with it, the hope of messianic deliverance. But here lay a snare. What if the next messiah, when he appeared, did not deliver them from foreign grasp but instead condemned them to greater privation?

4

IS THIS THE ONE?

ONE MIGHT HAVE expected the Messiah, when he appeared, to be of noble blood and well versed in the scriptures. Indeed, he must hail from the house of David as foretold by the prophets and be a Judean by birth. These were essential prerequisites. A scholar, perhaps a high priest or even a Pharisee, would be advantageous.

What if he were none of those? Then, of course, he must be rejected. No one would take such a person seriously. Or would they?

In parallel with the learned scholars and prophets of the Jewish faith, others played a more charismatic role. Derided by sages and priests, these holy men were usually of humble circumstances, living frugally and sharing their meagre possessions with the poor. Popular among the common folk, they performed "miracles," healed the sick, and cast out demons. Some preached, prophesied, and censured the wayward, warning that the "day of the Lord is at hand," reminiscent of the book of Zephaniah centuries earlier. Some claimed to be the Messiah.

It is perhaps easy to dismiss such men as charlatans, drifting from town to town with disciples in tow, freeloading off the affluent and the witless. But in a society devoid of physicians, ignorant of the cause of disease, exposed to the vagaries of climate, and rooted in superstition, they offered hope and perhaps some diversion. Ancient and not-so-ancient cultures abound with faith healers, medicine men, shamans, witch doctors, and the like.

Some were mentioned by a noted historian of the day, Flavius Josephus. Among them was Hanina ben Dosa, a "caring and compassionate man"[159] born near the town of Nazareth. Like most Galileans, his faith centred around prayer and good works rather than the Torah. According to Josephus, he cured the sick, performed exorcisms, brought rain in times of drought, fed the hungry, spent time teaching children, and attracted a group of faithful disciples.

Others, like Honi the Circle Drawer, could bring rain. Apollonius of Tyana healed the infirm, the blind, and the lame and raised a young girl from the dead. Simon ben Yohai cast out demons.

A VOICE CRYING IN THE WILDERNESS

Another such man was John, who began preaching in the backwoods of Perea, close to the river Jordan. Dressed in camel hair, eating locusts and wild honey, John lived a life of fasting and abstention in the desert. His practice of immersing himself and his followers in water for ritual purification in the manner of the Essenes earned him the title "the Baptist." As his reputation grew, so did the crowds who came to hear his words. This caused disquiet in higher places.

From 4 BC to AD 39, Herod Antipas governed the northern Palestinian province of Galilee and the eastern province of Perea as autonomous regions within the Roman Empire, paying tribute to Rome but otherwise relatively independent from it. Herod was dubbed "the Fox"[160] due to his perceived deviousness.

The Fox struggled to contain the social unrest in his domains, especially his northern province. The independent-minded Galileans "inured to war from their infancy"[161] vowed to serve no master but God and always seemed willing to fight.

Anxious to avoid conflict or give the Romans an excuse to impose direct rule, Herod was determined to root out any potential unrest before it had time to develop. Although the Baptist did not advocate an uprising, Herod feared his growing popularity might make him a focus for seditious groups and a challenge to his authority. Crowds were, in Josephus's words, "aroused to the highest degree by [the Baptist's] sermons."[162] The Fox watched with concern.

Among those who came to hear the preacher was a man called Jesus. Hailing from the village of Nazareth, he had a mother called Mary, four brothers, and several sisters. Early accounts do not mention a father.[163] By trade he was a *tektōn*, a woodworker or builder, and like most peasants in Galilee, he was most likely illiterate.

John's preaching had a profound effect on Jesus. The Baptist spoke of repentance and the remission of sins. He urged his followers to lead righteous lives and practise justice towards their fellow men and piety towards God.

Inspired, Jesus was baptised and spent some time in the wilderness, fasting and praying. This process of self-denial and deprivation favoured by ascetics often led to a semi-delirious state that they equated to a spiritual experience. Jesus reputedly entered such a state. Once initiated, he remained a disciple of the holy man. What drove him to this lifestyle is not known, but there is evidence of a rift with his family.[164]

Meanwhile Herod, fearing the Baptist's growing influence, decided to act. He had John imprisoned in Herod's fortress at Machaerus, east of the Jordan River, and eventually secretly executed. Popular belief[165] blamed his execution on Herod's wife Herodias and her daughter, Salome. In this colourful story, Salome demanded John's head on a platter as a reward for an exotic dance she performed at Herod's birthday banquet. John had publicly rebuked Herod for marrying the wife of his half-brother, which the Scriptures forbade. However, Tiberius, where the banquet was held, was many miles from John's prison, and it's unthinkable that an aristocratic woman would dance in front of guests, a task reserved for prostitutes and slaves. The story seems to be an adaptation of an earlier tale involving the Persian monarch Ahasuerus (probably a reference to Xerxes).[166]

JESUS GOES IT ALONE

Following the arrest of his mentor, Jesus decided to take the Baptist's message to the countryside of Galilee. He was initially accompanied by other disciples of John and later gathered a small core of followers. Scriptures assigned him 12 apostles to coincide with the symbolic 12 tribes of Israel.

Like the itinerant holy men of his time, Jesus moved from town to town preaching, casting out evil spirits, and healing the sick. He appeared to have considerable oratorical flair and delivered his message in simple parables like a storyteller. The underlying doctrine was John's uncompromising message of self-sacrifice and asceticism, though some of his pronouncements bordered on the absurd. Examples include "Let the dead bury their own dead,"[167] and the impractical "Turn the other cheek."[168]

Gradually, the emphasis of his preaching changed and became more self-focused. He mixed the new doctrine of John with the old Jewish faith, making repeated references to the Scriptures and particularly to passages relating to a messiah. "Repent!" he warned, for "the kingdom of God is near."[169]

Whatever the preaching, the practice was less abstentious. Taking advantage of his new-found notoriety, Jesus abandoned the frugal ways of the Baptist. He indulged the hospitality of "publicans and sinners," feasting and drinking in their company. This earned him some criticism and an unfavourable comparison with John.[170] It also caused disquiet to the Baptist while he was still living. From his prison confinement, he asked his followers to investigate.[171] When criticised for this behaviour, Jesus explained that he was above such matters.[172]

News of Jesus's activities reached his family, who felt he had gone mad or perhaps were just embarrassed by his conduct. They made an unsuccessful attempt to drag him back home.[173] When his wanderings eventually took him to his hometown, the charisma that beguiled the rest of Galilee had no effect. The locals, knowing Jesus well, were quite offended at his conceit: " 'Isn't this the carpenter? Isn't this Mary's son and the brother of James, Joseph, Judas and Simon? Aren't his sisters here with us?' And they took offense at him."[174] Jesus became bitter at their rejection: "A prophet is not without honour except in his own town, among his relatives and in his own home,"[175] he lamented.

If John had wished to restrain his disciple, his execution put paid to that. When news of the Baptist's death filtered to the outside world, it created panic among his followers, who, Jesus included, took refuge in the desert.[176] But the expected purge did not materialise.

Using the fishing village of Capernaum on the Sea of Galilee as a base, Jesus soon resumed his wandering, preaching sermons, exorcising demons, and drawing crowds. Wherever he went, the sick received him with hope and reverence. To these audiences, he continued his moralistic stories for those with "ears to hear,"[177] those destined for salvation. Not to the uninitiated, though, who were "ever hearing but never understanding."[178] His followers included patrons, many of them women who helped provide for him "out of their resources."[179] One such woman was Mary Magdalene.[180]

Meanwhile, Herod was somewhat dismayed that a second version of John the Baptist (as he saw it) was now doing the rounds. "Was there any end to these prophets?" he must have wondered.

Jesus believed, like the Essenes, that the kingdom of God would occur in his lifetime:[181] "There are some standing here who will not taste death before they see the kingdom of God arrive with power."[182]

In this new realm, the poor would triumph over the rich and, as in Psalms 37:11 and recounted in Matthew 5:5, "the meek will inherit the earth." The masters of this new dominion would be the children of God: the Jews. When approached by a Greek woman who implored him to cast out a devil from her daughter, Jesus replied, "First let the children eat all they want ... for it is not right to take the children's bread and toss it to the dogs."[183] For "children" read "Jews," and for "dogs," read "Gentiles." Jesus's entreaty to "Love your neighbour as yourself" from Leviticus 19:18 appears to refer specifically to the Jewish people.

TENSION IN JERUSALEM

As the feast of the Passover approached, Jesus set off towards Jerusalem with some companions. Among these was Mary Magdalene, who was intensely loyal and perhaps enamoured with the preacher. Joining with other pilgrims, they took the circuitous route along the river Jordan to Jericho to avoid the territory of the hostile Samaritans.

The Galileans were isolated from their fellow Jews of Judah in southern Palestine by the province of Samaria, which lay between the two districts. This isolation contributed to the distinctive manner they adopted towards the rituals of the Torah. The Judeans, who, like the Samaritans, were under direct Roman rule, regarded the Galileans as rough and uncouth. For this reason, they treated them with disdain. The scribes who adhered to the Judean code criticised Jesus and his followers for their coarse habits and Galilean irreverence to the traditional rituals of their faith. Their bad habits included eating bread with unwashed hands[184] and plucking ears of corn from fields on the Sabbath. Jesus tended to respond aggressively to such criticism.

The Passover feast threw these disparate groups and all the other fractious religious and political elements in Roman Palestine together. As the multitudes flocked to the city, it created a tense time for the Jewish authorities.

Arriving in the evening at Bethany near the Holy City, Jesus and his companions found lodgings. The following morning, they made their way to the cauldron of tension that was Jerusalem. On the way, a hungry Jesus lost his temper with a fig tree because it had no fruit.[185] He either did not know or had forgotten that the fruit season was several months away.

Making his way to the temple, still in a foul mood, he launched a physical attack on the merchants and money changers who operated there. Goods for sacrifice could be purchased only with Judean shekels. For a fee, these men provided an exchange service and collected the half-shekel temple tax, while other merchants sold the necessary sacrificial offerings. Galileans resented the fact that their currency was not accepted, and Jesus was frustrated that the poor, of which he was one, could ill afford the required items.

The high priests were furious at Jesus's behaviour but were afraid to intervene. His actions must have proven popular among the teeming masses of impoverished pilgrims, enough to cause a sympathetic riot if the authorities moved against him. He had aroused their interest as a potential trouble-maker and might have been oblivious to the danger his actions had placed him in.

The following day, he re-entered the city and again made his way to the temple, preaching to those who would listen. Some of the priests approached and asked him by what authority he had acted the previous day. His reply was to ask them by what authority John had baptised: divine or human? It was a loaded question. The late holy man, who had been severely critical of the priests, was still loved by the poor, and a denial of his divine authority in the highly charged atmosphere might have been risky. They declined to answer and wisely withdrew.[186]

Jesus had now identified himself as a disciple of John the Baptist and a possible focus for his despondent followers. He had openly challenged the authority of the priests by attacking the traders in the temple and had shown an ability for populist agitation.

Later that day, the priests and their agents posed several questions designed to trap him or determine his ideological position. For example, was it right to pay taxes? A no answer would indicate subversion. His reply, "Give back to Caesar what is Caesar's and to God what is God's"[187]—in other words, "yes"—was compatible with the Sadducee stance on Roman rule. However, an alternative meaning might be that, while the coin should be returned to Caesar, the land of Israel should be returned to God.[188]

Either way, the answer did not mollify the priests. They probably feared an organised coup against their authority over the temple. Such a move was not inconceivable and would have some degree of support. The wealth of this aristocratic elite and their pro-Roman sympathies made them unpopular, but an attack would provoke swift Roman retribution. Whether their fears regarding Jesus were justified or not (and they might well have been), they decided to take no chances. The haste and ruthlessness of their next move was designed to quell any such revolt before it began.

ARREST AND INTERROGATION

The following day, Jesus again entered Jerusalem with his companions. He seemed unaware his life was in danger. This was the first day of the Passover, when it was customary to partake of an evening meal after the day's fast. It was to be his last supper.

After the meal, he and three companions, filled with wine and bread, made their way to the Mount of Olives. Here they were set upon by an armed troop of the high priest Caiaphas. A man called Judas, who was present at the earlier supper, identified Jesus in exchange for a bribe. A short struggle followed before the holy man was dragged away to the house of Caiaphas, where the Sanhedrin, the supreme council of the Jews, had been hastily assembled. Other than Peter, who had followed from a safe distance, Jesus's companions fled.

In this intimidating atmosphere, Peter, who had entered the servants' quarters, came under suspicion because of his Galilean accent. When challenged by a maidservant, he denied he was a follower and bade a hasty retreat. Jesus, now alone and abandoned, was interrogated, beaten, and ridiculed. His grilling led to the accusation of blasphemy,[189] which would have merited the immediate sentence of stoning to death.[190] Instead, the priests sent him the following morning to the office of Pontius Pilate, the Roman prefect (governor) of Palestine.

Here, various charges were presented, allegedly prompting the question from Pilate, "Are you the King of the Jews?" Jesus's reply was, "You have said it."[191] To the other charge, of refusing to pay tribute to Rome, he reputedly said nothing. Surprising, considering what he had earlier said about giving back to Caesar.

Despite the narrative, Pilate is unlikely to have been present to interrogate a lowly prisoner. He resided in Caesarea, the seat of Roman jurisdiction in Judah, and would typically be represented by an agent in Jerusalem. In any event, the prefect—or his agent—lost no time condemning the prisoner. The authorities wished to make an example of Jesus early in the festival to dissuade any further disruption by unruly elements. In this, they succeeded.

Jesus was handed over to the soldiers, who ridiculed him, placing a crown of thorns on his head and a purple garment on him. Purple was the colour worn by royalty. They mockingly called him King of the Jews. They then led him to the place of execution with two *lestai* (bandits), who also mocked him for his pretensions.

Here, all three were crucified. Atop each cross, the soldiers pinned the titulus delineating the charges for which they were condemned. For Jesus, the inscription read, "Jesus of Nazareth, King of the Jews," indicating the crime of sedition.

By now, all his companions had absconded, fearful of sharing his fate. Only the faithful Mary Magdalene remained, accompanied by two other women. One was Mary, the mother of James and Joseph, and the other was Salome. On the ninth hour of the day (3 p.m.), six hours after his crucifixion, the sad figure on the cross passed away.

A STRANGE TALE UNFOLDS

Here the story of Jesus would have ended, a minor player in a great drama, his life confined to a brief reference by Flavius Josephus in his book *Antiquities of the Jews*. Like the other failed messiahs before him, none of Jesus's prophecies came true. The kingdom of God did not arise, the Jews were not liberated from Roman rule, and the meek did not inherit the earth.

As a wandering holy man, he was overshadowed by the Hasidim, miracle workers such as Hanina ben Dosa or Apollonius of Tyana. As a preacher, he was seen primarily as a disciple of John the Baptist. His stage was a mere sideshow in the great empire of Tiberius. But in death, his status rose above that of his contemporaries. His memory would endure long after the great men of his day were forgotten.

This remarkable outcome is due in part to the actions of several unrelated individuals, who, over the coming centuries, would play a role in transforming the lowly *tektōn* into a symbolic leader of a powerful religion. The first such person was Mary Magdalene, from whom he had cast out seven devils.[192]

Possession by demons was an archaic rationalisation for mental illness. Exorcism was the cure. Whatever comfort Jesus had given the troubled woman, she became his most loyal friend. When others had absconded in his final hours, she was one of the few to remain.

Mary, with her companions, had followed the procession to the place of execution. This entailed some risk since associating with a dissident could have led to her arrest. Near enough to see the torment, too far to touch, and afraid to address him lest she was noticed, she watched helplessly as the man she loved slowly expired in the agony of crucifixion. From a safe distance, she kept vigil until he passed away.[193] Mary's account of what happened next unintentionally sets the first step in his deification.

Typically, crucified bodies were left rotting on the cross for some time as a visible warning to others before being dumped in the nearest ditch.[194] However, according to the Scriptures, a man called Joseph of Arimathea, "an honorable counselor"[195]—in other words, a member of the Sanhedrin who is not mentioned previously in the narrative—approached Pilate and requested the body to be handed over to him for burial in his own tomb.

This was highly unusual. Joseph must have had sufficient social standing to obtain an audience with the prefect of Palestine or his agent. He also had enough wealth to have his own tomb ready at short notice. (Jesus had been arrested only the previous night and was sentenced that morning.) Why would such a man decide to bury a poor peasant from Galilee who had arrived in town only a few days previously and had been executed for sedition? It was a hazardous undertaking.

A later explanation, that Joseph of Arimathea was a follower of Jesus who also awaited the kingdom of God, implies his support for a revolution against the privileged group to which he belonged.

How Mary, a Galilean, knew Joseph's name is not explained either. There was no record of communication between them. However, his action neatly fulfils the prophecy of Isaiah that "he was assigned a grave with the wicked, and with the rich."[196]

Joseph took possession of the body, wrapped it in linen, placed it in the tomb, and rolled a stone over the door. From a distance, Mary Magdalene and her friends watched the proceedings. It was now late at night; it would soon be the Sabbath, when it was forbidden to anoint the dead. She would have to return two days after the Sabbath to perform this duty.

On the third day, when she and her two companions returned, they were astonished to discover that the stone had been rolled back and the body was gone. In its place sat a young man who told them that Jesus had risen. Terrified, the women fled the scene and reportedly told no one.

Various explanations have been put forward for this account. The first is that Jesus was still alive when taken from the cross. The second is that the three women, frightened, traumatised, and witnessing the burial from a distance in the blackness of night, went to the wrong tomb. They were strangers to the area, after all.

The third explanation is that the corpse was originally left in Joseph's tomb because it was convenient. Since this was Joseph's tomb, the body would have to be moved to a different resting place before decomposition set in. Joseph might have gotten there and removed the body before Mary and her friends arrived.

The final explanation is that Mary or some later narrator made it up.

Whatever the real story, a rumour circulated in Jerusalem that the body of the crucified temple agitator had disappeared. And with the rumour grew an expectation that he had somehow not died but would reappear among the living. Was it a reckless conspiracy theory by desperate people or a harmless fabrication gone viral?

Whether Jesus had claimed to be the Messiah (according to later gospels he did make that claim, as we shall see, but he had no intention of being crucified), there were faint murmurs that he was God's chosen one. In hushed tones and hidden pockets of Jerusalem, clusters of despondent men and women assured each other that he must indeed be the Messiah despite his lack of qualifications for the role. They prepared to convert others to this view.

5

THE ONE WHO IS REMEMBERED

The story of the empty tomb eventually found its way to Galilee, where the friends of Jesus had fled.[197] They had good reason to hide. Their former mentor had been brutally executed for sedition, and their lives, by association, might be in danger. It was safer to lie low and let the dust settle.

Yet the mystery of the missing body cried out for an explanation, and soon the unlikeliest solution was adopted. The holy man had risen from the dead and would return to create the kingdom of God on Earth. He must therefore be the Messiah! Emboldened, some of his former associates gathered to prepare for his arrival. It was a risky undertaking.

A SUBVERSIVE CULT

Few records were kept during this period. Jesus's followers had little reason to keep them, believing his return was imminent. The early years of the emerging sect are therefore obscure. What is apparent is that a movement came into existence in Jerusalem that prepared itself for his arrival. It was headed by James the Just, brother of Jesus, and it included some of his former companions, his other brothers, and his mother, Mary. Whatever misgivings his family previously had concerning his preaching, they now embraced the radical ideas of their dead relative.

They formed themselves into a commune like the Essenes. Those who wished to join had to sell their property and share their wealth among the brethren. The sect probably consisted of no more than 100 persons, if even that. The Acts of the Apostles, written more than 50 years later, gives the number at 120, a multiple of the symbolic figures 10 and 12.

They observed the practices of their Jewish faith as set out in the Torah. They prayed in the temple, read the Scriptures, circumcised their boys, and ate in the prescribed manner. The ritual of baptism, a precondition for admission, was one of the few outward deviations from mainstream Judaism. Even that was not unusual.

They consisted of Galileans, who, like Jesus, were Aramaic speakers, as well as poor Hellenistic Jews who spoke Greek. Neither group understood classical Hebrew nor possessed a profound grasp of the Torah. This left them open to less orthodox ideas.

Their beliefs did not sit easily with more conventional Jews, especially the Sadducees, who made several attempts to stop the "unschooled, ordinary men"[198] from preaching in the temple. Like his brother, James savagely attacked the Sadducees and the Jewish elite for their oppression of the poor: "Look! The wages you failed to pay the workers who mowed your fields are crying out against you. ... You have lived on earth in luxury and self-indulgence."[199]

The earliest violence against them came from the priests and was directed mainly at Hellenistic Jews. Many of these were unemployed immigrants, impoverished by the downturn in economic activity when the grand building programme initiated by Herod I ended.[200] Their disdain for temple rituals set them apart from Orthodox Jews and made them easy targets. One of their number, a deacon called Stephen, became the first martyr when he was stoned to death for his deviant interpretation of the Scriptures and his anti-temple rhetoric.[201]

This event set the prelude for an organised purge against the Nazarenes, as they were called. An enthusiast in this campaign was a Pharisee called Saul. He went from house to house, arresting members of the sect, mainly the militant Hellenes. Some were subsequently put to death, causing panic among the faithful. Those who escaped the clamp-down fled the city and took refuge in various locations, including Samaria, Cyprus, Antioch, and Damascus. They settled in these places and began preaching their beliefs to the Jewish diaspora. If the purge was intended to stamp out the new heresy, it had the opposite effect. Having escaped Jerusalem, the doctrine spread among the Hellenistic Jews in regions beyond the reach of the Sadducees.

DIVISION

Around this time, the cult fell prey to the old dilemma: dissension. Frustration with the obstinacy of the Jews to conversion led some members to advocate the inclusion of Gentiles. The problem centred on the prerequisites for a messiah. The Nazarenes failed to convince their fellow Jews, especially the more learned ones, that their prophet filled the necessary requirements. First, he should be of the house of David, as foretold or implied by Isaiah, Ezekiel, Nathan, and Jeremiah. Jesus did not qualify.[202]

Second, the prophet Elijah would return before the Messiah's arrival, as foretold by Malachi: "See, I will send the prophet Elijah to you before that great and dreadful day of the Lord comes."[203] But Elijah had not returned.

Third, he would be born in Bethlehem: "But you, Bethlehem Ephrathah ... out of you will come for me one who will be ruler over Israel."[204] But he was from Nazareth.[205]

Finally, the Messiah should be born of a virgin: "Therefore the Lord himself will give you a sign: the virgin will conceive and give birth to a son, and will call him Immanuel."[206] Mary, his mother, with her many other children, was not a virgin, and, at any rate, she had given him the name Jesus, not Immanuel. The writers of the Septuagint had mistranslated the Hebrew *almah*, meaning "young woman" to the Greek word *parthenos*, which implies "virgin." Although this was not a prerequisite for Jews who understood the ancient texts, it caused much hand-wringing among the Hellenists who did not.

The Gentiles, not having the Scriptures to guide them, could more easily be persuaded that the life and death of Jesus were fulfilments of ancient prophecies. Before admittance, however, they had to undergo circumcision and follow the rites of the Torah. Essentially, conversion to Judaism was a precondition for entry into the Nazarene community. Moderates advocated a relaxation of this precondition, but to purists, this was anathema. As the debate raged, a new camp emerged. Discord turned to argument, then hostility, and finally to violence.

The breakaway group included their former persecutor Saul, known more commonly by the Greek version of his name, Paul. After converting to the new faith, he soon realised that the cult was doomed to oblivion if it did not widen its focus. In opposition to Paul was James, the brother of Jesus, who insisted that salvation was reserved for the chosen people. Peter, weak minded and open to manipulation, wavered between the two and sided with whichever party he happened to be with at the time. Eventually, this led to a clash between him and Paul.

A REBELLIOUS ATMOSPHERE

Conflicts within the embryonic religion were set against the backdrop of a growing crisis in Palestine. Following the death of Herod Agrippa, grandson of Herod I, the provinces he had ruled under Roman vassalage came under direct Roman control. These provinces, Samaria, Judah, Galilee, and Perea, were subsequently administered by a succession of incompetent and corrupt governors, often representing emperors of even greater ineptitude. Emperor Caligula, for example, precipitated a political crisis by attempting to have his statue erected within the temple walls. This constituted an abomination to the Jews and a violation of the first divine commandment. His assassination by the Praetorian Guard in AD 41 averted a crisis and convinced the Jews that God had intervened.

Roman meddling in the appointment of the high priest, together with penal taxation and rampant unemployment, created a mood for rebellion. It also sparked heightened speculation that the coming of a messiah was imminent. Indebted peasants abandoned their holdings and swelled the ranks of the urban unemployed. Various factions emerged with unique grounds for sedition. Zealots prowled the countryside, stirring revolt. Sicarii assassins carried daggers beneath their cloaks and scoured the city streets, delivering swift justice to Romans and their sympathisers.

More would-be messiahs emerged. One promised to divide the Jordan River; another incited unrest in Jerusalem; two others engaged in lawless raids in Galilee and Judah. These are mentioned in the Acts of the Apostles or Josephus's *The Jewish War*. Most, like Jesus, suffered the terminal fate of seditionists under Roman law.

Josephus also mentions another Jesus, son of Ananias, who prophesised doom. He was arrested by the Romans. After torturing him, they decided he was a maniac and expelled him from the city. He continued preaching in the countryside, crying, "Woe to Jerusalem, woe to the people and woe to the temple,"[207] and finally perished during the coming uprising when struck by a stone from a ballista.

All these "deceivers and deluders of the people, under the pretence of divine illumination,"[208] together with Zealots and Sicarii, prepared their followers for the "great and dreadful day" to come.[209] Intense debate raged about the right preconditions for such an event and which of the competing parties were qualified to lead it. The Nazarenes were among the contenders. Their prophet was ready to return from the dead, and there would be no salvation for the rich in his new kingdom.

A FINAL PROVOCATION

Nothing could suppress the growing mood of discontent, however. It just needed a spark, which was duly provided by yet another incompetent Roman prefect, Gessius Florus. When he confiscated silver from the temple to compensate for unpaid taxes, the revolt of AD 66 began.

Rebels swept across the land. They overthrew the Roman garrisons and set up their administration, complete with coinage stamped with the year one. Nero sent his general, Vespasian, to quell the revolt. Leading an army of 60,000, Vespasian crushed all opposition in Galilee and prepared to move against the rebel strongholds of Judah.

In Jerusalem, the defenders were divided into various factions, all engaged in vicious infighting. Victims of their own fanaticism, they quarrelled over the Scriptures even as the Roman army approached. Anyone who spoke of surrender or tried to escape was killed. According to Josephus, as many as 500 were crucified in a day.

Meanwhile, back in Rome, faced with growing opposition to his reign, Nero took his own life, prompting a struggle for succession. Vespasian hastened back to join the contest, leaving his son Titus behind to undertake the siege, which began in AD 70.

Within Jerusalem's walls, the rival factions finally stopped quarrelling and agreed to face the enemy together. Partisans of both sexes resolved to fight rather than surrender and inflicted considerable damage on their attackers—all in vain. After a brutal six-month struggle, the legions burst through the defences and exacted terrible revenge. "Neither persuasion nor threat could check their impetuosity ... everywhere was slaughter and flight."[210] Alongside rebels and militants, the troops butchered the peaceful and unarmed.

As the last remaining Zealots fought to the death in front of the temple, the structure was set alight either by the attackers trying to take it or the defenders trying to prevent them. Amid the flickering flames, the bodies of the dead piled around the altars, and rivers of blood flowed down the sanctuary steps. Eventually, the Romans emerged triumphant and subdued all resistance.

Those who had survived starvation and the ensuing massacre were sold into slavery. The city and temple were razed to the ground, houses were reduced to rubble, and "those places which were adorned with trees and pleasant gardens, now [became] desolate."[211] Determined to root out any future sedition, the Romans obliterated any physical trace of the Jewish faith.

Later, in AD 130, Emperor Hadrian attempted to erase the city's very memory. During his reign, Jerusalem ceased to be a place of pilgrimage. He renamed it Aelia Capitolina and erected a new shrine to Jupiter atop the ruin of Yahweh's temple. All this he financed with Jewish taxes to symbolise the victory of the Roman God over its Jewish counterpart. This was the future that awaited the defeated city.

Meanwhile, sporadic resistance continued in eastern Palestine following the city's destruction. Within a few years, the revolt was over. The failure of the rebellion and the destruction of the temple created yet another watershed for the Jewish religion. The Zealots were exterminated, along with the numerous other seditious sects. And the temple's demolition ended the raison d'être for the Sadducees. That left two factions, Pharisees and Nazarenes.

The Pharisees survived because their ritual diet and observances focused on the home and synagogue rather than the temple. Their spiritual descendants were the rabbis who replaced the temple priests. These shepherds of the faithful laid the framework of the Jewish faith as it is practised today.

The Nazarenes, who resembled the Pharisees somewhat, survived because their prophet was executed at the behest of the temple priests. The temple's obliteration could be considered divine retribution against the same priests and their establishment. Unlike the messiahs who had perished in the revolt, this one had not. His earlier death ensured his absence. Many of his Hellenic followers, who were scattered in the earlier purges, were a safe distance from Jerusalem when the carnage took place.

The Aramaic-speaking disciples, who survived the siege, migrated across the Jordan River to Perea. Here they established a community, never mentioning their forlorn wait in the doomed city for the Messiah who never appeared.

The Pharisees and Nazarenes now competed for the hearts and minds of the chosen people. It was an unequal struggle. Apart from the few Hellenistic Jews, the Nazarenes had little impact on their co-religionists. They remained a tiny, uninfluential sect. The Jews, exhausted by their rebellion, had no stomach for yet another messiah. That included one returning from the dead, especially one who did not have the proper credentials.

CONFLICTING REPORTS

The first surviving written account of the life of Jesus was recorded around this time, 35 to 40 years after his crucifixion. Most witnesses to his life had passed away by then. This account would later be called Mark's Gospel (Greek *euangélion,* meaning "good news") and was probably partly based on an earlier account. Although Jesus is mentioned in the writings of St. Paul, which predate this story, Paul was more interested in interpreting the message than recounting the life of the holy man. Another early work, the Epistle of James, deals with the movement's ideology.

The opening line of Mark's Gospel, "the good news about Jesus, the *Son of God* [emphasis added]," underlines the context in which the cultists saw themselves. The Roman emperors referred to themselves as sons of God. The Jews also used the term to refer to a good or pious Jew. By using Roman terminology and style, the Nazarenes were setting themselves up as a counterforce to the empire. The Nazarenes were a subversive cult dedicated to revolution, and their battle would begin with the return of Jesus from the dead. However, since the failed uprising, they had tempered their message to avoid posing an obvious threat. Mark's Gospel reflects this by downplaying the radicalism of the earlier Epistle of James.

As with later gospels, the language used was Koinē Greek, the lingua franca of the Roman Empire. Koinē Greek was common among Hellenistic Jews but unfamiliar to the Galileans.

Mark's was the first and shortest gospel and is traditionally attributed to Mark the Evangelist. It begins with the conversion of Jesus by John the Baptist. It recounts Jesus's itinerant preaching, his warning that the kingdom of God was at hand, and his execution during Passover. The period from the outset of his mission to crucifixion takes one year, and the gospel ends with the two Marys and Salome fleeing from the empty tomb. Many years later, an addition was appended, Mark 16:9–20, introducing the idea of a resurrection. This appendage does not occur in the earliest manuscripts.[212] A later text gives Jesus a father called Joseph, also a *tektōn*, to allay rumours that Jesus's birth was illegitimate. Joseph is not mentioned in earlier accounts.[213]

Like most stories of its day, the account is full of miraculous events—healing of the sick and casting out of devils. At no point in the narrative does Jesus claim to be divine. In fact, he appears to deny any divinity.[214] Neither does he claim to be a messiah (although he infers the possibility), except once during his interrogation by the high priests. When they ask, "Are you the Christ?" (Greek *messiah*, "anointed one"), he answers, "I am."[215] Since this reply sealed his fate, we only have the word of the high priests that he gave that answer, Peter being too far away to have heard.

It is clear from this gospel that the kingdom of God is reserved for the Jews only. However, it acknowledges that Gentiles deserve kind treatment so long as they know their place.[216] The gospel also has Jesus prophesying the destruction of Jerusalem and its temple, much as Jesus, son of Ananias, had done. But this prophecy is made after the fact since the siege and capture had already occurred.

Written soon after the Jewish revolt, Mark's Gospel strives to distance Jesus from the charge of sedition. It achieves this by introducing the character Barabbas, a Zealot who had already engaged in an insurrection. Pilate offers an assembled mob the chance to grant amnesty to Jesus, but the crowd demands the release of Barabbas instead. "Why, what evil has he done?" pleads the governor. To this, they cry, "Crucify him!"[217]

Pilate was a ruthless governor who despised the Jews and their customs. According to Philo of Alexandria, his executions were so frequent that the Jews complained directly to the emperor.[218] It is improbable that such a man would offer to release a rebel who might be a future threat to Rome.

In any case, there is no historical record of such a custom, nor is there mention of Barabbas, whose name incidentally means "son of the father." The tale implies that the Romans did not consider Jesus a rebel, and Jews chose the son of a man in preference to the son of God.

The story contained enough gaps for the Pharisees to drive a herd of camels through. It did not meet the conditions prophesied for the coming of a messiah. Jesus was a Galilean peasant. He was not of the house of David, and the prophet Elijah had not reappeared on Earth, as already stated. Furthermore, the only witnesses to the incarceration in the tomb were three frightened and disoriented women who had seen events from afar and in the dark.

In the resurrection story (which, as stated, was inserted later), Jesus appears to the apostles as they sit together for a meal. He tells them to go, baptise, and preach to the world. He is then taken to heaven.

MORE CLARITY OR MORE DOUBT

The next surviving account of his life seeks to address these limitations. Written perhaps 10 to 15 years after Mark and attributed to Matthew, this story starts with a painstaking attempt to trace the lineage of Joseph, father of Jesus, through David and right back to Abraham himself, a span of 28 generations. This put Abraham's lifetime sometime after the actual historical death of David. It has Mary, a virgin, conceive by the Holy Spirit rather than by Joseph. Thus, Jesus becomes divine, making Joseph's ancestry irrelevant.

It gives Bethlehem in Judah as the birthplace of the infant Jesus, where he is visited by wise men who were guided there by a star. Herod the Great hears that a new king is born and orders a massacre of all male children under the age of two in the vicinity of the town. This sets the pretext for the family to flee to Egypt and return later to the safety of Nazareth in Galilee. Neither Herod nor his heir have jurisdiction there, thus justifying Jesus's Galilean address. However, there is no historical reference to Herod ordering a massacre of male children.

This account also gives a more elaborate explanation of the resurrection. "Many women" witness the crucifixion in addition to Mary Magdalene and two other Marys. Two of them are sitting opposite the sepulchre when Jesus is interred. The high priest, with approval from Pilate, places guards over the grave and later bribes them to say that the disciples carried the body away. These additions variously remove the doubt that the women got the wrong tomb or contrived the disappearance. It does not explain why the high priest would request a guard over the tomb in the first place. According to the gospel, even the apostles were not expecting Jesus to rise from the dead.[219] In fact, the final words of the dying Jesus, "My God, my God, why have you forsaken me?"[220] imply that his crucifixion was not part of any plan. Nothing in the Scriptures says the Messiah will suffer, die, and be resurrected from the dead. However, this does not prevent apologists from ascribing references in Psalms 16 and 22 and Isaiah 53 to a suffering messiah.

On the third day, in place of the young man, there is an angel who rolls back the stone and tells Mary Magdalene and her companion Mary that Jesus has risen. As the two women hurry away, Jesus suddenly appears and tells them to instruct the apostles that he will meet them in Galilee. Later, in Galilee, he instructs them to preach to all nations—presumably only to the Jews of all nations, since earlier in the same gospel, he had instructed them not to preach to heathens or Samaritans.[221]

As with Mark's Gospel, the ministry of Jesus takes one year, and salvation is reserved for the chosen people. Jesus is again quoted as prophesying events that occurred before the gospels were written: his betrayal, his execution, the story of the resurrection, the fall of Jerusalem, the destruction of the temple, and one event that does not occur—the end of the world within the lifetime of his listeners.[222]

But Matthew's Gospel was a poor attempt at covering the cracks in the messianic story, and the Jews were not buying it. The Nazarenes remained a minority sect. The Pharisees were winning the debate in the post-rebellion Jewish world. The gospels reflect this in the bitter recriminations Jesus makes against the Pharisees. Such arguments might never have occurred in his lifetime since very few Pharisees lived in Galilee. Disillusionment was creeping in, Jesus had not returned, and the Pharisees were getting stronger.

ANOTHER VERSION

Luke's Gospel is the third and last of the Synoptic (meaning "seen together") Gospels, which give a broadly similar account of the life of Jesus. Luke's story expands further on Matthew's and Mark's. Like Matthew's, it draws partially from Mark and partially from an earlier collection of the sayings of Jesus, a source known to scholars as Q. Now we are told that John the Baptist and Jesus are cousins. There is also the implication that John is Elijah in some form, thus fulfilling a messianic prerequisite. John is reduced to a lesser role, and Jesus is not baptised by him, nor does he become his disciple. These revisions seek to dispel the fascination Jesus held for John by reversing their actual relationship.

To explain how Joseph and Mary came to be in Bethlehem in Judah at the time of the birth, we are told it was necessary because Joseph, being of the house of David, needed to return there to register for the census. This presents an interesting picture of the poor *tektōn*, so keen to enrol himself for a taxation system his countrymen regarded as onerous that he travels from Nazareth in Galilee to the birthplace of his ancestors in Bethlehem. Not only that, but he drags his heavily pregnant wife along for the ride.

In fact, there was no obligation under Roman law for anyone to return to their ancestral homeland to register for a census.[223] The census referred to by Luke, the census of Quirinius, took place in AD 6, nine years after the death of Herod the Great, whereas Matthew and Luke have the birth of Jesus occurring during Herod's reign. In fact, there is doubt if such a census did actually take place.[224]

Much fanfare accompanied the birth, with shepherds, angels, and a heavenly host attending. After the infant's circumcision, the family returned to Galilee, not Egypt, as in Matthew's Gospel. One passage has the young Jesus reading aloud passages from the scriptures in the synagogues of Nazareth to awestruck listeners.[225] Jesus was almost certainly illiterate, and the small collection of mud huts that was Nazareth would not boast a synagogue.[226]

For the crucifixion, there are now many witnesses among Jesus's acquaintances. To overcome the problem that a woman's testimony would not be accepted in the Jewish courts of the time, Luke's story has Peter himself going to the tomb to verify it is empty, even though Peter was in Galilee, where he had fled after the crucifixion. Following his resurrection, Jesus appears to the apostles in Jerusalem, not Galilee, as in Mark and Matthew. He then ascends to heaven from Bethany.

All the gospels outline the seditious charges brought by the high priest. These include claiming to be King of the Jews and opposing the payment of taxes. However, during Jesus's interrogation, the Sanhedrin accused him of blasphemy,[227] something that would not have concerned Pilate. If he revealed a plot to seize the temple or any other alleged crime under interrogation, it is not mentioned—nor would it have been wise to repeat it in the gospels. The leader of a failed coup cannot be the Messiah, nor can one who makes confessions under torture.

Amid all these miracles—casting out demons, prophecies, and warnings of the imminent kingdom of God—there is a recurring theme in all the stories, expanded to its fullest in Matthew's Gospel. It advocates a brotherhood of sorts, sharing of wealth, and warnings against over-dependence on the material things of this life. This idea is central to the message of James the Just. It echoes previous scriptures and other outside influences prevalent at the time.

Between 272 BC and 230 BC, several hundred years after the death of Buddha, the Indian king Asoka reputedly sent missionaries to preach his doctrine. Their teachings are reflected in the gospels. Both Buddha and Jesus try out asceticism (Buddha in a Hindu monastery, Jesus with John the Baptist) and abandon it. Both fast for a period, one for 49 days, the other 40 days, during which time they endure temptation. Both appeal to the most vulnerable, criticise the shortcomings of priests of the old religion (Brahmins; Pharisees and Sadducees), and agree on women's equality (Buddha explicitly and Jesus implicitly), and both advocate selflessness.

But there the similarities end. The gospels use miracles and exorcism rather than reason to convert their listeners. While Buddha rejected the religion out of which his ideas developed (Hinduism), the gospels do not. Although Jesus criticises old laws "because your hearts were hard,"[228] he does not reject them. Quite the contrary. To convert the Jews to the new philosophy, the gospels and the Acts of the Apostles take great pains to point out that Jesus fulfilled the scriptures of the Old Testament and that he was a faithful observer of the ancient religion with its heaven and fiery judgement reserved for those who do not accept the word of God.[229]

The maxim "Do to others as you would have them do to you" in Matthew 7:12 and Luke 6:31 (BSB) emerged five centuries earlier in the writings of the Chinese philosopher Confucius.[230] Variations also appear in the Sanskrit *Mahabharata* of ancient India, in ancient Greek philosophies, and in the Persian Pahlavi texts of Zoroastrianism.[231]

While the influences of Zoroastrianism can be found in the Old Testament texts, an offshoot of that Persian religion, Mithraism, makes a singular mark on the gospels. When Mithra the Saviour was born, shepherds were present at his birth, and the rite of purification by water features in Mithraic rituals. Adherents practised brotherhood and humility, and their cult had found its way into the Roman Empire about 60 years before the gospels.

ALTERNATIVE ACCOUNTS

Other accounts of the life of Jesus, such as the Gospel of Philip, the Gospel of Thomas, and the radical Gospel of James, were written and rejected by the church when it catalogued the acceptable or orthodox versions in the fourth century. Among the accepted stories would be the Gospel of John, written long after the Synoptic Gospels and borrowing heavily from Greek philosophy. These four gospels (Matthew, Mark, Luke, and John) and other epistles and acts constitute the New Testament. Very little of this Testament is "new," and the inspiration does not appear to be divine.

A Roman called Celsus wrote an alternative account of the life of Jesus many years later. It is worth quoting an excerpt from it:

> He was born in a certain Jewish village, of a poor woman of the country, who gained her subsistence by spinning, and who was turned out of doors by her husband, a carpenter by trade, because she was convicted of adultery; that after

being driven away by her husband, and wandering about for a time, she disgracefully gave birth to Jesus, an illegitimate child, who having hired himself out as a servant in Egypt on account of his poverty, and having there acquired the arts of magic, on which the Egyptians greatly pride themselves, returned to his own country, highly elated on account of them, and by means of these declared himself a God.[232]

Celsus states that the real father of Jesus was a Roman centurion called Pantera.

The story is a rendition of the life of Jesus popular among Jewish opponents of the Nazarenes. Its reliability is therefore suspect, and it deserves to be treated with the same scepticism as the gospels themselves. But it reflects rumours about Jesus that were current in Palestine at the time.

An earlier and more impartial account comes from the hand of the great historian of the day. The author was the Jewish writer Flavius Josephus (mentioned in chapter 4), who was captured by the Romans during the revolt of AD 66. The significance is not what he says about Jesus but what he does not say. In *The Jewish War*, an account of events from the Maccabees up to and including the revolt of AD 66 and its aftermath, he fails to make any reference to Jesus at all. He finished the book around AD 78, somewhat coinciding with the time frame of the Synoptic Gospels.

Josephus's second great work, *Antiquities of the Jews*, was written around AD 93–94, when he was resident in Rome. He may have encountered the Nazarenes, who were active there. Through them, he would have learned about Jesus. Christians later altered parts of this book to enhance the prestige of their Messiah. Despite these forgeries, there is general agreement among scholars about which references formed part of the original text.[233]

Among those deemed authentic is a reference to Jesus as a "wise man" and "performer of paradoxical deeds" in Galilee ("paradoxical" meaning "impossible or miraculous"). Later, when referring to four misdeeds committed by Pilate, Josephus includes the sentence of crucifixion issued against Jesus, implying it was unjust.

Finally, on the execution of James by the Sadducees, Josephus refers to him as "the brother of Jesus, who was called Christ, whose name was James."[234]

These fleeting references to Jesus, when set against his longer passages on John the Baptist and other faith healers of the time, such as Hanina ben Dosa, show that Josephus considered him a relatively insignificant man who made little impact on the affairs of the time.

This flies in the face of the partisan accounts in the Synoptic Gospels (although it is close to the original Mark). It especially conflicts with the Gospel of John, which, as we will see later, portrays Jesus as a noteworthy prophet who engaged the attention of Sadducees and Pharisees and the adoration of multitudes. In reality, Jesus was hardly known outside Galilee. He only came to the attention of the temple priests following his altercation with the money changers. Had he been well known, there would have been no need for Judas to identify him with a kiss.[235]

A PARTING OF WAYS

Luke's Gospel highlights a split that had grown in the Nazarene community over the admission of Gentiles. Unlike Mark and Matthew, Luke opens the door to non-Jews. The phrase "a light for revelation to the Gentiles"[236] and the good Samaritan story represent the breakaway group's views.

Paul, the Nazarenes' new man and a friend of Luke, had begun a wide-ranging mission to convert the Gentiles. He was well equipped for the task. Unlike the Jerusalem apostles, he was literate and conversant in Greek[237] and Latin,[238] the two main languages of the empire. A new faith, Christianity, began to emerge. It was supported by Hellenised Jews and Gentiles who saw Jesus as a supernatural being because of his resurrection and elevated him to the level of a god in the Greek tradition. Through this faith and the efforts of Paul, Yahweh the war god would be introduced to the peoples of the world.

In Perea, the Aramaic Nazarenes comprising the original followers of Jesus and John the Baptist remained steadfast to the Torah and Mosaic law. With the temple gone, they prayed in the synagogue.

They rejected the virgin birth, believing that God chose Jesus to be the Messiah and that he was anointed by the Holy Spirit at his baptism. Apart from a shortened Aramaic version of Matthew, they rejected the gospels, the divinity of Jesus, and the later notion of a Trinity. In their view, the crucifixion of Jesus was not an atonement for the sins of humankind, Paul was a false prophet, and Peter was not the head of the church. Only the *desposyni* (blood relatives of Jesus and their descendants) were the legitimate apostolic successors.

They remained a small, isolated community caught between the growing Christian movement and reconstituted rabbinic Judaism. Rejected by both, their descendants, known as Ebionites ("the poor ones"), were confined mainly to Perea and the neighbouring districts of Palestine and Antioch. There they lived in relative obscurity, practising their faith, maintaining a vegetarian diet, and waiting patiently for the return of the man from Nazareth.[239]

Within 400 years or so, this tiny sect that preserved the original message of Jesus almost completely disappeared from the pages of history—but not without first imprinting their beliefs among the Arab tribes who roamed the deserts east of the Jordan River.

Their beliefs re-emerged as part of a new and virulent ideology in the seventh century. Then followers of Jesus were presented with a quandary. Which version of the crucified preacher should they believe in: the simple prophet from Nazareth or the anointed Christ? But this would be a question for later.

First, their nemesis Paul would take his unique version of Jesus to the world. In the process, he introduced the concept of a messiah to people unfamiliar with the term. His message, not the Nazarenes' message, would triumph against all expectations.

PART TWO

CHRISTIANS

"Think not that I am come to send peace on earth:
I came not to send peace but a sword."

—Matthew 10:34

6

GAMEKEEPER TURNED POACHER

THE DISCIPLES OF Jerusalem could never have imagined that their tormentor would become the champion of their new faith. After first persecuting the followers of Jesus, Paul hijacked their mission and rewrote their doctrine. From a narrow Jewish-centred creed, he transformed it into a universal faith for humanity. It was a bold move, with no guarantee of success.

A betting man at the onset of the first century AD would have given long odds on a heresy from Palestine becoming the supreme religion of the empire. The Christians, or Galileans, as they were also called, were merely a breakaway group from a heretical sect called the Nazarenes. And the Nazarenes were just a small part of a minority religion, Judaism.

Judaism itself was just one among a multitude of creeds such as the Egyptian cults of Isis and Serapis or the Persian cult of Mithras and a host of local divinities that the Romans embraced within their expanding borders.

By the third century AD, only one of these would prevail. The journey that took it there entered its next phase through the mission of Paul. This unlikely ambassador elevated the faith from its humble origins to a global religion.

Paul hailed from Tarsus in Asia Minor. Tent merchant by profession[240] and Pharisee by conviction, he was strong minded and energetic. In appearance, he was short of stature, bald, and bow legged.[241] In spite of this, he was also supremely self-confident. The fact that he never met Jesus or heard him speak did not restrain his passion, although his concept of the holy man was more abstract than human. Prone to long-winded sermons that sometimes sent his listeners to sleep,[242] he spread the new doctrine with the same fervour and certainty that he had previously devoted to its persecution.

His conversion was the result of miraculous intervention, rather than rational deliberation. As described in Acts, it happened en route from Jerusalem to Damascus, where he had intended to purge the Hellenistic Nazarenes who resided there.

First, a flashing light knocked him to the ground, then a voice of reproach cried, "Saul, Saul, why do you persecute me?"[243] Finally, he was struck blind. For three days, he lingered sightless in Damascus until his conversion to the new faith, much to the relief of the local Nazarenes. He repeated this story to incredulous Jews who had heard it all before,[244] and he was smuggled out of the city at night before they could stone him to death.

Using Antioch as a base, he embarked on three remarkable and exhausting journeys to spread his version of Jesus throughout Asia Minor, Greece, and the Mediterranean islands. He suffered hardship, shipwreck, and imprisonment. He sometimes experienced the hostility of his fellow Jews for preaching to the Gentiles, and in one incident, he faced the hatred of the Greeks for preaching the "Jewish doctrine."

Violence followed him everywhere. He was beaten and stoned several times and was once left for dead. Conversions varied from the many to the few. In some places, as few as one or two joined the new cult.

During his travels, he wrote endless letters, or "epistles," to the nascent communities he had established. Some epistles survive in edited form; others were written by his followers but attributed to him. With the support of Luke and other missionaries who accompanied him, he tirelessly followed up his mission by revisiting his converts or corresponding with them. Part of the groundwork was already set by Hellenistic Nazarenes who had gained conscripts among the Jews of Rome, Antioch, and Alexandria. They in turn spread the message in Ephesus and other towns of Asia Minor and Egypt.

CONFLICT WITH THE DISCIPLES OF JESUS

Paul was not interested in the ideas of Jesus and made no attempt in his early mission to meet with those who had seen him in the flesh. He was heavily criticised by the Jerusalem Nazarenes, especially James, for allowing non-Jews and the uncircumcised into the flock. Paul ignored their criticism and bullied Peter into accepting his policy. But Peter was an unreliable convert and wavered between both camps.[245]

Paul, ever confrontational, publicly attacked Peter in Antioch: "I opposed him to his face."[246] He accused Peter and his companions of spinelessness when they backed down after a delegation of Jerusalem Nazarenes confronted them.[247] This incident exacerbated the division. It was here in Antioch, according to Acts 11:26, that the term "Christian" was first used to describe the Pauline followers of Christ.

The second Epistle of Peter, written between AD 80 and 90, wherein he calls Paul "our beloved brother"[248] and implies that he eventually acquiesced to Pauline policy, is regarded by many scholars as a forgery.[249] Peter was dead by then, having expired sometime between AD 64 and 68. In any case, he was probably illiterate and could not speak Greek.

Paul was brutally critical of the Nazarenes for insisting that Gentile converts be circumcised and conform to Judaic law. His language in various epistles is strident: "Watch out for those dogs, those evildoers, those mutilators of the flesh."[250]

The Jerusalem church countered Paul's missionary work by dispatching preachers of their own to the communities he had converted. Upon arrival, the missionaries urged them to conform to the Jewish rituals. Paul bitterly describes them as "false apostles, deceitful workers," comparing them to Satan masquerading as an angel of light.[251] As the conflict intensified, he was twice recalled to Jerusalem to answer their accusations.

On the first occasion, a resolution between the opposing camps seems to have been reached at a special council. However two versions of the event, Luke's in Acts 15 and Paul's in Galatians 2, differ somewhat. Both versions point to an amicable solution. According to Paul's, the council agreed to separate missions—Peter to the Jews and Paul the Gentiles. James the Just is shown to have conceded that Gentile converts could be exempted from circumcision provided they adhered to the Jewish dietary laws and refrained from worshipping idols or committing adultery. Only Jewish converts would continue to follow the strict Mosaic law as laid out in the Torah.

Later events cast doubt on an amiable reconciliation. Paul continued to attack his Jerusalem brethren and their Judaizer missionaries.[252] He ignored the ruling to refrain from non-kosher food, telling his listeners to "eat anything sold in the meat market without raising questions of conscience, for 'the earth is the Lord's, and everything in it.' "[253] He talked disparagingly of James, John, and Peter: "Whatever they were makes no difference to me … they added nothing to my message."[254]

Apocryphal writings such as Pseudo-Clementine homilies and recognitions confirm the hostility between the two factions. James, John, Peter, and the other followers of Jesus viewed Paul with wariness and suspicion, if not open derision, and the Epistle of Barnabas strongly condemns the Judaizing teachers. Although these texts would be excluded from the Christian biblical canon, they support evidence of a severe split.

Further evidence of an enduring rift was provided almost a century later by the Christian writer Justin Martyr. He distinguished between Jewish Christians who observed the laws of Moses (but did not require others to do so) and those who insisted that Mosaic law was obligatory for all converts. Justin Martyr regarded the second group as heretical.[255]

PAUL CHASTISED

In AD 57, eight years after his first summons to Jerusalem, Paul was recalled again. On this occasion, he went there with some companions, fully expecting to be attacked or even killed by the Nazarenes: "I am going to Jerusalem, not knowing what will happen to me there."[256]

Luke's Acts of the Apostles contains the accounts of his visits to the city. There is no surviving Jerusalem-church version. This final meeting started peacefully—"brothers and sisters received us warmly"[257]—before turning sour. The Nazarenes accused Paul of turning away from the law of Moses and insisted he make a demonstration of his faith. They wanted Paul to visit the temple with some of their community, so "then everyone will know there is no truth in these reports about you, but that you yourself are living in obedience to the law."[258]

In what must have been a humiliating concession, Paul complied with their instruction. He dutifully performed the rites and even shaved his head as a token of repentance. The rituals continued for several days and had almost concluded when some Jews from the province of Asia (modern Turkey) recognised Paul. Presumably, they had heard him preaching there, but it is not clear whether these were Nazarenes, Pharisees, or both.

They grabbed him and incited their fellow worshippers by declaring he had preached against the Mosaic law and brought a Gentile into the temple. This was enough to provoke a general assault by the congregation. He was beaten and dragged out of the building.

News of the commotion reached the Roman garrison, and their timely arrival saved Paul from a certain lynching. He was arrested for his own safety and to prevent a riot. The commander initially mistook him for an agitator who had instigated a recent revolt. He had no desire to antagonise the populace further. The commander hastily confined Paul to barracks with instructions that he be tortured. Paul might have met the same fate as Jesus had he not played the citizenship card.

Aware of his predicament, Paul informed his captors that he was a Roman citizen and appealed to Caesar. The Romans would not execute one of their own without formal and sustainable charges, which, of course, they could not produce. They had no choice but to give in to his request.[259]

After being informed of an assassination plot, the commander sent him out of harm's way to Caesarea. He was accompanied by a note to the Roman prefect Felix explaining the reasons. To placate his accusers, the prefect kept Paul under confinement.

During Paul's two-year detention, while awaiting the call to Rome, Herod Agrippa II and the new Roman prefect Festus visited him. After listening, with some humour, to a long-winded sermon from the preacher, Herod was inclined to release him but could not, as Paul had already appealed to the higher authority of Rome. Festus thought he was insane and, like his predecessor Felix, regarded him as a trouble-maker and "a ringleader of the Nazarene sect."[260] Neither of them felt he deserved death.

After two years of incarceration, Paul was sent to Rome. When he finally arrived after an eventful journey that included a shipwreck, he contacted the local Jewish community. They already knew of the Nazarene cult but not of him. He rented a house in the city and spent two more years there. He was free to preach without hindrance, provided he did not attempt to leave Rome. Here, in the Acts of the Apostles, the story ends.

Christian tradition holds that Paul was executed. But he had committed no crime to warrant such a fate, and the Roman authorities in Palestine seemed not to have desired it. In his epistle to Philemon, written while in Rome, Paul implies that he expected an acquittal: "Prepare a guest room for me, because I hope to be restored to you in answer to your prayers."[261]

The account of his life ends around AD 64, coinciding with the great fire of Rome. He could have perished in the fire or the purge of Jews in its aftermath. Or perhaps he died a natural death, possibly in Spain, where he intended to travel: "So after I have completed this task ... I will go to Spain and visit you on the way."[262] A natural death is more likely, as the next surviving account of his life, written 30 years later in AD 96 by Clement, bishop of Rome, ends with "having reached the farthest bounds of the West; and when he had borne his testimony before the rulers, so he departed from the world and went unto the holy place, having been found a notable pattern of patient endurance."[263] There is no mention of a violent death.

Later, as we will see, when Christianity developed a martyrdom fixation, accounts of his execution and the martyrdom of other apostles began to emerge.

CHANGING THE MESSAGE

Paul's ideas recounted in his epistles are like his sermons: long-winded, rambling affairs. He urges his followers to lead righteous lives and to avoid fornication, homosexuality, idolatry, and theft. These were the standard moralistic fare of the times and compatible with the Scriptures. The faithful will be rewarded and the unfaithful punished.

Although sometimes stressing continuity with the Torah,[264] he more frequently refutes its tenets, which precipitated the conflict with the Jerusalem church. Salvation will come to those who believe in Jesus, whom he declares has "redeemed us from the curse of the law,"[265] the "law" being "the ministry that brought death, which was engraved in letters on stone."[266]

However, he was not above modifying his hard-line stance on the old law when it suited: "To the Jews I became like a Jew, to win the Jews. To those under the law I became like one under the law (though I myself am not under the law), so as to win those under the law. To those not having the law [Gentiles] I became like one not having the law (though I am not free from God's law but am under Christ's law), so as to win those not having the law."[267]

In other words, he rejected Jewish law, "I myself am not under the law,"[268] except when it was convenient for him to pretend otherwise, usually in the presence of traditional Jews.

Most of his writings concentrate on controversies current in the church at that time, especially the question of admitting Gentiles. This becomes, for him, almost an obsession. There is considerable anger in his words, usually directed against his fellow Jews. This includes those who reject Jesus and those who believe in Jesus but reject the Gentiles—in other words, the Jerusalem church. His message differed significantly from the ideas of Jesus himself.

Jesus preached of an earthly kingdom of heaven[269] where, according to Matthew and the later gospels, he would reign as the Messiah.[270] Faithful Jews would receive baptism, observe the laws of Moses, repent of their sins, and gain salvation through him.[271]

Paul's writings ignore the teaching of Jesus. Instead, he preached of salvation by faith—that is, faith in the spiritual Jesus, his death and resurrection, and a more abstract heavenly kingdom.[272] While the followers of Jesus saw his death as a terrible tragedy[273] that could only be redeemed by repentance, Paul saw it as a great event, the fulfilment of a divine plan.[274] For him, the resurrection of Jesus ushered in a new age as foretold by the prophets.

What made Paul so assured in his beliefs? Well, it seems Jesus had communicated this message directly to him.[275] This gave him authority to dismiss the interpretations of those who actually knew Jesus and had heard him speak.

He does not explain why the son of God, after finally coming down to Earth "to seek and to save the lost,"[276] did not make a point of meeting Paul himself. Instead, he chose other apostles who did not believe he was divine. These apostles did not expect him to be executed or to rise from the dead, and they rejected communion with Gentiles. This omission underlines the conflict between the followers of the earthly Jesus and the followers of Paul. Paul did not concern himself with the physical Messiah, whom he rarely quoted. His Jesus was an abstract concept.

Favouring faith over wisdom,[277] Paul held that man's physical state binds him to evil, which can be overcome only by belief in the spiritual Jesus. It can best be summed up by the sentence, "With my mind I am a slave to the law of God, but with my flesh I am a slave to the law of sin."[278] Perhaps a worthy diagnosis of the human condition, but a deadly prescription for its cure, since it implies that those who refused to convert remained slaves to sin—evil by choice, one might say.

This message contrasts with the views of James the Just, who favoured action over faith: "Be doers of the word and not hearers only."[279] "What good is it, my brothers and sisters, if someone claims to have faith but has no deeds? Can such faith save them?"[280] "Faith by itself, if it is not accompanied by action, is dead."[281] In a statement that appears to be a personal attack on Paul, he continues, "You believe that there is one God. Good! Even the demons believe that—and shudder. You foolish person, do you want evidence that faith without deeds is useless?"[282]

The radical ideas of James would sound plausible under a red banner in the chill October of St. Petersburg 1917. Paul's followers need not wait so long. Faith in their lifetime would secure their reward in the afterlife.

PAUL PREVAILS

Paul spent his last years dealing with the concerns of his new community, corresponding with them, and preaching the word through his various epistles. One of the main apprehensions of the fledgling church was the failure of Jesus to return to begin the heavenly kingdom as promised. In his letters, Paul urges the faithful to remain patient. If he himself entertained doubts, there is no trace of it in his writing; his kingdom was less tangible.

Throughout his life, Paul remained focused on a single goal. Outwardly, this goal seemed to change after his epiphany on the road to Damascus. In substance, though, it never changed. Jesus, moulded to his image, became a vehicle for preaching his doctrine of a universal moralistic society based on faith and inspired by Jewish monotheism. He did not see himself as the agent of a new religion, nor would he have desired that. Yet that was the outcome of his mission.

By the end of his career, he had planted this doctrine in several cities throughout the empire. Numerically small and still predominantly Jewish, it remained a sect within a sect. But among the members were non-Jews, and this was Paul's main achievement. He had brought a reconstructed Hebrew faith to the Gentile world. This fulfilled a prophecy of Zechariah: In the last days, the Gentile nations would come to the God of Israel as Gentiles.[283]

Without Paul, this might never have happened, and perhaps this was his primary intent. Since before the birth of Jesus, some Pharisees had acquired a missionary zeal to create a race of God-fearing Gentiles worshipping under the priestly guidance of the chosen few, the Jews. These *ger toshav* ("righteous Gentiles")[284] needed only to adhere to the seven so-called Noahide Laws that would allow them to share the kingdom to come. According to the Talmud, these laws were first given to Adam and later to Noah. They specified prohibitions against blasphemy, idolatry, fornication, and theft, as well as adherence to strict dietary rules. Although, as we have seen, Paul even allowed latitude on the dietary laws.

He may have wanted to prepare the *ger toshav* for this purpose, but his unsightly appearance worked against it. While a diminutive, balding, bow-legged preacher might struggle to inspire his listeners, a martyred prophet is a different matter. Such a man can be moulded into a sublime being whose aura transcends the drab human frame. It was only necessary to alter the message, replacing the exclusive Jewish earthly kingdom of Jesus with Paul's inclusive heavenly one. A prophet, after all, can claim to speak for the divine, knowing the divine will never refute his message. Could this have been his eureka moment on the road to Damascus? If so, it was a stroke of genius.

Paul could not have foreseen the outcome this would have for his fellow Jews. As the Hebrew God became the god of the Gentiles, the Gentiles came to see the Jews as complicit in the brutal execution of His Son, *their* Saviour. To exonerate the Romans and avoid the charge of subversion, the Scriptures, in their final form, placed the guilt for the crucifixion on the shoulders of the Jews. This was to condemn the chosen people to centuries of persecution, torture, and murder in retribution for an atrocity of divine proportions. A salvation born out of violence and death cried out for vengeance—someone had to pay.

Paul had transformed the subversive message of the dead preacher into a universal doctrine for all humanity. He had done that against opposition from the Jews, polytheists, and the original followers of Jesus. It was a remarkable achievement. Believers see the divine hand at play; his detractors see only a reappropriation of the man-god myth. The impartial observer must decide for themselves.

The seed he planted would soon lead to the birth of a powerful religion—but not without labour pains. Small though this community was, it managed to split again, perhaps due to its Gentile converts and the failure of Christ to reappear on Earth. Those who formed the new breakaway group were called Gnostics.

7

THE MESSIAH BECOMES GOD

ANYONE WHO WASN'T bewildered by the writings of Paul and the gospels was probably not paying attention. These messages raised as many questions as they answered. What was the nature of Jesus, why was he executed, what was his relationship to God, and how was humankind to be saved?

The wisest converts attempted to address these imperfections and propose an explanation. As might be expected, they did not all agree on a formula. Their efforts generated more ambiguity and dissent. This prompted numerous redefinitions of Christian doctrine.

For example, how did one explain evil? Was it the absence of good, a dark side of God, human nature, or the work of a malevolent God? Gnostics opted for the latter explanation.

They believed that God, the Creator, was an inferior being, the "devil" that had tempted Jesus in the wilderness in Matthew 4:1–11. The Torah was an account of this God's efforts to keep humanity immersed in ignorance, and to punish any attempts to acquire knowledge. The expulsion of Adam and Eve from Paradise, the flood, and the destruction of Sodom and Gomorrah were acts of vengeance by this lesser God against those who pursued enlightenment. Gnostics could not reconcile the brutal invasion of Canaan and attempted genocide of its inhabitants with a benevolent deity.

Gnostics believed that a divine spark or soul was trapped inside every individual's physical body. Escape from this bodily prison could be achieved through "knowledge" (*gnōsis*) or insight by which people discover the divine within themselves.

The most notable proponent of this philosophy was Marcion. In the next century, he was the first to catalogue the various writings of what would later become the New Testament. This was something the official church did not complete until the fourth century AD.

The many accounts of the life of Jesus and different interpretations of his message contributed to an accumulation of divergent beliefs. These accounts include the Gospels of Mark, Matthew, Luke, Thomas, Philip, and Barnabas, the Acts of Thomas, and other writings lost to history.

Marcion limited the collection to 10 letters of St. Paul and a version of the Gospel of Luke and rejected the rest. He listed the moral contradictions between the Jewish Scriptures of the Torah, or the first five books of the Old Testament, and the new revelations of St. Paul and Luke. Marcion believed the god who sent Jesus to Earth was not the aggressive war god Yahweh. In fact, Yahweh was Satan, and all earthly things were part of his domain. The gospels had been corrupted by persons determined to keep Christianity Jewish, and the apostles had misunderstood the intentions of Jesus.

Not all Gnostics believed that Jesus was the Saviour, but Christian Gnostics did. The movement grew in parallel with Christianity and might initially have been indistinguishable from it. Most were simply Christians who embraced Jesus but rejected the old Scriptures. However, as Gnosticism began to pull the faith away from its Jewish roots, a counter-challenge came in the form of a new message called the Gospel of John. This work was most likely written by one or two Greek scholars sometime between AD 95 and 150. John, the apostle of Jesus, was long since dead and, in any case, had most likely been illiterate.[285]

THE MESSAGE IS CHANGED AGAIN

By this time, the centre of the faith had shifted from Palestine to Asia Minor. Following the failed revolt, the destruction of the Jerusalem church removed any restraints against the Pauline doctrine. At that point, the faith began to take on a decidedly Greek character. John's Gospel leans heavily on Greek philosophy to explain the nature of Jesus, replacing the Greek idea of Logos, "the divine will," with "the Word." This was a concept partially inspired by the Hellenistic Jewish philosopher Philo. "In the beginning was the Word, and the Word was with God, and the Word was God."[286] "The Word became flesh and made his dwelling among us."[287] Jesus becomes the incarnation of the Logos, and Greek philosophy again enters the fog of Hebrew theology.

The term "Son of God" now came to mean literally the son of God rather than its original reference to a pious Jew. Jesus becomes part of a divine triad alongside God the Father and the Holy Spirit. The latter was a spiritual manifestation of God on Earth existing through the church. Early Church Fathers like Theophilus of Antioch (died AD 185) and Tertullian (AD 160 to 220), gave this triad a new name: *trinitas*, "the Trinity."

Other than a series of arguments between Jesus and learned Jews on whether he is the Messiah, probably reflecting debates between Pharisees and Christians of the day, the Gospel of John contains no significant ethical philosophy. It also appears to have abandoned the shared-wealth idea of previous writings.

In it, John the Baptist identifies Jesus as the Messiah. This contrasts with Matthew's Gospel, which has the Baptist sending his disciples to question Jesus on his behaviour. Jesus himself talks extensively of his vocation on Earth and clearly identifies himself as the Christ. His mission lasts three years instead of one, as in the Synoptic Gospels, and his followers are numbered in the thousands. They proclaim him everywhere he goes, a scenario quite at odds with the historical records of the day, as recounted by Josephus, for example.

The Gospel of John has Peter present at the interrogation by the high priest. The witnesses to the crucifixion are now increased to include Mary, the mother of Jesus, and an unnamed disciple (traditionally held to be John). Joseph of Arimathea and a friend, Nicodemus, collect the corpse. Mary Magdalene goes alone to the tomb and finds it empty. She rushes to the apostles, declaring, "They have taken the Lord out of the tomb, and we don't know where they have put him."[288]

This contrasts with the Gospel of Matthew, where an angel at the tomb tells Mary that Jesus has risen. She returns to the tomb with Peter and another disciple, who verify that it is indeed empty except for the linen garments used to wrap the body. Mary sees two angels, who tell her the body was taken. She then sees a man she believes to be the gardener and asks him what he has done with the body.[289] The man reveals himself to be Jesus. We must assume there is no resemblance since this comes as a surprise to her. The character of doubting Thomas is introduced, and Jesus appears to the disciples several times after his death. They, too, fail to recognise him.

We now have four gospels giving four contradictory accounts of the death and resurrection of Jesus. All the accounts come from Greek writers of a later generation who did not witness these occurrences. They also had strong motivations to sell a particular message: that the least likely explanation for these events, a miracle, was the correct one.

From the simple holy man described by Josephus and Mark, Jesus gradually morphs into something quite different with each successive telling. Of all the gospels, John's would be unrecognisable to the original followers of Jesus. This marks the final break between Christians on the one hand and the Nazarenes (Ebionites) and Pharisees on the other. John's Gospel is rabidly anti-Jewish, treating them as a hostile race. It frequently describes enemies of Jesus as "the Jews," as if Jesus and his disciples were not. One stark passage has Jesus telling the Jews, "You belong to your father, the devil, and you want to carry out your father's desires."[290]

As with the other gospels, it portrays the Roman prefect Pilate as a reasonable man pleading with the irrational mob and with their persistent demands for the crucifixion of Jesus. This is at odds with the real Pilate, who, as we have seen, sent thousands to their deaths without due process. The Jews, not the Romans, are the bad guys. The sentiments of this gospel, together with passages from Luke, represent a sinister trend in the new faith: blaming the Jews for the death of Jesus.

Ironically, despite its anti-Jewish ranting, this version is faithful to the Hebrew Scriptures. In opposition to Gnosticism, it emphasises continuity with the Old Testament and the first divine commandment: "No one comes to the Father except through me."[291]

The Gospel of John is the one most frequently quoted by evangelists and fundamentalists. It represents the character of Jesus as understood by most Christians today and completes the deification of the humble *tektōn* from Galilee. If Jesus somehow returned from the dead and read this account of his life, he would be horrified. As a devout Jew, he would have considered his deification blasphemous and contrary to the Scriptures. The Greek and later Roman man-god was a concept alien to Judaism. Equally repulsive was the idea of dying for the sins of humankind as a kind of human sacrifice.

It is unlikely that he would have recognised the central characters or many of the events described, including the marriage feast of Cana, the woman accused of adultery,[292] and the raising of Lazarus from the dead,[293] all of which are unique to this account of Jesus's life. The latter story had a significant impact on contemporary Christianity and was probably added for that purpose.

GOD'S KINGDOM, ON EARTH OR IN HEAVEN?

Although this gospel, like those before it, proclaims the imminent coming of Christ, many years had passed since the crucifixion. The original followers were dead, and a new generation had come and gone, yet no kingdom of God on Earth was in sight. Disillusionment was setting in. The gospel sought to redefine the kingdom of God as the church. Through the Holy Spirit, the church represented the divine power on Earth.

However, for the less theologically inclined, the story of Lazarus offered hope that believers who were already dead would be raised up to share in the kingdom. This tale profoundly affected those waiting patiently for the second coming. Its importance can be attested by the frequency with which images of the event appear on the tombs of early Christians in the catacombs of Rome. Next to the mission of St. Paul and his heavenly kingdom, it contributed significantly to the growth of the new faith.

Following from this gospel, the Christians became more confident and dogmatic but less united. The idea of three divine beings proposed in John's Gospel presented an enigma. This concept was later challenged by a Libyan presbyter called Arius. He believed Jesus was not divine but a human created by God and infused with a godly spirit. This would create a bitter division among Christians, but more on that later.

Despite these divisions, the Christian message continued to spread. Missionaries had initially avoided the urbane and high born, concentrating instead on those "best disposed to receive the impression of superstitious terrors."[294] Early non-Jewish converts included outcasts of society. These were slaves and peasants alienated from the mainstream social order with little hope of advancement or reward. From these, the missionaries, typically educated Hellenistic Jews, exacted absolute submission to the new doctrine "without being able to produce a single argument that could engage the attention of men of learning."[295]

In attempting to explain the writings of Paul and the gospels, Christian scholars had pushed their doctrine even further from its simple origins. This opened the way for theological disputes that would forever vex their religion, as any churchgoer today will confirm.

No longer confined within the community of the faithful, this would play out in full view of an empire slowly awakening to the hostile sect in its midst.

8

SUICIDE MARTYRS

THE ROMAN EMPIRE had evolved to counter enemies beyond its borders. It was ill prepared for the Christian threat from within.

When the empire awoke to the danger, its response was inconsistent and erratic. The Christian reaction tested their resilience. A fight for survival began.

Local governors did not become aware of the new movement for some time. Disputes between the various sects of the "Jewish superstition," as they saw it, were of little interest. When they did become aware, it seemed nothing more than a family quarrel. However, the exclusivity of the Jews and the ongoing unrest in Palestine before the revolt of AD 66 marked them out for suspicion. This prompted Nero's predecessor, Claudius, to close one of their synagogues and expel some Jews from Rome in AD 49.

The Roman writer Suetonius attributed the expulsion to an agitator called Chrestus.[296] This sounds like *Christus*, the Latin version of "Christ." Suetonius might have assumed this to be a living person, so Jesus's Jewish followers, the Nazarenes, were included in the expulsion.

Clearly, Romans did not yet distinguish between the two groups and knew nothing of Jesus. This is underlined in the Acts of the Apostles. When quarrelling Jews and Nazarenes brought their disagreement to the Roman proconsul in Corinth, he responded, " 'If you Jews were making a complaint about some misdemeanor or serious crime, it would be reasonable for me to listen to you. But since it involves questions about words and names and your own law—settle the matter yourselves. I will not be a judge of such things.' So he drove them off."[297]

Tacitus gave the first account of Christian persecution. In AD 64, a great fire destroyed part of Rome, following which Nero embarked on a massive rebuilding project. Rumours circulated that the emperor had started the fire as a novel way of compulsory purchase in the densely populated centre: "Neither human resources, nor imperial generosity, nor appeasement of the gods, eliminated the sinister suspicion that the fire had been deliberately started. To stop the rumour, Nero made scapegoats ... and punished with every refinement the notoriously depraved Christians (as they were popularly called)."[298]

Christians generally accept this as the first organised persecution under Roman rule. However, there is no certainty that it was.

First, Tacitus, sympathetic to the faction that precipitated Nero's downfall, was writing 50 years after the event. He was also deeply hostile to the former emperor. Contrary to Tacitus's claim, the group was not "popularly called Christians" in AD 64. The Nazarenes, as they were called, were numerically tiny and indistinguishable from the Jewish community of which they were part.

Nero had no apparent reason to single out the Nazarenes, even if he knew of them. Paul had urged his followers to be law abiding: "The authorities that exist have been established by God."[299] If Nero did punish any group for the fire, it was most likely to have been the Jews as a whole, some of whom might, by coincidence, have been Nazarenes. Poppaea, Nero's second wife, who was sympathetic to Jewish priests, could have helped them to scapegoat the Nazarenes.

The next account of persecution occurs during the reign of Domitian (AD 81 to 96). He reinvigorated the idea of the divine emperor, which had been introduced under Augustus, and enforced penalties against "atheists." Ironically, considering its modern usage, "atheists" meant those who rejected the Roman gods—Jews and Druids, for instance. According to Eusebius of Caesarea, a Christian author writing centuries later, some fellow worshippers were caught up in the persecution.

REVELATION

Christians reacted with the publication of their most subversive document, the book of Revelation (also called the Apocalypse.) This set the tone of resentment against Roman authority that would persist for 200 years. The origin of this discontent was Ephesus in Asia Minor, where the building of a new temple dedicated to the emperor imposed a civil obligation on the populace to partake in its ceremonies. Christians and Jews refused to comply.

Revelation employs symbolism and allegory to get its message across. It uses vindictive language drawn from Old Testament prophecies and pre-Christian subversive texts, like the *Sibylline Oracles*.

Angry words leap from its pages. The Roman Empire is described as a "great whore"[300] and the emperor a "beast."[301] Coded Greek text and numerals seem to identify the emperor as Nero. When translated into Latin and later English, the combination becomes a meaningless 666 that naive Christians later misinterpreted to mean Satan. Originally designed to deceive the Romans, it continues to deceive the gullible and superstitious.

The text reveals the still predominant belief that the end is nigh, citing things that will "soon take place."[302]

Despite the bluster, Revelation reveals little about actual persecution aside from the banishment of the author to a nearby island, the execution of another individual, and the expectation that some Christians would be arrested. One feels that the writer was a trifle melodramatic.

This subversion was not universal. Another Christian document written at the same time urges obedience to authority: "Submit yourselves for the Lord's sake to every human authority: whether to the emperor as the supreme authority or to governors."[303]

A DEGENERATIVE CULT

By the reign of Trajan (AD 98 to 117), Christians could be identified as a sect distinctive from the Jews. Tacitus, in his annals, describes them as "depraved" with their "deadly superstition" and "hatred for the human race."[304]

The Greco-Roman satirist Lucian was equally disparaging: "The poor wretches have convinced themselves that they are going to be immortal and will live for all time by worshipping that crucified sophist and living under his laws. Therefore, they despise the things of this world and consider them common property. They believe their doctrines by tradition without any definite evidence. So, if a character or trickster comes among them, he quickly acquires wealth by imposing on the simple folk."[305]

In AD 111 a more judicious account comes from Pliny the Younger, governor of the province of Bithynia-Pontus in western Asia Minor, where Christians had become numerous. Their habit of holding religious services in private gave rise to conspiracy theories. It was rumoured they practised incest and cannibalism and plotted subversion.

Pliny noted with despair that many temples were practically deserted owing to the conversions to the new faith. His investigations quashed claims that Christians held bizarre ceremonies in which they consumed the flesh and blood of sacrificed children. This was a misinterpretation of the eucharistic consumption of the body and blood of Christ. He found that "the sum total of their guilt or error amounted to no more than this: they had met regularly before dawn on a fixed day to chant verses alternately among themselves in honour of Christ as if to a god, and also to bind themselves by oath, not for any criminal purpose, but to abstain from theft, robbery and adultery, to commit no breach of trust and not to refuse to return a deposit upon demand."[306]

Pliny concluded they were a harmless but misguided folk: "I found nothing but a degenerate sort of cult carried to extravagant lengths."[307] Like Tacitus, he suggested that they deserved some form of punishment for refusing to obey Trajan's edict banning *collegia illicita* ("political gatherings").

Trajan, in his response, urged caution: "These people must not be hunted out," he declared, insisting that anyone brought before the court should not be punished, provided they denied they were Christians and proved it by making a token offering to the gods. "He is to be pardoned as a result of his repentance, however suspect his past conduct may be." He warned against false accusations, stating that "pamphlets circulated anonymously must play no part in any accusation. They create the worst sort of precedent and are quite out of keeping with the spirit of our age."[308] Clearly, moderation and the rule of law were important to the emperor.

For the next 150 years, persecution remained sporadic, more often prompted by popular anger rather than imperial decree. Christians were sometimes blamed for natural calamities like poor harvests, droughts, and floods, which were seen as signs of divine wrath, making them convenient scapegoats for localised retribution.

Yet government and citizens harboured deep suspicion towards the Christian sect. This was evidenced by the need for Pliny to carry out his investigation in Bithynia-Pontus. There were several reasons for this mistrust.

THE ROMAN PERSPECTIVE

The empire was a multi-ethnic society with different communities venerating the local deities of the regions or cities where they lived. Temples served as centres of worship and social bonding. The Romans were tolerant of this diversity. Citizens were free to practise their chosen religion, provided they also respected the state religion.

From the earliest times, Rome integrated religion with the civil system. Ritual observance was linked to the Senate and central to the welfare and safety of the people. The Romans did not consider worship a private matter, so

Christian secret gatherings aroused suspicion. Insurrections throughout the empire, including the Jewish and Celtic (under Boudica) revolts, prompted legislation that declared such *collegia illicita* treasonable (*laesae majestatis*) and subject to severe penalties. Christianity, Judaism, and Celtic Druidism were mistrusted for that reason.

The Christians' refusal to offer token deference added to this distrust. It smacked of treason and sacrilege. While not all Romans believed in the divine nature of emperors or intervention of the gods, they considered displays of reverence crucial for national unity, akin to the modern practice of saluting the flag or standing for the national anthem. Judaism was eventually granted the status of *religio licita* when rabbis agreed to include the emperor's name in their prayers. No such accommodation was reached with the other cults.

Superstitious Christians considered the Roman gods as fallen angels, malevolent demons that had come to Earth to deceive humanity. They harboured a genuine fear of the malign influence of these beings. Since every aspect of Roman life, from birth to marriage and festivals, involved reverence to these spirits, Christian refusal to partake in such acts distanced them from friends and family.

The faithful would not allow burial in pagan cemeteries. Converted spouses couldn't be interred with their polytheist partners, and children couldn't rest beside their non-Christian parents. To the Romans, this created the perception of a fanatical cult that brainwashed children, tore families apart, and divided entire communities.

Christian doctrine reinforced these fears: "For I have come to turn 'a man against his father, a daughter against her mother, a daughter-in-law against her mother-in-law. A man's enemies will be the members of his own household.' Anyone who loves their father or mother more than me is not worthy of me; anyone who loves their son or daughter more than me is not worthy of me."[309]

And, "Do not call anyone on earth 'father,' for you have one Father, and he is in heaven."[310]

Romans regarded the Christian pursuit of personal salvation as an evasion of public duty, contrary to the sense of noble self-sacrifice that had built the Republic and empire. Christians avoided public employment and military service. The eschatological nature of Christianity was in part to blame for this. Since the end of the world was nigh, wealth accumulation was pointless, and defending the empire counterproductive. Their propagation of poverty as an ideal, even if largely ignored in practice, was at variance with Roman enterprise.

A church that anticipated the "day of God," when the temporal rulers would be overthrown, put its loyalty to the state in question. Their secret ceremonies added to the suspicion.

Slaves and migrants did not share an attachment to deities that bore no relation to the gods of their homeland. Freed slaves (*libertes*), many of whom became successful entrepreneurs or teachers, resented the local gods, symbols of their former oppression. Others alienated from the community or the state felt likewise. Thus, Christianity became a kind of globalist faith that united these disaffected people.

Teachers in particular, despised by the rich parents of their pupils, returned the contempt in equal measure. They quietly moulded the young minds with their faith and their distaste for the empire and its traditions.

Tertullian, who initially urged the faithful to support the state, had a change of heart and began to encourage passive subversion: "There is no agreement between the divine and the human sacrament, the standard of Christ and the standard of the devil, the camp of light and the camp of darkness. One soul cannot serve two masters—God and Caesar."[311]

"THE SILLY, THE MEAN, AND THE STUPID"[312]

A second-century AD work, *The True Word*, penned by Celsus, unleashed a scathing criticism of the new faith. The book was later banned, and all copies systematically eradicated after Rome became Christian. However, Origen of Alexandria (AD 185–254), one of the early Church Fathers, had already composed a rebuttal called *Contra Celsum*. By extensively quoting Celsus in his *apologia* ("defence"), Origen effectively preserved some of the arguments in *The True Word*.

Celsus accused the Jews and Christians of separatism and of asserting superior wisdom when, in fact, they had merely borrowed ideas from Plato, Socrates, and the Stoics. The kingdom of God was a distortion of Plato's doctrine. The miracles ascribed to Jesus were mere fictitious yarns, no more astonishing than the magic tricks performed by Egyptian con artists at the time. The tale of the resurrection was invented by Jesus's disciples, "a group of notorious publicans and fishermen." Celsus argued that "Should God … on awakening from a lengthened slumber, desire to rouse the human race from evil, why did he send his spirit into one corner of the earth? Why … did he not send it out into the whole world … and why did the resurrected Jesus only appear to the apostles?"[313]

Christian belief that the world was created for the benefit of humankind ignored our common bond with nature. The human spirit, Celsus believed, had sprung from the animal spirit. Christians should give thanks to the powers of nature by sacrificing to the gods since they also enjoyed its bounties.

He criticised Christians for excluding the educated and wise from their community. They preferred to convert "the silly, the mean, and the stupid with women and children,"[314] fearing to challenge men of authority or learning in debate.

To Celsus they were freeloaders who stayed at home and left the burden of state defence to others. He begged them to abandon their hope of a kingdom of God on Earth and instead "Help the king with all your might and labour with him in the maintenance of justice," otherwise "the affairs of the world will fall into the hands of the wildest and most lawless of barbarians."[315]

Origen countered that Christianity would unite all the peoples of the world under one faith. If everyone converted, there would be no more wars. Such is the hopeless optimism of the righteous!

"THE BLOOD OF CHRISTIANS IS THE SEED OF THE CHURCH"[316]

The pleadings of Celsus fell on deaf ears; Christians clung to their dogmatic separateness. Thus, the eye of suspicion remained focused on the cult and prompted varying degrees of persecution throughout the second and third centuries AD.

The charges for which Christians were tried and punished varied. One prominent martyr from that period was St. Ignatius of Antioch (died AD 107). On his way to Rome for execution, he wrote letters to his followers, describing the structure of the Christian community, which now included bishops, deacons, and subdeacons.

Although he fails to specify the charges against him, it seems that discord within the Antioch church was the reason. Disagreements over scriptural interpretations had intensified, and he might have been denounced by members of a rival faction. Regardless, he welcomed the opportunity to die for his faith and urged Christians in Rome not to intervene on his behalf, expressing a willingness to face death for his belief: "Allow me to be eaten by the beasts, through whom I can attain to God."[317]

Another account written by an unknown Christian author tells of the martyrdom of Polycarp, bishop of Smyrna. Officials had begged him to say "Caesar is Lord" and offer incense to save his life, but he refused. Later, in the arena, the governor asked him to swear an oath "by the luck of Caesar." He declined again, eager to meet his death.[318]

Repeated examples of "stage heroics," as Marcus Aurelius described them, appear in accounts of the time.[319] Rather than persecuting helpless Christians to death, Roman officials frequently tried to talk some sense into these reckless fanatics. Pleading with one would-be martyr, the presiding official told him to "Cease this foolishness and be of good cheer." In yet another case, the magistrate asked, "What is so serious about offering some incense [to the gods] and going away?"[320]

Following the example of Trajan, emperors Hadrian and Antoninus Pius continued to uphold the law. They issued proclamations forbidding the persecution of Christians if the persecutions were merely a response to popular clamour. Concrete evidence of wrongdoing was required. Even when faced with such evidence, the accused could obtain pardon by performing a token gesture such as casting a few grains of incense at the temple altar.

The need to make these rulings implies that the faithful were sometimes victims of arbitrary and localised justice. But the edicts did not halt persecution, and a martyrdom cult began to develop. Fuelled by the belief that the victim's soul ascended directly to heaven, many refused to avail of the legal escape routes. Deluded die-hards offered themselves to the authorities, confessing their faith and demanding punishment. Some were fired by excessive zeal; others simply wished to escape a life of hardship or debt.

"No sooner had the first batch been sentenced," gushed Eusebius, "than others from every side would jump onto the platform in front of the judge and proclaim themselves Christian. They paid no heed to torture."[321]

This mania for self-destruction perplexed the Roman authorities. When approached by Christians who demanded persecution, the proconsul of Asia, Arrius Antoninus, granted the request to a few and dismissed the remainder. He declared that if "you ghastly people" were so weary of life, there was plenty of rope available to "hang yourselves" or cliffs to jump off.[322]

As this form of militant Christianity spread, it gained a strong foothold in the provinces of North Africa. Here the self-destructive mania is best exemplified in the martyrdom of saints Perpetua and Felicitas, along with three male companions, in Carthage in AD 203. The following account gives an insight into the mindset of those involved.

Perpetua stood before the court, her child in the care of friends, her pagan father by her side, tearfully pleading with her to recant. "What!" exclaimed the weary magistrate, "Will neither the grey hairs of a father you are going to make miserable nor the tender innocence of a child, which your death will leave an orphan, move you? Sacrifice to the prosperity of the emperor." She replied, "I will not."[323]

SUICIDE MARTYRS

Her slave Felicitas, eight months pregnant, was distressed that this condition might cause her sentence to be revoked: "She was inconsolable … fearing that her martyrdom should be deferred on that account." It was against the law to execute a pregnant woman. So, the five accused unanimously joined in prayer to obtain of God that she might deliver her baby before the shows. Scarcely had they finished their prayer when Felicitas went into labour and gave birth to the immense delight of the would-be martyrs.[324]

They were condemned to be torn apart by wild beasts in the arena in Carthage.

The day of their triumph having come, they went out of the prison to the amphitheatre full of joy. Perpetua walked with a composed countenance … Felicitas went with her, following the men, unable to contain her joy. … Perpetua sang, as being already victorious; Revocatus, Saturninus and Saturus [their male companions] threatened the people that beheld them with the judgements of God. … They rejoiced exceedingly in being thought worthy to resemble our Saviour in his sufferings. God granted to each of them the death that they desired.[325]

Various wild beasts attacked the five, including a bear, a leopard, and a "wild cow." Any survivors were finished off by gladiators. The one assigned to Perpetua was "a very timorous and unskilful apprentice who, with a trembling hand, gave her many slight wounds which made her languish a long time."[326] "Thus," according to St. Augustine, "did two women amidst fierce beasts and the swords of gladiators vanquish the devil and all his fury." Their execution date, March 7, is remembered in the Christian calendar.[327]

Tertullian, who hailed from Carthage, welcomed these theatrical suicides, which he termed *secunda intinction* ("second baptism"), boasting, "It is bait that wins men for [our] school. The oftener we are mown down … the more in number we grow: the blood of Christians is seed of the church."[328]

A calendar of the saints who died was drawn up, and their anniversaries celebrated. Veneration brought prestige to the local church, and pilgrims travelled to the holy places where the martyrs once lived.

The pilgrims brought money, creating a cult industry in the process. Common criminals executed for transgressions against the state suddenly acquired a piety in death that they had never known in life. Miracles abounded. A felon released from prison would claim to incredulous believers that the limbs torn from his body by his torturers were miraculously restored by the intercession of some saint.

MARTYRS REMAIN FEW IN NUMBER

Most Christians, however, avoided the ultimate penalty and, when given the option to recant, did so only to return to the faith later. Some bought off the magistrates, and others absconded, quoting Matthew 10:23: "When you are persecuted in one place, flee to another." Tertullian was not impressed. He accused them of using Matthew as a cloak for cowardice: "Persecution, from which it is evident we must not flee, must in like manner not even be bought off."[329] Tellingly, Tertullian never offered himself for martyrdom but remained an enthusiastic cheerleader for those who did.

Despite Tertullian's exhortations to self-sacrifice, the numbers of those executed remained small. Origen of Alexandria, writing shortly before Emperor Decius (AD 249–251) launched a more systematic persecution, stated: "And these individuals who can be *easily numbered* have endured death for the sake of Christianity—God not permitting the whole nation to be exterminated but desiring that it should continue and that the whole world should be filled with this salutary and religious doctrine."[330]

As the religion spread, it gained converts among the professional classes and even some of the nobility. Initially these were mainly female,[331] attracted by the creed's mystical nature and alienated by Rome's masculine religions. Through these women, as well as ex-slave teachers, Christianity gradually infiltrated the upper classes, and by the end of the second century AD, it could number the educated and wealthy among its members.

This somewhat raised the intellectual level of the church. Miracles, apparitions, and even the raising of the dead, all common events among the faithful, were discouraged and later banned by a more rational hierarchy.

The belief in a second coming waned, and theologians, some of them former polytheists, used their philosophical training to debate the tenets of their new-found faith.

Not all Christians approved of the trend, and once again, a breakaway sect emerged. Montanists held fast to traditional Christian superstitions. Visions, miracles, and new prophecies remained on their agenda, as did public displays of reverence, all of which attracted undue attention, prompting persecution and martyrdom. This seemed to suit their aspirations. Tertullian nodded approvingly, despite his legal education. He was the first to claim that St. Peter was martyred,[332] an apparent contradiction of an earlier account of Peter's death by Clement, bishop of Rome.

Conflict with the Roman establishment forced Christians to transform and adapt. Despite the tension, the movement persevered into something quite distinct from the scattered communities of its early years. While not yet openly defying the establishment, some were goading it as a matador to a bull, daring it to strike, inflicting small wounds, and rejoicing in the danger to itself. Traditionalists pondered whether they were dealing with deluded mystics or unhinged fanatics—a question some still ask today.

As it grew, the movement diverged into opposing sects and faced the challenge of new religions as it competed for converts.

9

RIVAL FAITHS

THE MEEK SHALL inherit the Earth, so long as they obey the strong.

To counter pressure from the authorities, competition from emerging creeds, and their inclination to fragment, Christians required resolute leadership to survive and persevere against competing sects. This led to the development of a more proficient organisational structure and a hierarchy of authoritative leaders.

AN ASSERTIVE CHURCH

The democratic nature of the church slowly yielded to autocracy. Local bishops had previously been poor and sometimes uneducated artisans or slaves. As wealthy professionals entered the fold, ecclesiastics increasingly came from that class. They often attained the role by purchase rather than election. This is reflected in the sentences passed to such men in times of persecution. In the second century AD, low-bred martyrs like St. Ignatius of Antioch were torn apart by the jaws of wild beasts in the arena. High-bred Romans were beheaded, a sentence passed down to later bishops such as Cyprian of Carthage in the third century AD.

The position of women was also downgraded. In the early church, they served as deacons, read the Scriptures at gatherings, and even wrote gospels (the Gospel of Mary). A woman called Prisca, mentioned in Romans 16:1–4, may have been a deacon. Romans 16:12 cites two female co-workers, Tryphena and Tryphosa. Pliny also mentions women *ministrae* in his accounts. Women also established religious institutions. One example was Amma Syncletica of Alexandria, who founded a monastic order in Egypt. Another was Eudocia, an Athenian writer of Christian literature. Soon, however, they would be confined to a secondary role or no role at all.

Changes were initially informal and local. Some churches forbade menstruating women from participating in the sacraments. Minor alterations were made to the Scriptures. For example, in Romans 16:7, St. Paul sends greetings to fellow disciples Andronicus and Junia, who had been in prison with him. Junia was changed to Junias, a man's name, in several later manuscripts to hide the concept of a female apostle.[333]

Pope Clement I (AD 35–99) was among the first to formalise these moves with a decree that only men could serve as priests or hold authority in the church. He could point to Paul's Epistle, 1 Timothy 2:11–14, as justification. Although outlying communities ignored the order, other prohibitions on women followed in later church councils.

With the influx of learned scholars, a self-confident hierarchy began to challenge the traditional philosophers. The commissioning of a counter-argument to Celsus's critique 80 years earlier was an example of this intellectual assertiveness. As we have seen, Origen of Alexandria, one of the most accomplished biblical scholars of the early church, was given this task. His prolific writings demonstrate that neither education nor wealth nor his denunciation of the Montanist superstition were guarantees of rationality.

Origen was a strict ascetic who sold all his non-Christian books. According to Eusebius, he also castrated himself in order to instruct female pupils without temptation. He believed miracles could be worked through precise incantations invoking the name of Yahweh. He explained the raising of the dead by stating, "many others were known to have risen out of their graves after they had been buried,"[334] thereby assigning the rank of commonplace occurrence to the singular miracle upon which Christianity placed its trust.

In *Contra Celsum*, he asserts that the mass of contradictions in the Bible are signposts to spiritual allegorical exegesis. Thus, he rationalised the irrational.

Origen conceded that before the time of Christ, some philosophers such as Heraclitus or Aristotle might have grasped the concept of Logos. But afterward, only Christians were blessed with true knowledge.

The influx of wealthy converts empowered the church to care for, and by that means control, the poor, making it a self-governing entity within the state. This became an important factor in the ascendancy of the faith and posed a direct challenge to traditional nobility. Aristocrats had hitherto patronised polytheist temples and distributed largesse to the poor. This enhanced their prestige and influence. Suddenly, they faced competition from the church. Charity was not an incidental adjunct to Christianity. It was a central theme that made it attractive to the underprivileged, particularly in times of turmoil.

A TIME OF UNCERTAINTY

Such a period of unrest was the Crisis of the Third Century, which began in AD 235 following the assassination of Emperor Severus Alexander. In the anarchy that followed, any dissident group was bound to raise suspicion and become a target for state-sanctioned violence. Christians would be no exception. The most extensive persecution occurred under Decius (AD 249–251) and was short lived. It was not just aimed at Christianity but rather was an attempt to force social uniformity amid the prevailing chaos.

A proclamation was made that every citizen must offer sacrifice to the gods and the emperor on a fixed day. A *libellus*, or certificate, was issued to all those who obeyed the command. Christians could, and indeed did, obtain these certificates through various means, like sending a slave to sacrifice on their behalf, bribing officials, forging certificates, and making a token offering themselves followed by repentance and absolution. Others simply got them from polytheist friends or arranged to be out of town on the appointed day.

Bishop Cyprian was not impressed, condemning those who "polluted their hands and mouths" and "infected their consciences with wicked certificates," bemoaning the fact that "thousands of certificates were daily given."[335]

The purpose of the edicts was to unite the empire at a very challenging period. The most severe penalties were aimed at the church's new affluent leaders rather than the general congregation. Pope Fabian was martyred. Origen was arrested, tortured, and later released. Cyprian was exiled and later beheaded during the reign of Valerian. Instead of random and localised attacks, persecution had become more centralised.

The successors of Decius, Gallus (AD 251–253) and Valerian (AD 253–260), continued the process. They confiscated church property, closed Christian cemeteries, and banned gatherings of the faithful. Valerian went further with the execution of several bishops, presbyters, and others, including Pope Sixtus II. Governors pursued the policy with varying degrees of lassitude, which were often resisted with subterfuge by the faithful. As Cyprian lamented in a letter to Donatus, bishop of Carthage, "There is no fear about the laws; no concern for either inquisitor or judge; when the sentence can be bought off for money, it is not cared for."[336]

Although persecution of the clergy continued to some extent, the church survived. Finally, Emperor Gallienus (AD 253–268), son, co-ruler, and eventual successor to Valerian, allowed Christians to worship freely and restored confiscated church properties.

For the next half century or so, during the Peace of Gallienus, persecution ceased and the faithful flourished. Christians continued to infiltrate Roman society and gained high offices in the administration of the empire. Some even joined the army.

They no longer met in caves, private homes, and courtyards but constructed special buildings for worship. In almost every major town or city, these stone-built,[337] sometimes windowless, churches began to appear as the faithful grew in wealth and confidence.

Success relaxed the austerity and discipline of early Christianity, and a hierarchy developed where bishops were as much temporal as religious rulers. They held their own courts, collected taxes, issued edicts, and became a parallel power within the empire.

VYING WITH THE COMPETITION

Christians also absorbed the customs and traditions of the polytheism they sought to replace. They appropriated the Egyptian cult of Isis, beloved by Roman women, and the more ancient cult of the Mother Goddess in the portrayal of Mary as Mother of God. The Festival of Goddess Diana became the Festival of the Assumption of the Virgin. The ancient Feast of the Dead in November, or Samhain, as the Celts called it, was changed to the Feast of All Souls (Hallowe'en). Rituals dedicated to the resurrection of Attis at the equinox were replaced by the resurrection of Christ at Easter. The word "Easter" itself derives from the Germanic goddess Eostre or the Babylonian goddess Ishtar.

Assimilation of these ancient traditions had already begun at the time of the early gospels and continued up to the third century AD. However new emerging religions presented a more formidable challenge. One of those was Mithraism.

Introduced to Rome by pirates captured by Pompey circa 68 BC, this cult originated in Persia as an offshoot of Zoroastrianism. While in Rome, it adopted quite distinctive Roman characteristics. Here, Mithraic devotees used holy water and shared a ceremonial communion of bread and wine. As the religion spread throughout Italy and the provinces, it found common currency with ancient European traditions.

Mithraism's association with Sol Invictus ("invincible sun") made it popular with the army, especially in Europe. It grew to become the main religion of the legions. The handshake, the symbol of a contract in Persia, was adopted as the ritual greeting. (For Christians, it was the kiss.) And the Sun's Day (Sunday) became a holy day. Priests were addressed as "father," a term forbidden to Christians by Matthew 23:9, and prelates wore a red cap and carried a staff.

In AD 274, the emperor Aurelian made Sol Invictus the state's official religion. It would be celebrated on December 25, to correspond with Saturnalia. This was an occasion for feasting, merrymaking, and giving gifts and would sometimes last for a week. It is closely related to ancient winter solstice festivals that abounded throughout the empire and beyond, such as the Germanic festival of Yule or the Irish celebration of *Grianstad an Gheimhridh* (winter solstice).

Later Christian apologists complained that the polytheists were doing the devil's work by counterfeiting the true faith, ironically unaware that the reverse was the case. Tertullian accused Mithradian priests of mocking the communion rites with their ceremonial consumption of bread and wine. He declared angrily, "The devil [is the inspirer of the heretics] whose work it is to pervert the truth, who with idolatrous mysteries endeavours to imitate the realities of the divine sacraments."[338]

St. Justin Martyr proposed an even more bizarre explanation: that time travellor demons had come down to Earth centuries before the birth of Jesus and created parodies of the rites and traditions of the true Christian stories. "The wicked devils have imitated in the mysteries of Mithras, commanding the same thing to be done [holy communion]."[339]

Adherents of Mithraism, like Christians, believed in the immortality of the soul, the last judgement, and the resurrection. These were all ideas derived from Zoroastrianism. But there was a difference between the faiths.

Mithraism's followers bore no prejudice towards other creeds. They were careful to demonstrate their loyalty to the emperor and empire. In contrast to this, and despite its adoption of polytheist traditions, Christianity held fast to two overriding features: the belief in Jesus as Redeemer and an unshakeable intolerance.

These two religions now competed for supremacy—that was, until yet another sect emerged from that same reservoir of mystic cults as the other two.

Manichaeism was a form of deviant Christianity. When its adherents fled persecution in Persia, they mainly settled in the urban areas of Asia and North Africa. Their founder, Mani, was a member of a Gnostic Christian sect. He experienced heavenly visions and died in a Persian prison while awaiting execution. His followers revered Jesus, Zoroaster, and Buddha and held dualistic (Gnostic) beliefs.

They divided themselves into two groups, the Elect, who refrained from eating meat, drinking alcohol, having intercourse, or bathing themselves, and the Hearers, who played a lesser supportive role.

Like Christians, Manichaeans were exclusivist, intolerant, and devoted to missionary work. In the latter activity, they were very successful, and they competed vigorously with Christianity for new converts in the regions where they settled.

During the Crisis of the Third Century, and perhaps because of it, these eastern faiths consolidated their influence. Germanic tribes infiltrated from the north. Persians attacked from the east. Migrating tribes spread disease, instability, and economic hardship within the borders. Amid the chaos, as the empire fought for its very existence, citizens sought solace in cults that offered personal redemption.

In the 50 years before Diocletian ascended the imperial throne in AD 284, no fewer than 23 emperors reigned, each for a brief period, usually ending with their murder, assassination, or execution. The Crisis ended with his rise to power.

Christians had endured partly by assimilating the customs and rituals of the cultures they initially confronted. This included not only the rites of the traditional faiths but some of the rites and beliefs of the new rival religions. Many endure to this day.

Despite this, Christianity retained enough distinctiveness to present a counterculture to traditional Roman values, and its growing influence posed an ongoing threat. It would soon face the greatest challenge to its survival.

10

THE GREAT PERSECUTION

"**M**AKE ROME GREAT Again" might have been the motto of the new administration. Following the crisis that nearly tore it apart and undermined the old certainties, the empire needed to reassert its traditional values. This included upholding the sanctity of the family, reverence to the gods, and respect for the emperor and Senate.

But the prevalence of Asian religions, especially in the eastern provinces and Africa, threatened these values. Eventually, the authorities sought to obliterate the most dangerous ones. That included Christianity. So began a brutal contest between opposing belief systems. Only one could triumph.

STABILITY RESTORED

Diocletian was a conservative man of humble origins who had risen through the ranks. The early years of his reign were absorbed with restoring order in the beleaguered empire. Like his recent predecessors, he permitted Christians to serve in his administration. Many were promoted despite their refusal to partake in traditional Roman ceremonies. His wife and daughter were both sympathetic to the faith, if not actual converts.

The new emperor divided his realm into four parts and appointed co-rulers: Maximian, who, like Diocletian, held the title Augustus, and Galerius and Constantius, who held the lesser title Caesar. Known collectively as the Tetrarchy, they governed their appointed regions with him, but Diocletian retained supreme authority. The fourfold division was supremely successful, achieving victories against external enemies, securing borders, and restoring peace and stability for a time.

To combat economic decline, the government imposed price and wage controls, delegated tax collection to professionals, and curtailed free enterprise. This led to the rise of monopolies that stifled competition. Great tracts of land, some in far-flung corners of the empire, came under the control of a wealthy urban-based elite. This widened the wealth gap and alienated citizens from the government.

The following extract from a letter written to Donatus around that time encapsulates the situation:

> And thus, the empire having been quartered, armies were multiplied ... There began to be fewer men who paid taxes than there were who received wages; so that the means of the husbandmen being exhausted by enormous impositions, the farms were abandoned, cultivated grounds became woodland, and universal dismay prevailed.[340]

It was fertile breeding ground for recruitment to dissident creeds. So what if the emperor is indifferent? Jesus cares and he loves you!

Having centralised the earthly power, Diocletian conceived something similar for the heavenly. He renewed ties between the traditional Roman religions and the state. The army and citizens were encouraged to unite in temple worship and uphold the sanctity of the family.

Non-traditional cults were tolerated so long as they supported these goals. Sol Invictus conformed to his policy; Manichaeism did not. In fact, the rapid growth of the latter sect was causing alarm.

In AD 302, the proconsul of Africa, Amnius A. Julianus, wrote to the emperor seeking assistance against Manichaeism's troublesome followers. The response of the Tetrarchy reveals that they shared his concern. They issued a pronouncement, *Collatio Legum Mosaicarum et Romanarum,* stating that this "new and unexpected monster" from Persia was disturbing peaceful and innocent people "with the poisons of their wicked deeds."[341] Membership of the cult was incompatible with virtuous Roman character. Its Persian origins increased their distrust despite Sassanid persecution of Mani and his followers.

The celibacy of the Manichaean Elect was especially repulsive to family man Diocletian. In the words of the rescript, "We order that their organizers and leaders be subject to the final penalties and condemned to the fire with their abominable scripture." The persecution was aimed at the Elect hierarchy rather than their Hearer underlings. They were burned alive together with their scriptures.

TOLERATION TURNS TO HOSTILITY

We don't know if the Christians were alarmed at this clamp-down. If not, they should have been. The following year, the Tetrarchy turned its attention to them. Although some of the factors that made Manichaeism a security concern also applied to Christianity, it is not clear why Diocletian decided so late in his reign to turn against them. He had previously shown no hostile inclination and tolerated their growing influence in the administration.

Records of his motives are unavailable, possibly destroyed along with many other censorious documents when Christians came to power. The main surviving accounts come from two Christian writers.

Eusebius of Caesarea declared it was a punishment from God for infighting among Christian sects. Lucius Lactantius, a professor of rhetoric and member of the imperial circle, gives a more rational, albeit biased, account. According to Lactantius, Galerius was the instigator.

Among the Tetrarchy, Galerius was responsible for eastern affairs. His mother was a priestess of the temple who complained bitterly at the hostility of the Christians. No doubt they were poaching members of her flock, and her frustration might have rubbed off on Galerius.

Tensions arose as missionaries taunted non-believers with threats of hellfire and damnation, boasting that only the faithful would gain eternal bliss. Their conceit is reflected in the pejorative term *paganus* that Tertullian used to describe polytheists. Originally a reference to non-military citizens, it eventually came to mean a country bumpkin or redneck. Christian gangs mocked and desecrated the temples of the "pagans."

Polytheists returned the insults. The philosopher Porphyry accused Christians of worshipping a man instead of God. He suggested they should honour Apollonius of Tyana, who was credited with more impressive miracles than Jesus but never called himself God.

And so the war of words continued, underlying a cultural rift within the empire. Senators and aristocrats who had not converted shared the frustration of the traditional priests at the diminution of their flocks. An assertive Christian hierarchy was usurping the influence they once wielded through good works and patronage of the temples. Church ministers were undermining their authority.

EXTERMINATE THE SECT

It was not just the hostility of Christians and their growing independence that troubled Galerius. His military mind worried that their infiltration of the army could undermine the supplies to troops on the eastern front. It is unclear whether this concern was based on specific intelligence or conspiratorial paranoia.

According to Lactantius, the initial spark came from a seemingly minor incident. It occurred during a ritual where diviners called haruspices sought to predict the future by examining the entrails of sacrificial animals. For a traditionalist like Diocletian, this was an important ceremony. In a solemn atmosphere, as the emperor and his attendants awaited the celestial verdict, some Christian officials placed a sign on their foreheads. Perhaps this was to ward off the "evil spirits" that frequented such occasions. Distracted by their action, the chief haruspex declared himself unable to make a prediction.

Diocletian flew into a rage. He ordered the frightened attendants to offer sacrifice to restore the *pax deorum* ("peace of the gods"). He then extended the order to all administration and army personnel. Senior figures who ignored the instruction were either demoted or fired.

Once the necessary rituals were accomplished and his anger abated, no further punishments were issued—with one exception. While visiting the court, a deacon called Romanus interrupted another ceremony by loudly denouncing the sacrifice under preparation. His tongue was cut out in punishment, but his audacity troubled the emperor.

While wintering in Nicomedia (modern İzmit, Turkey), Galerius urged Diocletian to take further measures. As they strolled among the imperial gardens, they could not ignore an imposing stone structure that overshadowed their brooding tranquillity. On an adjacent hill, Christians had constructed a brand-new church. Its freshly cut stone reminded them, if they needed reminding, of the religion's growing self-assurance.

Initially, Diocletian resisted, preferring a policy of tolerance. Eventually, Galerius prevailed, and on February 24, AD 303, 19 years into his reign, Diocletian issued an edict against the Christians that initiated the first systematic attempt by Rome to exterminate the sect throughout the empire.

Under the edict, all Christian houses of worship were to be destroyed, scriptures burned, and property confiscated. Christian officials were removed from office, and those of low birth were deprived of freeman status. The imposing church in Nicomedia was the first to be demolished. The Great Persecution had begun.

The edict aimed to limit the wealth and influence of the church and deprive the faithful of its leadership. However, the reaction of the Christians fuelled the suspicion that they were seditious. Sporadic rioting erupted throughout the realm. In Nicomedia, a man called Eutius tore down the edict, ripped it up, and cursed the emperor's name. He was executed for treason, making him the first martyr of the new decree. Christian mobs retaliated. They made two attempts to burn the imperial palace but only managed to destroy a section of it. The alleged perpetrators were executed in retaliation.

Uprisings took place in Asia Minor and Syria. The Tetrarchy responded with a second edict ordering the arrest of all the clergy. This, however, placed a considerable strain on the penal system, as prisons were filled to capacity. According to Eusebius, common criminals had to be released to make room for bishops, priests, deacons, and exorcists.

To deal with the overcrowding, a third edict was passed permitting the release of prisoners provided they offered sacrifice to the gods. Many availed of the opportunity and offered token sacrifices. Some refused and were tortured into doing so. Others were released by sympathetic officials who falsely reported they had performed the required service.

The three edicts targeted church property and the clerical elite. A fourth and final edict in AD 304 was aimed at the laity. It decreed that all subjects, under penalty of death, must assemble at a designated place and offer an annual sacrifice to the emperor, much like the earlier decree of Decius.

INCONSTANT CAMPAIGN

The imperial authorities had never previously carried out such widespread persecution of Christians. But the success and severity of the persecution varied from province to province, depending on the zeal of the prefect or local magistrate. Some were content to close the churches. Others accepted texts on medicine, recipes, or any random subject for burning while reporting it as Christian literature. The enduring practice of box-ticking by indifferent officials prevailed.

The attitude of Diocletian's co-emperors was also a factor. In Africa and Italy, where Maximian held sway, the persecution was short and violent, and it provoked strong resistance. Although he did not enforce the fourth edict, there was much bloodshed. This was especially true among those Africans who regarded an agonising death as a kind of vocation. Many had already achieved martyrdom during periods of no persecution.

In the east so many abandoned their faith that Eusebius wrote of apostates becoming "countless in number."

By contrast in the west, under Constantius, suppression was mild and confined to demolishing churches and confiscating property. Or at least, that's what the records would show after his Christian son gained power. In any event, Christians were fewer there than elsewhere.

The persecution was still in progress when Diocletian resigned as emperor in AD 305. This unusual step was partly due to ill health. He persuaded his senior co-ruler Maximian to resign with him and promoted Galerius and Constantius to the rank of Augustus. Two new junior emperors, Severus and Maximinus Daza, were appointed Caesars to make up the four members of a new tetrarchy. The sons of Constantius and Maximian, respectively Constantine and Maxentius, were overlooked. This would soon provoke a contest for power.

Diocletian retired to Salonia in Dalmatia (modern Split, Croatia), where he grew cabbages "with his own hands," as he wrote to friends. He might have expected to enjoy a well-deserved repose. After all, he had inherited an empire in crisis, secured the borders, defeated external enemies, reformed the taxation system, and disciplined errant religious cults. In his own words, he had initiated an era of peace and security. Alas, how easily a leader can misjudge his legacy.

His choice of successors frustrated that optimism. It began with a power struggle in Italy and the west. The rival aspirants needed all the friends they could get, even if they were Christian. Persecution thus ground to a halt in that region.

Galerius and the new Caesar, Maximinus Daza, persisted for a while in the east.

Eventually Galerius finished the persecution in eastern Europe with the Edict of Serdica (modern Sofia, Bulgaria) in AD 311: "Wherefore it will be the duty of the Christians, in consequence of this our toleration, to pray to their God for our welfare, and for that of the public, and for their own; that the commonwealth may continue safe in every quarter, and that they themselves may live securely in their habitations."[342]

By this decree, he permitted Christians to resume their "foolish practices," provided they refrained from subversion and prayed for the welfare of the emperors. Although Christianity was not exterminated, Galerius felt he had curtailed its threat to the state.

But it was not over. Maximinus Daza escalated oppression in Egypt, Syria, and Asia Minor. This was a particularly vicious campaign by a man motivated more by sadism than conviction. Thousands were mutilated or dispatched to the mines. In an atmosphere of increasing intimidation, people were punished for merely conversing with or showing sympathy to Christian prisoners.

PERSECUTION ENDS, DIVISION INTENSIFIES

Daza's policy had a negative effect on labour supply, and his position as ruler was coming under pressure as the power struggle extended to the east. In AD 313, he belatedly issued his own edict of toleration, allowing Christians the right to worship freely.

With that edict, the Great Persecution was over. Ultimately, it had failed. Christians were too numerous to be fully exterminated.

Although more widespread and systematic than previous programmes, it was not implemented uniformly across the empire. Many Christians had avoided punishment.

Where persecution was severe, it elicited sympathy from the polytheists, who felt pity for the Christians and revulsion at their tormentors. The autocratic nature of the regime under Diocletian and the harsh economic conditions of the underclass did not help his cause. Christianity had the allure of a counter-establishment movement in an oppressive state.

It is difficult to estimate the total number executed in the Great Persecution. Many tales of martyrs were exaggerated, embellished with miracles and angelic interventions. Most were simply forgeries.

In his essay *De paucitate martyrum*, written in 1684, Henry Dodwell exposes the fiction of so many martyrdom tales. This view was echoed by his near contemporary Edward Gibbon:

> A convenient distance of time or place gave ample scope to the progress of fiction; and the frequent instances which might be alleged of holy martyrs, whose wounds had been instantly healed, whose strength had been renewed, and whose lost members had miraculously been restored, were extremely convenient for the purpose of removing every difficulty, and of silencing every objection. The most extravagant legends, as they conduced to the honour of the church, were applauded by the credulous multitude, countenanced by the power of the clergy, and attested by the suspicious evidence of ecclesiastical history.[343]

Gibbon estimated the figure for those killed at 2,000.

A later writer, ecclesiastical historian and Anglican priest W. H. C. Frend, put the figure between 3,000 and 3,500. Frend reckoned the total executed since the death of Jesus up to Daza's edict of AD 313 was between 5,500 and 6,500. However, there is no method to define the exact number. It is impossible to distinguish between those who sought martyrdom, those who merely refused the option to evade execution, and unwilling victims of the purge.

In addition to execution, untold numbers suffered imprisonment, torture, mutilation, and forced labour, especially under Maximinus Daza.

However, when compared to the punishment of common criminals, mutineers, and rebels over the three-century span, the number of Christian executions is not excessive. It would be overshadowed by the multitudes destined to perish when Christians later took control.

Whatever the numbers, Christianity had endured the most concerted attempt at its extermination and survived. One may ponder whether this was due to the unwavering conviction of the faithful or an administration that had not been sufficiently merciless. Having failed to crush them, Diocletian had unwittingly exposed his own weakness or the obsolescence of his ideals.

Severely wounded by the onslaught, Christianity was further divided between those who embraced persecution and those who avoided it. Each side could quote the Scriptures in defence of its position. Each side would defend its position to the death. Christians would now become both the persecutors and the persecuted.

11

CHRISTIAN VS. CHRISTIAN

"**M**ANY ARE CALLED, but few are chosen."³⁴⁴ Who, then, are the few?

Ironically, the ending of persecution sowed the seed for the first major inter-Christian violence. Since the injunctions of Decius, the church had fiercely debated the treatment of *lapsi* and *traditors*—those who avoided martyrdom. Some viewed the abjuration of one's faith for whatever expediency as a mortal sin punishable by exclusion from the fold. Others advocated leniency.

TROUBLE IN AFRICA

Mensurius, bishop of Carthage, was among the latter. He had no truck with martyrs and avoided becoming one himself by surrendering heretical documents to the authorities. In a letter to Secundus, bishop of Tigisi of Numidia (roughly modern Algeria), he criticised those who willingly embraced persecution. They were nothing more than "criminals and debtors" who thought they might "rid themselves of a burdensome life or wipe away remembrance of their misdeeds."[345] In his view, by inviting imprisonment, they exploited the generosity of fellow Christians who brought them gifts and food.

Secundus, in his reply, strongly disagreed and implied that Mensurius himself was less than holy for avoiding punishment.

Undeterred, Mensurius prevented sympathisers from bringing alms to Christian prisoners in Carthage during the persecution. His deacon, Caecilian, seized their donations and trampled them underfoot.

Two opposing camps emerged: *traditors* such as Mensurius, who believed it was acceptable to evade martyrdom, and *rigorists* such as Secundus, who regarded such behaviour as unforgivable. Tensions escalated; conflict was inevitable.

The rift erupted in AD 311, when Mensurius died. His deacon Caecilian was consecrated bishop at Carthage. One of the three consecrating ecclesiastics was himself believed to be a *traditor*. Although the evidence was flimsy, an opposition group of 70 bishops formed a synod presided over by Secundus. Declaring that *traditors* could neither receive nor administer the sacraments, it pronounced the consecration invalid.

They summoned Caecilian to appear before them. They had not forgotten his thrashing of their food donations. The new bishop wisely refused, stating, not unreasonably, that "If I am not properly consecrated, let them treat me as a deacon, and lay hands on me afresh, and not on another"—the laying of hands being the act of consecration. The reply came, "Let him come here, and instead of laying [hands] on him, we will break his head in penance."[346]

Denied the opportunity to "break his head," they settled for excommunicating him instead.

Excommunication was a severe punishment. It involved exclusion from the church and the sacraments and, in extreme cases, could only be revoked at death. If not revoked, it condemned the recipient's soul to eternal punishment. A sentence that extended to the afterlife presented a potent psychological weapon in the hands of the hierarchy. It was designed to keep dissenters in line.

The dispute was submitted to several ecclesiastical councils, each of which revoked the excommunication and upheld the appointment of Caecilian. This was not surprising.

The problem with the *rigorist* position was that the sins of an individual clergyman could invalidate any sacrament he performed, including baptism, marriage, or ordination. This would render the blameless recipients unbaptised, unmarried, or un-ordained. So, for example, if a man was ordained to the priesthood, and unknown to him, the ordaining priest was a *traditor*, then in the eyes of the *rigorists,* he remained a layman. Any sacrament he subsequently performed, such as baptism or marriage, would be invalid, thus initiating a chain of errors impossible to trace.

However, it was impossible to reason with *rigorists*. They stubbornly refused to accept the decision of the councils. From their perspective, the issue was one of free choice and the right to resist force when used by the state or by other Christians against them.

The movement flourished in Numidia and spread to adjoining provinces, especially Mauritania. They elected a bishop of their own, Donatus, who himself had been imprisoned and tortured during the purge of Diocletian. Henceforth they were known as Donatists.

Their symbol was the Ark, wherein dwelt the righteous, while outside were lost souls, drowning in a sea of sin. After all, according to the Bible,[347] only the few would be chosen, and they were the few.

The dispute engulfed the Roman provinces of West Africa. It descended into violent confrontation, with the combatants burning each other's villages, raping each other's women, and torturing each other's clergy with the zeal of the righteous. Each side was consumed by a divine justification to kill their foes, the enemies of the true God. Each side was equally ready to die the death of martyrdom if it came to that.

Bands of armed Berber Donatists, calling themselves *agonistici* ("fighters for Christ") but known to their enemies as *circumcelliones* ("scroungers"), terrorised the countryside, murdering and robbing their rivals, "living as bandits" and "honoured as martyrs."[348]

Their weapons of choice were wooden clubs, which they called "Israelites." They advocated debt cancellation, freedom for slaves, and above all, martyrdom, "because they love the name martyr and because they desire human praise more than divine charity."[349]

Polytheists looked on in astonishment. The historian Ammianus Marcellinus remarked, "No fury of the savage beast against man can surpass the hostility of the Christians towards each other."[350] It was a taste of things to come.

THE FAITH ENDURES

The Donatist controversy brought to the forefront underlying fractures in the Christian community. More fractures would soon appear. Could internal strife triumph where external oppression had failed?

It would take a ruthless man to meet this challenge. The fate of Christianity depended on the outcome.

12

AN UNEXPECTED TRIUMPH

WINNERS GET TO write history. So, the victors have recorded the next phase in our narrative. Their version, which is now enshrined in legend, owes more to spin than truth, as we shall see.

Their hero was a skilled manipulator who brooked no dissent. Such a man could readily align with a religion that shared his authoritarian tendencies. So it was when Constantine met Christianity. Against such opposition, a tetrarchy built on consensus was doomed.

POWER STRUGGLE

A battle for succession began among the new Tetrarchs, reminiscent of the conflicts that plagued Rome during the Crisis of the Third Century. This was precisely what Diocletian had tried to prevent by relinquishing power. His former co-rulers and their sons or nominees now vied for control. He could only watch in dismay from his Dalmatian estate as the armies of the combatants trampled across the empire, bringing destruction in their wake.

When his former co-emperor of the west, Constantius, died in AD 306, the troops immediately declared his illegitimate son Constantine as successor. A furious Galerius, who favoured another, had little choice but to accept the fait accompli. The rebels were in far-away Britain, outside his control.

Constantine was about 32 at the time. Born in Naissus (modern Niš, Serbia), his mother Helena was a "camp follower," one who made a living providing services to the Roman army. His father abandoned her when he married a woman of higher birth.

Like most soldiers, Constantine revered Sol Invictus, the physical manifestation of divine Mithras. He was a skilled commander, highly respected by his troops. This ability, combined with ruthless ambition, helped to bind his fate with that of the empire.

Though devoted to his mother, his illegitimate birth and her former occupation were an embarrassment to him and a source of much jibing by his enemies. He needed legitimacy and sought it by creating a fake ancestry. Henceforth the orators proclaimed his dynastic connection with the former Emperor Claudius II, an illustrious warrior of the third century AD.

If this were not enough, Constantine claimed to have seen a vision of Apollo at a temple in Gaul. Images of Mars, which previously appeared on his coinage, were now replaced by those of Sol Invictus (associated with the sun god Apollo). This move appealed to both the troops and the Roman elite.

Having secured heavenly endorsement, the young Caesar revealed a cold-blooded streak. At his command, a captive Frankish king and his troops were torn apart by wild animals in the arena. His calculated decision not to support the rebellion of his brother-in-law Maxentius in Italy enhanced his popularity and preserved his forces.

It did not make him very popular with Maxentius, who might have benefited from his assistance. Despite this, Maxentius had managed to take control of Italy and North Africa.

The two western co-emperors signed a treaty, but there was little trust between them. Though Constantine was married to Maxentius's sister, Fausta, he had sent their father to the grave for an attempted mutiny. It was too much to hope that a treaty would last. By 312, Constantine was leading his Gallic army across the Alps into Italy for a showdown. They soon arrived at the outskirts of Rome.

Maxentius decided to risk everything on a single encounter. Advancing out of the city, he positioned his forces on the north side of the Tiber near the Milvian Bridge. With their backs to the river and too close to its banks, his army had little room for manoeuvre. Constantine, the shrewd general, saw the mistake and ordered a full-scale attack.

Pressed by the sudden onslaught, the defending troops were forced to withdraw across a pontoon bridge, which collapsed under the pressure. In the confusion, many were drowned, including Maxentius. The victorious Constantine entered the Eternal City as the sole emperor of the west. However, it was not enough to satiate his lust for power.

THE EDICT OF TOLERATION

Following the victory, Constantine allied with Licinius, the leading contender in the east. The two met in Mediolanum (modern Milan) in 313. They jointly issued the Edict of Milan, which granted liberality to all religions, including Christianity. It went further than the Edict of Serdica in ordering confiscated property to be restored to the church.

To cement their friendship, Licinius married Constanta, sister of Constantine, before rushing back to confront his rival, Maximinus Daza, who had just invaded Thrace. Licinius overcame Daza, forcing him to flee back to Asia Minor. Eventually, in the words of Eusebius, "God granted him victory" when the fugitive Daza died of an illness. Licinius was now the sole emperor of the east.

The chronicler Lactantius described the new eastern emperor as a champion of Christ who was visited by an angel before the battle against Daza.[351]

Eusebius, in his earlier writings,[352] was equally flattering towards Licinius. It appears he was a Christian and might have been instrumental in persuading Galerius to issue the Edict of Serdica, which ended the Great Persecution.

Two of his first acts after defeating Daza were to destroy a temple to Zeus at Antioch and to execute the resident priest, Theotecnus, who had unwisely predicted that Daza would triumph.

Licinius then set about hounding the family members of Galerius and Diocletian. They were labelled "the persecutors" by Christian chroniclers, although some had been either Christian themselves or sympathetic to the faith. Among those was Prisca, wife of Diocletian, who was thrown into the Orontes River, "where she had often herself ordered chaste women thrown,"[353] implying she had killed Christians, which is hard to credit. Licinius then had her daughter beheaded to the enthusiastic applause of the Christian mob.

CONSTANTINE'S VISIONS

Constantine's beliefs at that time are less clear. The Arch of Constantine erected to commemorate his victory at the Milvian Bridge makes no reference to Christianity. The images show sacrifices to Apollo, Hercules, and Diana. An inscription reading *instinctu divinitatis* ("inspired by the divine") can be seen as a reference to whatever god one chooses—deliberately ambiguous, perhaps. The coins minted for the next eight years continued to bear the symbol of Sol Invictus.

As a gesture to Sol Invictus, Sunday became the official day of worship and was designated a day of rest. This encouraged Christians to abandon the traditional Sabbath (Saturday) and thus distance themselves further from the politically unpopular Jews. It also made their religion more attractive to non-believers.

In parallel with his reverence toward Sol Invictus, Constantine sought favour with the church and would later grant the clergy exemption from certain taxes. This is a privilege the church enjoys to this day. Additionally, he granted them freedom from compulsory service and the right to inherit property. In correspondence with bishops, he adopted a friendly tone, even crediting their god with a role in his success.

There was political advantage in the strategy. Various estimates place the number of Christians in the west at between 2% and 20% of the total population.[354]

This contrasts with the eastern empire and Africa, where estimates vary from 20% to almost 50%.[355] They were a highly organised and wealthy minority. They had enough political power to have caused Diocletian to attempt their downfall and for Galerius to realise it was impossible. Furthermore, their numbers were increasing at a rapid rate.[356] It was partly through their influence that Armenia, a Roman protectorate, officially became the first Christian kingdom with the baptism of its King Tiridates III in 301.

Constantine had spent his early years in the court of Galerius at Nicomedia. There, he had seen first-hand the power of the movement and the concern it caused the emperor. At that time, he did not object to the Great Persecution. However, he would subsequently go to great lengths to pretend that he did.

If he wanted to conquer the east, he must portray himself as the divinely ordained champion of the Christians. Perhaps with this in mind, he recounted a story to his secretary that his victory over Maxentius was secured by the intervention of the Christian God. Lactantius included this in *De Mortibus Persecutorum*, written or edited while he was in the court of Constantine.

On the eve of the battle of Milvian Bridge, the story goes, Constantine had a dream where he saw the letter *X* sideways with the top portion shaped like a *P*, thus ⚹. The next day, he ordered his troops to place this sign, the *Chi-Rho*, on their shields. Lactantius asserts that the symbol represented Christ.

Eusebius included a similar story in his sycophantic biography of the emperor, *Vita Constantine*. (In an earlier book, he gives a slightly different account.) In this version, Constantine and his troops see a vision of the cross in the sky with a Greek inscription, Εν Τούτω Νίκα. This is roughly translated as "By this, conquer." Later that night, Christ appears to the emperor, instructing him to adopt the symbol to protect his troops. The time and location are not specified. It was probably in his later campaign in Asia. However, popular myth came to associate it with the battle of the Milvian Bridge.

Constantine was not above seeing visions when political expediency demanded it, as with his earlier vision of Apollo in Gaul. However, this new apparition, albeit in a dream, helped foster the myth of divine intervention analogous to Moses and the burning bush or St. Paul on the road to Damascus. It was another shrewd manoeuvre by a devious self-promoter.

What is certain is that he placed the symbol on his standard during the wars in the east, where he now turned his attention. He calculated that it would dishearten the Christian troops of his opponent.

Using the excuse that Licinius had sent an agent to assassinate him, Constantine launched his first attack in 314. After a brief conflict, they agreed on a truce. Constantine had no intention of honouring it.

Over the next 10 years, he repeatedly invaded the territory of Licinius on the pretext of pursuing barbarian intruders only to retreat following a ceasefire. He was merely testing the waters, waiting for an opportune time to deliver the final blow.

This came in 324, when he led his army into Asia Minor and, in a decisive battle near Chalcedon on the eastern shore of the Bosphorus, routed the army of Licinius. His position hopeless, the eastern emperor, accompanied by his wife and the bishop of Nicomedia, surrendered to his brother-in-law on the promise that his life would be spared. Six months later, Constantine ordered his execution by strangulation. His young son Licinianus, despite being Constantine's nephew, was flogged to death. This was a humiliating execution normally reserved for slaves.

A CHRISTIAN EMPEROR

Constantine now needed to discredit his dead rival and portray the war as a struggle between a Christian ruler and his heathen opponent. Enter Eusebius, the bender of truth. Earlier versions of *Historia Ecclesiastica* were edited to change or remove laudatory comments. Licinius was now portrayed as a tormentor of the faithful. No longer the Christians' champion, he instead closed churches, executed bishops, and secretly plotted widespread persecution.

There are no specifics, and the writer fails to name any martyrs. However, he correctly identifies three factual "persecutions" that did occur. Licinius ordered Christians to pray outdoors. (The churches were overflowing with new converts.) He passed a law forcing men and women to sit separately during services, and he required bishops to remain in their appointed sees rather than switch to new ones.

Rather than the actions of a persecutor, the measures indicate a man engrossed in church affairs. In fact, church councils and Christian rulers later endorsed these decrees.

In contrast, Constantine was depicted as a pious Christian who ordered the removal of his statues from all polytheist places of worship and enacted anti-pagan laws, including the destruction of temples and the banning of sacrifices. The struggle between the two emperors was portrayed as a victory of Christianity over polytheism. Thanks to Constantine, Rome became a Christian empire.

The fact that this perception survives to the present day is testimony to Constantine's mastery of spin. The past was rewritten, his future legacy secured. In reality, the transition from a polytheist to a Christian empire was a process that cannot be assigned to a specific time or event. Although Christianity was not yet the official religion of the empire, a significant milestone had been achieved.

On matters of faith, Constantine was ambivalent. Though he seemed genuinely to favour Christianity later in his life, he fully understood the political advantage of presenting himself as a figurehead for their cause.

Whatever Constantine's true motives, Christians were ecstatic. Within living memory of the Great Persecution and despite their minority status, they now savoured the sweet taste of imperial favour. The Edict of Milan had given them universal toleration. A champion of their faith, as many saw it, was now the sole and undisputed ruler of the empire.

The writings of Eusebius reflect this Christian triumphalism: "Our Saviour's mighty power destroyed at once the many governments and the many gods of the powers of darkness, and proclaimed to all men, both rude and civilized, to the extremities of the earth, the sole sovereignty of God himself."[357]

Constantine was compared to a sacred being: "His ministers are the heavenly hosts; his armies the supernal powers, who own allegiance to him as their Master, Lord, and King. The countless multitudes of angels, the companies of archangels, the chorus of holy spirits, draw from and reflect his radiance as from the fountains of everlasting light."[358]

There was a pervasive sense that ancient prophecies would be fulfilled, signalling the imminent realisation of God's kingdom on Earth. Quoting extensively from Isaiah and the other scriptures, Eusebius announced, "He shall have dominion from sea to sea and from the river to the ends of the earth."[359]

TRUE FAITH OR TYRANNY

There was no historical precedent for a cult assuming political control in this manner. Only later, with the triumph of Christianity's sister religion Islam, would something analogous be repeated. In fact, one must arrive at the 20th century with the triumph of Bolshevism in Russia and National Socialism in Germany to find appropriate parallels. The conditions were the same: social unrest, economic depression, political insecurity, a fanatical but well-organised minority, and a stark, inflexible philosophy.

Once in power, the first victims of the inevitable purge were the closest ideological allies. Thus, the Bolsheviks destroyed the Mensheviks and the Nazis destroyed Röhm's Sturmabteilung. Christians would likewise initiate a similar eradication of their nearest competitors.

The church owes its subsequent survival to the lack of a potent enemy, at least until the rise of Islam. There was no free world to unite against this philosophy and no power within to challenge it. Tolerant polytheists were not equipped to counter its fire; even the powerful cult of Mithraism, nurtured to fight foes from without, was no match for the foe within. Manichaeism was too recent to have developed a structure or amass the numbers that Christianity possessed. Barbarians knocking on the empire's borders, largely ignorant and unrefined, would be ripe for indoctrination when the time came.

With the emperor's support and administration, Christianity could destroy all opposition to its doctrine, both physical and intellectual. Books were burned, along with the ideas they contained. Through terror, Christianity removed all challenges to its authority so that for the coming centuries, only one truth would be known or tolerated.

A tyrant had given power to a tyrannical creed. Or a ruler, blessed by God, had brought the true faith to humankind. Take your pick.

The most optimistic believers had reason to suppose the kingdom of God was at hand. Soon, however, disputes concealed within the movement would emerge to trouble their emperors.

PART THREE

HERETICS

"I shall give thee the heathen for thine inheritance and the uttermost parts of the Earth for thy possession."

—Psalm 2:8

13

CHRISTIANS DIVIDED

THE TRIUMPHANT CHURCH soon displayed its intolerant character. Its first targets were not unbelievers but rather fellow Christians. Victory exposed an underlying animosity among the faithful that threatened to tear them apart.

In his attempts to mediate between the warring Christian factions, Emperor Constantine entangled the state in the tortuous field of theology and set a dubious precedent for future governance. The state could henceforth arbitrate on matters of private conscience. Was this the victory Christians had sought?

VENOMOUS ERRORS

Despite its outward power, Christianity was divided from within. Contemporary writers put the number of Christian sects at between 80 and 128.[360] Different interpretations of the faith, ritual, organisation, and lifestyle, some relatively trivial, gave rise to fierce dispute and occasionally open violence. The Donatist controversy in North Africa was one such example.

The church could not endure this diversity. Selective interpretation of the Scriptures was incompatible with the dogmatic spirit of the first commandment and "far more evil and dangerous than any kind of war or conflict."[361] Those who deviated were guilty of heresy or free thought (Greek *hairesis*, "choosing for oneself"). And these heretics were "pernicious enemies of the human race," "pests of society," "false prophets," and "ravening wolves."[362]

In his exhortation to doctrinal unity, St. Cyprian of Carthage declared that "outside of the Church there is no salvation."[363] Heretics were outside, but doctrinal unity within the church did not exist. There was no established orthodoxy. Each faction considered that it alone practised the true faith, and each accused the others of heresy.

In the inevitable struggle that followed, the first losers would be Manichaeans, Monarchians, Montanists, and Gnostics. These sects were either less organised or politically weak. Gnostics, though once numerous, had been reduced by sustained attacks from an organised hierarchy long before Constantine came to power. Divided into several conflicting subsects, their elitism, emphasis on knowledge rather than faith, and mystic rituals set them apart from other Christians. Manichaeans had already suffered persecution at the hands of the state. However, they still retained some influence, especially in Africa.

The edicts of Diocletian, which had lapsed, were now reinvigorated to oppress those sects. The language of the persecutors leaves no room for compromise: "All ye who devise and support heresy by means of your private assemblies, with falsehood and vanity, with what destructive and venomous errors … through you the healthy soul is stricken with disease, and the living becomes the prey of everlasting death."[364] Provincial governors received orders to confiscate their property and banish the leaders.

Donatism was a different matter. Several ecclesiastical assemblies were convened to resolve the controversy. In each case, the Donatist position was overruled, and in each case, the Donatists refused to relent. They would have no truck with apostate bishops, and neither would they accept the pleas of the pope when he was compelled to intervene. Finally, having appealed to the emperor, they cursed his name when he also upheld the previous rulings.

For a ruler accustomed to victory on the battlefield and the power of life or death in court, this was a new experience. How could some inconsequential African peasants challenge his authority?

In 317, Constantine attempted to suppress them by force. He dispatched troops to Carthage, where they seized some churches and killed a few stubborn dissenters. However, beyond the cities, Donatism prevailed. Secure in their rural strongholds and unafraid of martyrdom, they were not easily intimidated. The empire, preoccupied with internal strife and external security, was not prepared to commit the resources necessary to overpower them. The conflict dragged on.

Constantine was dismayed at these divisions. Although he had not yet fully embraced Christianity and his coins still displayed Sol Invictus, he was concerned about the destabilising effect of Christian infighting. Even such trifles as the appropriate date for Easter were the source of furious debate. Should he intervene? Well, whether he should or not, it seemed he could.

By appealing to the emperor, the Donatists had invoked the civil authority to adjudicate on a matter of Christian doctrine. In accepting his right to arbitrate, the hierarchy endorsed the precedent. On that basis, Constantine felt emboldened to arbitrate once more.

On the advice of Bishop Hosius of Cordova, he decided to call a synod to discuss and resolve the various disputes. The aim was to establish a universally accepted creed, a common interpretation of the Scriptures by which Christianity would define itself.

Matters had come to a head in Alexandria. Here, a presbyter called Arius argued that Jesus did not exist from eternity but was created by God the Father. Therefore, he was not of the same divine substance as God but a separate being existing by the will of God.

It was not an entirely novel idea, but the hostile reaction of the local patriarch and his archdeacon Athanasius elevated it to the public domain. Soon, a fierce controversy raged and rapidly spread beyond Alexandria. A bemused Constantine dispatched Bishop Hosius with an open letter to the antagonists, urging reconciliation and asking them to forgive each other: "I find the cause to be of a truly insignificant character, and quite unworthy of such fierce contention."[365] The statement reveals a certain naivety on his part. Constantine would soon appreciate the ferocity of the theologians.

As with the Donatists, his intervention did not subdue the conflict. Worse, there were whispered rumours of insults directed at his statue. Bishops and clergy ranged themselves as partisans on either side, and the fury of their controversy threatened to engulf the east. On one side was the Platonic concept of an aloof entity, the Creator dispatching his intermediary, Jesus, to intercede with humankind. Opponents preferred a friendlier God who deigned to dwell among them for a time and in their own image.

Meanwhile, the polytheists enjoyed the spectacle of Christian squabbling and openly poked fun at their divisions and debates. Emperor and bishops agreed that this could not continue. Something must be done.

THE COUNCIL OF NICAEA

In 325, Constantine called the great synod at Nicaea in Asia Minor (modern İznik, Turkey) to address these vexatious divisions. It promised to be a momentous event.

Holy troops of bishops in white linen tunics arrived from all corners of the empire and even far-off Persia. They were accompanied by presbyters, deacons, and an assortment of officials and attendants "beyond computation."

Transport was provided courtesy of the empire, and generous provisions were furnished daily for the delegates at the emperor's command. Constantine, himself in lavish attire and seated on a throne of gold, addressed the delegates at the opening ceremony. Together they would decide what Jesus had meant when he said the things he mostly didn't say.

They aspired to a consensus of doctrine but failed even to reach a consensus on their number. Eusebius of Caesarea, who was present, reports that 250 bishops attended. Athanasius of Alexandria, who was also there, quotes 300. Socrates Scholasticus puts the figure at 318.

For two months, the assembly debated the various issues before it. Topics included the admission or expulsion of clerics castrated by choice or by violence, whether women should be permitted to cohabit with church ministers, and the election and authority of bishops. Pronouncements were made concerning Novatians, Docetists, Paulians, and other perceived deviants.

A decision was made on the date for Easter, taking the church further from its Jewish roots, for it was, according to Constantine, "an unworthy thing that in the celebration of this most holy feast we should follow the practice of the Jews."[366] It was moved to loosely coincide with the traditional Roman spring equinox. However, the failure of the council to provide a precise definition would lead to further disputes in the centuries to come.

At the top of the agenda was the Arian controversy. Arius was summoned before the council and given several opportunities to air his views, which he did. He argued that any creation must be less than the creator and the son less than the father that begot him. Putting it simply, in the beginning was the father, and the son came later, as indeed sons generally do.

To understand the physical characteristics of Jesus relative to the Father, wise beards pondered terms such as *ousia* ("essence"), *hypostasis* ("substance"), *physis* ("nature"), and *hyposōpon* ("person"). Words that once waxed the minds of long-dead Greek philosophers now found new life in Christian theology.

To Arius and his followers, "born," "created," and "begotten" had comparable meanings. To his opponents, they did not.

Although some bishops supported his reasoning, the majority rejected it. Foremost among the latter was Athanasius, advisor to the Patriarch of Alexandria. His position as archdeacon did not allow him to participate in the debates directly. However, he provided the counter-arguments for those anti-Arian delegates who could participate. He possessed the inflexible mindset of the fanatic and an aversion to those who sought compromise. Not for him, any of this Greek rationalism. The truth could be found only in the Scriptures, or at least his interpretation of them, and the early church traditions.

So heated was the debate that, at one point, an agitated bishop struck Arius in the face. This might have hurt him less than the final verdict. The assembly denounced him as a heretic and his beliefs as anathema. His writings were condemned, and an order was issued to burn his books. For good measure, Constantine banished him to Illyria and pronounced capital punishment for anyone found in possession of his works. By this measure, the emperor stamped the seal of civil authority on religious orthodoxy, uniting secular law and church canon.

At the conclusion of the council, most bishops agreed on a set of laws that outlined the church's position on the matters discussed. They also agreed on the formulation of a statement of belief setting forth the fundamental doctrine of the church, known henceforth as the Nicene Creed. The following is an excerpt from the original (it later underwent minor modifications): "We believe in one God, the Father Almighty, maker of all things visible and invisible; and in one Lord Jesus Christ, the Son of God, begotten of the Father as only begotten, that is from the essence of the Father. God from God, Light from Light, True God from True God, *begotten not created*, of the same essence [Greek *homoousion*] as the Father [emphasis added]."

The Nicene Creed is not only a statement of doctrine but also a carefully worded refutation of many of the divergent Christian beliefs of the day, especially Arianism. After much persuasion, all except two bishops signed the accord, many out of deference to or fear of the emperor.

"SUPERSTITIOUS AND SENSELESS MEETINGS"[367]

But the joyous optimism of clerics and the emperor was short lived. The faithful did not immediately embrace the Creed. The followers of Arius did not disperse. They became more numerous and allied themselves with the Melitians, another group denounced at the council. The Donatist controversy escalated in Africa, the Novatians held firm in Asia Minor, and other heretical sects continued their defiance. They would be sorely tested later but not without considerable resistance. Many heretical sects were localised and enjoyed fervent support in the regions or cities where they resided.

CHRISTIANS DIVIDED

An angry Constantine issued a threat: "Since it is no longer possible to bear with your pernicious errors, we give warning by this present statute that none of you [heretics] henceforth presume to assemble yourselves together. We have directed that you be deprived of all the houses in which you hold your assemblies: and ... forbid the holding of your superstitious and senseless meetings, not in public merely, but in any private house or place whatsoever."[368]

It sounded remarkably like previous salvos directed at the Christians by former emperors. He invited the faithful "who are desirous of embracing the true and pure religion" to unite in "one holy fellowship, whereby you will be enabled to arrive at the knowledge of the truth."

However, as far as Arianism was concerned, Constantine began to soften his stance. This was due to the influence of Eusebius of Nicomedia, who after initially refusing to sign the creed, publicly recanted and expressed agreement with it. The recantation smacked of opportunism; his next act was to persuade the emperor to rescind the sentence of exile against Arius if he also recanted.

Grateful for the opportunity, Arius composed a declaration of faith that seemed to satisfy the emperor. Nonetheless, the wary monarch sent the document to some bishops assembled in Jerusalem and asked for their opinion. The bishops, who sympathised with Arius, pronounced the declaration sound.

Satisfied, Constantine decreed that the former presbyter be readmitted into the congregation in Alexandria. The old patriarch had died, and archdeacon Athanasius, his chosen successor, now occupied the episcopal chair. His promotion had neither diminished his inflexibility nor improved his tolerance. There would be no compromise with those who did not conform fully to the Nicene Creed.

In the interests of peace and harmony, Constantine asked Athanasius to allow Arius and his followers to worship in the Egyptian churches. But the young patriarch doubted the sincerity of Arius's declaration and refused the request. Arians were out, and for Athanasius, the term "Arian" included anyone who rejected the Nicene Creed, whether they agreed with the ideas of Arius or not. It was a bold challenge to the emperor, but Athanasius possessed the intellect and the political acumen to uphold his cause in Egypt and beyond.

Constantine did not press his case. He allowed Arius to re-join the Christian community in Constantinople instead of Egypt. On the day appointed for his triumphal return, as he made his way to the basilica, Arius suddenly had a violent seizure accompanied by "evacuation of his bowels and a copious haemorrhage,"[369] according to Socrates Scholasticus, who saw it as divine vengeance. If the vengeance was divine, it was likely aided by an agent of the local bishop and a vial of poison. The condition proved fatal; Arius expired almost immediately.

For denying them admission to his Egyptian churches, the Arians retaliated with a synod in Tyre that deposed Athanasius. But the obstinate cleric would not go quietly and instead hastened to Constantinople. The emperor was astonished when the wide-eyed bishop suddenly appeared before him on the highway, seized his horse by the bridle, and demanded a hearing.

Constantine convened another meeting and heard the arguments of both sides. He heeded warnings from the Arian faction that Athanasius was a violent man who had committed criminal acts against Arians and Melitians and would use his power to cut off essential Egyptian grain supplies to the empire. Whether this was true or not, Constantine suspected Athanasius of sedition[370] and exiled him to Gaul. From there, the obstinate bishop maintained correspondence with his flock in Egypt and Libya, learned the Latin of the western clerics, and bided his time.

Meanwhile the drive for universality continued. In an atmosphere of intimidation, specific Christian communities were targeted, and any writings considered "deviant" consigned to flames. Countless letters, gospels, sermons, and theological treatises were destroyed as various sects were marginalised into obscurity.

Once the temporal power of the state became aligned to the spiritual authority of the bishops, the fates of both were entwined. Henceforth every citizen must submit not just to one faith but one specific interpretation of it.

Inevitably, many would challenge this imposition. The state might have better served the church by ignoring its disputes so long as it followed the laws. It seemed neither Constantine nor the bishops were capable of that.

The process begun at Nicaea would continue for endless centuries amid bloodshed and division.

14

ONE EMPIRE UNDER GOD

NICAEA GAVE TO Caesar what rightfully belonged to God, and the righteous gratefully received from Caesar in return. From now on, despite internal disputes, the church gave almost unequivocal support to Constantine. For the emperor, this provided the means to consolidate his power, distribute largesse, and secure an enduring legacy.

Fervent Christians viewed these developments with concern. They feared that a faith characterised by sacrifice and self-denial might succumb to greed and corruption.

From the time Constantine made Christianity the favoured religion, it was easier to be a Christian than not. Sensing the winds of change, the more astute now flocked to the church. Concessions on taxation and compulsory service attracted the avaricious. Episcopal posts became highly sought after.

Ambitious men saw the opportunity for wealth and the avoidance of duty these offices could provide. They enjoyed security, prosperity, and privilege in exchange for a questionable contribution to an empire that sustained the idle at the expense of the productive. If they misbehaved, they could always seek forgiveness.

The devout saw the influx of these opportunist converts as a dilution of the faith. Fearing that sinners would outnumber the pure, some sought a more mystical existence away from the community.

DEMONS IN THE DESERT

One such man was St. Anthony, the son of a wealthy Egyptian family. When his parents died, he gave away his possessions and farm to the local villagers, renounced the pleasures of wine and women, and sent his young sister into a convent. We don't know how his sister felt about this. He willingly forsook his comfortable home to set up residence in a pigsty.

Under the guidance of the hermit Paul of Thebes, Anthony maintained an ascetic lifestyle for 15 years before venturing alone into the desert. Here, where evil spirits lurked, he occupied an abandoned fort and remained there for nearly 20 years, living off scraps of food thrown over the walls by devoted followers.

Bread and salt were his regular fare and water his only drink, and many a day passed without either. There were no books to relieve his boredom, nor did he need them. He disdained scholarship of any sort, "for he could not endure to learn letters nor associate with others" but rather "to live like a plain man."[371] Although he could read and write, these ranked in usefulness below prayer, fasting, and sleeping on a hard floor.

In solitude, he battled demons in their various forms. Wild beasts tried to devour him, a soldier attempted to murder him, and a savage fiend almost beat him to death. On one occasion, a woman tried to seduce him, and when that failed, a young Black boy reclined at his feet. When the hunger pangs disturbed his dreams, a friendly monk tempted him with food. These "heralds of Satan" he repelled with prayers and abstinence.

Eventually, he left the fort to instruct his followers, who had encamped in nearby hills and caves. He organised them into a community of monks near the Red Sea. On two occasions, he visited Alexandria, where he proved a staunch ally of Athanasius in his campaign against heresy. Inspired by the monk's spiritual struggles, the patriarch wrote his biography, *The Life of Saint Anthony*, complete with demonic encounters.

It became a bestseller, turning the humble hermit into a household name. The story inspired many to seek refuge and spiritual salvation in the wilderness. Like Anthony, some became aggressive defenders of the Trinity, frontline warriors in the conflict against pagans and heretics. Others supported Arianism with equal ferocity. Colonies sprang up all over Egypt, neighbouring Libya, Syria, and Asia Minor. In the coming centuries, they spread to Ethiopia, Europe, Britain, Ireland, and as far away as Iceland.

Over time, a formalised monastic order developed. Novices, many poor and illiterate, including runaway slaves and fugitive criminals, vowed perpetual obedience to the monastery. Some shaved their heads, and others allowed their hair to grow without constraint. They lived in solitary cells, weighed down by chains, with nothing to cover their naked bodies except long manes. Fasting, sleep deprivation, silence, and penance were among their routines. Blind submission to the abbot was required, and once initiated, a monk could not leave. Those who tried were pursued and restored to confinement.

Manual labour was the order of the day. Free will was replaced by submission, and free thought by blind credence. Retaining a "savage enthusiasm which represents man as a criminal and God as a tyrant,"[372] the monks held that pleasure was synonymous with guilt. The thousands who entered these monasteries believed that the stark life they embraced on Earth would spare them the torments of hell in the afterlife. Pioneers like Amma Syncletica of Alexandria established similar colonies for female hermits. Whether male or female, they contributed to the expansion of Christianity within the empire and beyond.

Another type of hermit, Stylites (Greek "of a pillar") sought a more extreme form of asceticism by living in lonely isolation atop pillars. Numerous such eccentrics were venerated as saints for their pointless virtue. One of the more notable was St. Simeon Stylites.[373]

Departing from his monastery, he established an address in the desert 50 kilometres east of Antioch on a pile of rocks and stones. He gradually upgraded it to a two-metre column. To avoid the attention of visiting pilgrims, he erected a succession of pillars, each one higher than the last, until his final abode was a post 18 metres high. Here he remained, perched on the top, chained to the structure. For 30 years or more, he prayed, sometimes standing on one leg, and other times bowed in supplication. But he never once descended to the ground.

His zeal prompted the admiration of Christians near and far, who journeyed to pay their respects. It was said that the example of his devotion converted many non-believers. His mind, if it ever had been rational in the first place, must have been fried to a rare insanity under the hot Syrian sun. Or perhaps he found an inner peace that rendered the mortal world superfluous to his needs.

When, while bent in prayer, the life departed from his body, he was mourned by emperor and subjects alike. The Patriarch of Antioch, various bishops, tribunes, and a guard of several thousand soldiers attended his funeral. His relics were preserved in a special basilica built in his honour.

MAGIC RELICS AND MYTHIC MARTYRS

Relics themselves were a vital fabric of the faith. Innumerable mementos of the martyrs, including items of their clothing or bones or ashes wrapped in linen cloth, interred in tombs and churches, became a focus for pilgrimage.

The process began with Tertullian, that champion of martyrdom who declared 140 or so years after the deaths of Peter and Paul: "How happy is the church on which apostles poured forth all their doctrine along with their blood, where Peter endures a passion like his Lord's [crucifixion] where Paul wins his crown in a death [beheaded] ... where the Apostle John was first plunged, unhurt, into boiling oil, and thence remitted to his island-exile."[374]

Tertullian offers no evidence for his assertions. There is no reference to martyrdom in the earlier narratives of Peter and Paul.

The remainder of the apostles did not escape either. Most were posthumously martyred, executed sometimes in the most appalling circumstances, as were other invented saints. Men who had never lived endured terrible deaths. Only John could be reprieved to allow for the late appearance of his gospel in the second century AD. Thus, having survived immersion in boiling oil, he lived to a ripe old age of 120.[375]

Earnest believers flocked to these sepulchres, praying for the intercession of saints to cure a sickness, improve the harvest, or grant them success in some difficult venture. Enterprising clergy converted gullible pagans with claims that saints could intervene just as their former gods had done—and for a price.

When Constantine passed an edict transferring ownership of tombs and cemeteries to the church, there was nowhere for this industry to go but up. Because the heathen Romans had not been sufficiently thorough in their persecution—the number of martyrs was limited. It was necessary to fabricate more.

The poor, including Christians, were often buried in the catacombs beneath a city. The commercial advantage of granting sainthood to random corpses was not lost on the local churches. With some encouragement from the bishops, monks invented fictional accounts of exquisite tortures and brutal rapes to glorify the dead. The "venomous errors" of many a martyr were overlooked. If any succumbed to heresy in life, in death it was conveniently forgotten. In this, the church showed remarkable tolerance. There were enough stiffs to maintain a thriving business for centuries to come. Pilgrims came on cue.

One notable pilgrim was St. Helena, mother of Constantine, who embarked on a journey to Aelia Capitolina, the former city of Jerusalem. Since the emperor Hadrian made the name change to deter seditious zealots, it became a centre of polytheist worship prohibited to Jews. So effective was the obliteration of its memory that its original name was lost to Roman officialdom. When early pilgrims arrived in Palestine searching for Jerusalem, no one knew what they meant. Constantine restored the old name, and soon it became a destination for the faithful.

Family strife in the emperor's household prompted his mother's mission. Constantine had been married three times. Crispus, the eldest son by his first marriage, who had distinguished himself in the wars with Licinius, was accused of immorality. The details are unclear, but gossip at the time suggests a liaison with his stepmother, Fausta, Constantine's second wife. Whatever the particulars, Constantine ordered his execution by strangulation. Later the same year, apparently prompted by his mother, the emperor next turned his anger towards Fausta herself. He had the unfortunate woman boiled alive. Both victims suffered *damnatio memoriae*, obliteration of their names from all records.

Armed with a large purse and a heavy conscience, St. Helena made her pilgrimage to the Holy Land. Here, she commissioned the building of two churches, one on the site of the nativity in Bethlehem and the other on the place of ascension, the Mount of Olives in Jerusalem. Whether the "discovery" of these sites owes more to local entrepreneurship than reverence may be debated. The unearthing of some old timbers, which her guides assured her were the True Cross on which the Saviour died, was surely a triumph of credulity over common sense, as was their discovery in a nearby sepulchre of the very nails used to crucify him.

CONSTANTINE SECURES HIS LEGACY

She had the holy wood and metals transported in ceremony to Byzantium on the Bosphorus, where Constantine had established his new headquarters. The location was well chosen. Situated between the Balkan Peninsula and Asia Minor, it afforded easy access to the western and eastern frontiers. This positioned it ideally to control trade and administration. It recognised that the most advanced, wealthy, and densely populated eastern part of the empire was strategically more secure.

Renaming it Constantinople in honour of himself, Constantine instigated a massive building programme to transform the town into a new imperial capital. Settlers were brought in and, like the citizens of Rome, subsidised with bread and circuses to keep them compliant.

In every way, the city imitated Rome, complete with a senate, hippodrome, magnificent streets, and royal palace. It retained its acropolis with pagan temples and new shrines to the Dioscuri—that is, Castor and Pollux—and the goddess Tyche (Fortuna), the latter being a kind of presiding deity over the city. In this role, she would later be replaced by Mary, mother of Jesus. These actions contradict Eusebius's portrayal of the emperor as a devout destroyer of pagan images.

Christians who had begun serving in the army since the third century were inclined to join in more significant numbers when the empire embraced their religion. They now had a vested interest in its defence. Yet, as a career option, the army could not match a religious vocation. Better to be a priest than a centurion. The empire had to rely on recruiting barbarians, in the process training their enemies in the arts of Roman strategy.

To discourage reliance on outsiders, Constantine mandated that sons of veterans serve in the army, a decision that did little to improve morale. He made the policy universal so that all sons had to follow in their fathers' footsteps in whatever trades or occupations they pursued. The law aimed to control the movement of labour, extending the centralised control begun by Diocletian. The seeds of serfdom can be discerned in these restrictive laws.

The drive for religious universality was part of this process, a counter to innovation and free thought, which are anathema to those of an authoritarian mindset.

In his efforts to secure the collaboration of the faithful, Constantine plundered the empire's diminishing wealth. Lavish church-building programmes, expensive synods and ecclesiastical councils, generous donations of lands and money, and tax exemptions all helped to fill the coffers of a wealthy religion. This generosity gave him uncritical backing from the official church, as the sycophantic praises of his biographer, Bishop Eusebius, make clear. Constantine's support for their dogma gave them the opportunity and the means to attack the "ungodly."

Whatever his original purposes for adopting Christianity, there seems little doubt in later years of the sincerity of his convictions. Christianity appealed to his monolithic sense of order: one God, one emperor, one dominion. Although he might have considered making Sol Invictus the supreme religion of the empire, the power of Christianity in the east and his close association with its bishops probably swayed him in favour of the latter.

He remained a strong champion of the faith even after the security of his office no longer depended on it. In the later years of his reign, if we are to believe Eusebius, Constantine spoke out against pagan sacrifices, magic, divination, and "misguided rites."

However, there is little evidence of a systematic programme against ancient cults or their places of worship at this time. His subjects still spoke of the divinity of the emperor, the sacred palace, the sacred chamber, and the sacred altar of the emperor without reproach. These phrases were associated with traditional Roman beliefs.

He deferred baptism until the final days of his life, a common practice at the time that aimed to secure a sinless entry to heaven. The choice of an Arian bishop, Eusebius of Nicomedia, to administer the sacrament underlines his modified attitude towards the sect. Maybe he hoped for a reconciliation between the two factions, or perhaps the Arians had convinced him their deviance was insignificant. Perhaps he was hedging his bets before the final journey. Like many who wrestle with their faith, he, too, may have sought the pathway to heaven. A difficult task, but for Constantine perhaps less challenging than a pathway to his conscience, if he had one.

Shortly after baptism, he was dead.

Eusebius of Caesarea compared him to Moses, and the comparison has some merit. Both men were bloody generals who faithfully served God by the sword. Constantine's perspective on his own legacy is evident in his funeral arrangements.

After his body was escorted to the imperial capital, where it lay in state, it was taken to a final resting place in the Church of the Holy Apostles. Here, the remains were placed in a coffin, as he had directed, and surrounded on both sides by 12 other tombs. Each one was a memorial to an apostle, making

Constantine, by inference, the 13th apostle, faithful servant, and associate of his Lord Jesus Christ.

This self-indulgent statement was not entirely inappropriate. The mission to convert the world was firmly established and unhindered in his domain. The apostles might envy his success, if not his principles. They would surely recoil at the collection of grasping opportunists, oddball ascetics, and gullible relic hunters that comprised the faithful.

The peace that Constantine had brought to the warring factions was illusory. In truth, the conflict had just begun.

15

AN ELUSIVE PEACE

CAIN HAD A novel solution to sibling rivalry: fratricide. The sons of Constantine extended this policy to the wider family. Only one bloodstained survivor would rule the empire.

Ruling proved rather challenging. Political consensus among the diverse population was nearly impossible. Religion poisoned the debate and hampered the search for compromise. Ambition and theology set the agenda. In the ensuing conflict, bishops, priests, and their congregations became energetic participants.

BROKEN FAMILY, BROKEN EMPIRE

The heretical disputes that dogged Christianity did not stop outside the palace gates. The late emperor left a family divided between followers of Arius and supporters of the Nicene Creed.

In the purge that followed, Constantine's nephews Dalmatius and

Hannibalianus were the first to die, along with uncles, cousins, and their supporters. Later, Constantine II, his eldest son by his second marriage, succumbed to the assassin's blade. This left his sons: Constantius II, who had Arian sympathies, governing the east, and Constans I, a Trinitarian, ruling as emperor of the west. Having destroyed their family, they now assailed those whom they considered heretics.

Although subsequent Trinitarian writers condemned Constantius II as an Arian, he can be more accurately described as semi-Arian—that is, one who sought a middle way between Arianism and the Nicene Creed. For a hardline Trinitarian such as Athanasius, that simply made him an Arian.

Following the death of Constantine, that grand champion of the Nicene Creed regained his episcopal office. Back in Alexandria, his mind was still set against any reconciliation with heretics. This put him on a collision course with the new eastern emperor. Constantius was determined to achieve toleration and compromise and would not tolerate or compromise with anyone who disagreed. In 338, he renewed his father's order of banishment against Athanasius. It was part of a policy to establish a more compliant hierarchy.

It didn't stop the conflict of ideas. Constantinople became a hotbed of theological intrigue. An amusing description by a visitor to the city is recounted by Gibbon, quoting a contemporary scribe: "This city is full of tradesmen and slaves, who are all of them profound theologians, and preach in the shops and in the streets. If you desire a man to change a piece of silver, he informs you wherein the Son differs from the Father; if you ask the price of a loaf, you are told, by way of reply, that the Son is inferior to the Father; and if you inquire whether the bath is ready, the answer is, that the Son was made out of nothing."[376]

It was no laughing matter. A civil conflict arose when the pro-Nicene faction appointed a Trinitarian called Paul as patriarch without the emperor's consent. The Arians responded by nominating one of their own, Macedonius, also without the emperor's consent. Constantius, engaged on the eastern front at the time, convened a synod on his return. The assembly rejected both nominees and appointed Eusebius of Nicomedia instead.

Paul fled to the court of Constans in the west, only to sneak back again when Eusebius died. This reignited fighting between Arians and Trinitarian mobs, and "many lives were sacrificed in consequence."³⁷⁷ A furious Constantius issued an order to remove Paul again.

But the order proved more harmful to the general tasked with its execution than to Paul. A pro-Nicene mob attacked and set fire to his house. They dragged the unfortunate general by the heels through the streets of Constantinople and displayed his corpse for their derision. An angry emperor punished the city by cutting the corn allowance and sent Paul packing once more.

Meanwhile, the exiled Athanasius was a bigger nuisance abroad than he had been in Alexandria. Allying with Paul and others of similar outlook, he encouraged the Trinitarian Constans I to enforce the universal doctrine in his dominions. With the support of the pontiff and the western emperor, Athanasius attempted to reconcile the churches to a stricter interpretation of the Nicene Creed. The venue was a council in Serdica (modern Sofia, Bulgaria).

Instead of reconciliation, the discussions descended into hostile dissension. Fearing they would be outvoted or worse by the more numerous Latins, the eastern bishops demanded that Athanasius, Paul, and other suspended clerics be ejected from the council as a condition for their continued participation. When this request was rejected, they abandoned the meeting and convened a separate council in Philippopolis (modern Plovdiv, Bulgaria) in Thrace. From this safe distance, the rival delegates dispatched abusive missives to each other.

Overriding any division of theology or language was the character of Athanasius himself. To the Trinitarian westerners, he was a saint; to the Arian easterners, a scheming villain. It was not surprising then that they failed to agree on his reinstatement, one of the reasons the synod was called in the first place.

Constans felt obliged to intervene. In a letter to his brother emperor, he issued a threat. If Athanasius and Paul were not restored to their respective dioceses, he would intercede. Constantius, troubled by fighting on the Persian front, had no wish for a confrontation with the west. He wrote to Athanasius and Paul, permitting them to resume their tenures without retribution. We can assume he dictated these concessions with gritted teeth and silent curses.

CONSTANTIUS GETS A BREAK

Meanwhile, Constans had his own problems. His Trinitarian credentials might have endeared him to the pro-Nicene pope and, indeed, most western bishops. His anti-pagan legislation should have earned him the love of the Christian laity. However, his flagrant homosexuality and attachment to "handsome barbarian hostages" disgusted them.

An overbearing demeanour alienated the troops and ultimately sealed his fate. His Christian convictions carried little weight among the barbarian pagans of the western legions. A usurper, Magnentius, declared himself emperor and incited a mutiny. Constans was on a hunting trip in Gaul and isolated when he heard the news. Too late, he tried to flee to Spain before being trapped in a fort in the Pyrenees and subsequently killed.

With his brother out of the picture, Constantius could move against his troublesome bishops. Paul was banished again from Constantinople. This time there would be no return. He was imprisoned in a dark cell in Cappadocia, weighed down in chains, deprived of food, and finally strangled by an impatient jailer. Other Trinitarian bishops, who had been reinstated at the request of Athanasius, were either exiled or imprisoned.

For the moment, Athanasius himself was safe. The eastern emperor needed support in his life-and-death struggle against the usurper. He could not afford to alienate the influential bishop of Alexandria. After all, he controlled Egypt, the richest and most fertile of Romes provinces.

Following a three-year struggle, the rebel Magnentius eventually committed suicide after being defeated by legions loyal to the eastern emperor. Constantius now inherited his father's mantle and became sole ruler of the empire, east and west. He was now free to mould Rome to his version of the true creed.

BATTLE OF THE POPES

This put him on a collision course with Pope Liberius. The obstinate pontiff refused to allow any amendment to the Nicene Creed or publicly condemn Athanasius. Frustrated, Constantius sent him packing and appointed as replacement the pro-Arian Felix II.

That done, the emperor made his first visit to Rome. On arrival, he was confronted by a delegation of noble ladies. (Presumably their husbands thought it wiser to stay at home.) They made it clear that removing Pope Liberius was widely unpopular among the upper echelons of Roman society.

Meanwhile, Liberius in exile was not quite as unrelenting as Liberius at home. He missed the luxury of his office in Rome, he missed his privileges, he missed his comforts. In distress he seems to have agreed to some wording to the effect that the Son was of similar substance (*homoiousios*) to the Father rather than the same substance (*homoousios*)—a kind of soft semi-Arianism. Or perhaps he just signed a document condemning Athanasius. Trinitarian writers would not admit their pope could be bought so easily. Liberius didn't care; he got to go home.

His capitulation created a new dilemma for the emperor, however. Rome now had two popes. What was he to do?

Constantius devised a compromise. Each pope should govern his respective congregation. Satisfied with this novel solution, he headed for the circus, where he planned make a public pronouncement during the games.

The crowd did not like it. Up went the chant, "One God, one Christ, one bishop!" No mention of one emperor. Violence erupted, and the losers, mainly Arian, were massacred in the streets, the public baths, and even the churches. Felix was forced to retire to the suburbs, where he continued ministering to his Arian flock. Damage done, Constantius skipped town.

When both popes died within a year of each other, trouble erupted again.

Opposing mobs battled each other for several weeks, leaving a toll of dead. Power and wealth determined the outcome: the pro-Nicene Damasus I emerged victorious. The Arians accused him of hiring thugs to slaughter his rival's supporters. It didn't matter. Heedless of the simmering resentment, Damasus endured.

CONSENSUS IS FUTILE

In Constantinople, following the final departure of Paul, the Arian bishop Macedonius was back in control. He now had a free hand to indulge his prejudices. Employing persuasion or coercion as needed, he sought to convert the wayward to the "true faith." His clerics issued the sacraments by force, thrusting the eucharistic bread down the throats of unwilling recipients with a wooden device. Red-hot eggshells were used to burn the skin of reluctant communicants, according to the Trinitarian Socrates.[378] The persecution, "more grievous that under the pagan emperors,"[379] extended to other cities in the east.

Macedonius next turned his attention to the Novatians, a sect that, like the Donatists, refused readmission to *lapsi* who had dodged martyrdom. They extended this exclusion to anyone who had committed a mortal sin, "a sin unto death."[380] Absolution was out, as were fornication and adultery. At Nicaea the Novatians had been condemned for refusing to accept the forgiveness of sins. This provided Macedonius the pretext to attack them.

He started with the congregation in Constantinople, where they had three churches. Then, with the emperor's permission, he dispatched a military force to attack their communities near the Black Sea. He could have tried conversion, but why waste time with missionaries when you have an army?

The troops sent to deliver death or salvation were met by angry locals armed only with scythes, axes, and holy passion. In the brutal contest that followed, an untold number of peasants were massacred, and their villages destroyed. But the troops fared no better. A handful managed to flee, leaving behind 4,000 dead comrades in the fields.[381]

So much for Origen's hope that Christianity would unite all the peoples of the world. It failed even to unite the peoples of Constantinople and its vicinity. "Many were imprisoned, persecuted, and driven into exile. Whole troops of those who are styled heretics were massacred, particularly at Cyzicus and at Samosata. In Paphlagonia, Bithynia, Galatia, and in many other provinces, towns and villages were laid waste and utterly destroyed."[382]

However, Macedonius went too far when he attempted to repair the sepulchre where Constantine was buried. Without consulting Constantius, he ordered the corpse to be temporarily removed to allow work to proceed. Trinitarians were aghast at this blatant disrespect to the emperor's remains, even though he had been baptised an Arian. More likely, they needed a pretext to get even with the patriarch. In the riot that followed, a well in front of the church "overflowed with a stream of blood, which filled the porticos and the adjacent courts."[383]

This was too much for Constantius. He deposed Macedonius, who retired to a quiet suburb—but not before leaving a parting gift. In addition to rejecting the divinity of Jesus, Macedonius also denied the divinity of the Holy Spirit. His followers, called Macedonians, upheld these views long after his demotion and death. Thus, he bequeathed to the empire something it hardly needed: another deviant sect.

Constantius continued his campaign for a universal doctrine. He called endless councils and synods, alternatively persuading and threatening those who did not accede to his views. At one such event in Milan in 355, he hid behind a curtain, then rushed into the assembly, sword drawn. It had a persuasive effect on the reluctant delegates.

The polytheist historian Ammianus Marcellinus, who served in Constantius's army, described him thus: "Instead of reconciling the parties by the weight of his authority, he cherished and promulgated, by verbal disputes, the differences which his vain curiosity had excited. The highways were covered with troops of bishops galloping from every side to the assemblies, which they call synods. While they laboured to reduce the whole sect to their own particular opinions, the public establishment of the posts was almost ruined by their hasty and repeated journeys."[384]

The endless conferences almost bankrupted the diminishing resources of the dispatch services. Every new synod (14 took place between 341 and 360) seemed to raise new interpretations, additional innovations, and further debate. New words such as *anomoios* ("dissimilar"), *homoios* ("similar"), and *homoion* ("of like substance") were introduced, pondered, dissected, and disputed.

Bishop Sophronius summed it up best at the Synod of Seleucia when yet another revision of the Nicene Creed was read out: "If to express a separate opinion day after day, be received as the expression of the faith, we shall never arrive at any understanding of the truth."[385] He might also have suggested that, since they could never advance beyond speculation, they could never arrive at the truth anyway.

ATHANASIUS THE OBSTINATE

Meanwhile, that ever-present thorn in the emperor's side, Athanasius, remained enthroned in Alexandria. Having subdued his clerical opponents through persuasion, threats, or exile, Constantius felt confident enough to confront his old enemy, whom he suspected of supporting the revolt of Magnentius. Fearing that Alexandria, might arm itself in defence of it's patriarch he proceeded with caution.

In February, 356 armed troops infiltrated the city. They burst open the doors at the basilica of St. Theonas, where the patriarch was officiating, and set upon the cramped worshippers with drawn weapons. In the bloody chaos, Athanasius escaped into the darkness, aided by faithful monks who had prepared for such an event.

The violence spread as various factions took the opportunity to settle old scores. In the following days and weeks, cities and towns throughout Egypt witnessed retaliatory attacks by vengeful heretics and heathens. But the ultimate prize, the head of Athanasius, evaded their grasp. He had fled to the desert, where he remained among the devoted monks for the next six years. Safely hidden from the outside world, he lived in inaccessible monasteries. From such places, bands of holy fanatics emerged to challenge any troop of soldiers foolish enough to attempt his capture.

EGYPT'S NEW BOSS

Athanasius's replacement as patriarch was one George of Cappadocia. A devious character with an acquisitive inclination, George began his career as a humble cloth worker. Later, he moved to Constantinople, where he displayed a flair for commerce. Detractors accused him of shady practices and claimed he fled to Palestine to avoid investigations by local magistrates.

Like many ambitious men, he saw the advantages of a religious career and the profit of aligning with the dominant faction of the day. He used his wealth to gain influence and his influence to gain more wealth. As a self-made entrepreneur, he was precisely the kind of man the establishment Trinitarians despised.

For supporting the emperor against the troublesome Patriarch of Alexandria, he was granted the episcopal see. He used the position to enrich himself by embezzling the assets of widows and orphans. Such conduct was not uncommon among bishops, but his greed set new boundaries.

George placed a special tax on the extraction of nitre. He acquired a monopoly in trades like papyrus production, reed cutting, and undertaking. Ever the opportunist, he advised the emperor that the city's buildings, which had been constructed by Alexander the Great at considerable public cost, ought to be taxed. Their affluent owners were not impressed.

Polytheists learned with dismay that the new patriarch was even harsher than his predecessor. He zealously enforced the decrees of Constantius against their ancient traditions, exiling a prominent physician, Zeno, and torturing pagan priests. George had their temples ransacked or converted to churches, and he banned ancient festivals and sacrifices.

Following Pentecost, an armed detachment of his followers set upon a gathering of Trinitarians. In a "not my patriarch" style protest they had chosen to pray in the cemetery rather than receive communion in his churches. George's thugs beat them so severely that a few died of their wounds. Further attacks were made against pro-Nicene churches and congregations throughout Egypt and Libya. According to Athanasius (quoted by Socrates Scholasticus), more than 30 bishops were banished, some dying of hardship in exile.

Through a combination of greed and tyranny, George ensured that his enemies well outnumbered his friends. Inevitably, they revolted, forcing George to flee for his life. He spent a fruitful time abroad, addressing the conflicts that beset the emperor before being reinstated under armed protection in Alexandria.

One might have expected a degree of caution, given his recent expulsion. But no. He immediately resumed his persecution of polytheists and anyone else whose distress might give him profit or power. The disgruntled citizens could only wait for another opportunity. They would not have to wait long.

THE ONE THAT GOT AWAY

Flavius Julian and his older brother Gallus were among the few members of the extended royal family to survive the massacre following Constantine's death. One was too sick, and the other too young. The younger, Julian, subsequently avoided the jealousy of Constantius by laying low. When Julian's considerable intellect drew praise from the royal tutors, he wisely dissipated the attention with a shaven head and monkish disposition. He received a sound Christian education and became familiar with the Scriptures.

When his older brother Gallus was executed on the charge of abusing his position, Julian also came under suspicion. He subsequently spent a year under house arrest. The troubled conscience of the emperor, haunted by memories of the family members killed in the early purges, spared Julian a similar fate. He was eventually granted permission to attend the schools in Athens, where he studied philosophy.

In 255, Constantius dispatched the reluctant scholar to Gaul, where Germanic tribes were running amok throughout the Rhineland and pillaging Roman property. It was a dangerous mission. The western legions had suffered heavy losses during the uprising of Magnentius and were vulnerable.

AN ELUSIVE PEACE

The young Julian read *Bellum Gallicum*, Julius Caesar's account of his campaigns in the region. In the process, he discovered a talent for war and put his learning into practice.

He occupied and garrisoned the fortified town of Colonia Agrippina (modern Cologne, Germany), which the Franks had overrun, and went on to rout a 30,000-strong army of the Alemanni at Argentoratum (near Strasbourg, France). Returning to Paris, he set about an efficient overhaul of the tax and administration system of the province.

When Constantius was hard-pressed dealing with yet another assault from Persia, he ordered the western commanders to dispatch four legions to the eastern front. However, these local troops feared their absence would encourage the barbarians to make fresh attacks. So, they mutinied and proclaimed Julian emperor in Paris. Julian accepted the honour, and as he led his forces towards Constantinople, Constantius was obliged to quit the Persian front and march westward to confront him.

A bloody conflict was averted when Constantius took ill with a fever before the two armies met. Nearing death, he received baptism and nominated Julian as his successor, thus discouraging any rival claimant and the inevitable bloodshed that would follow. It was the final gesture of a well-meaning, if sometimes naive, leader.

Doctrinal disputes had vied with naked greed and ambition to thwart the peace of the empire. Opportunists thrived, idealists were persecuted, and polytheists were reduced to impotent spectators. Those of a reflective nature, whether Christians or non-believers, could only watch and follow their consciences in secret. One such person was Julian.

During his student years, he had carefully hidden a passionate hatred for Christianity. Now he could emerge from the shadows to challenge their hard-won power. Fear of renewed persecution chilled Christian hearts.

16

EMPEROR STRIKES BACK

CHRISTIANS AWOKE TO the horror that the new emperor, despite his religious training, was no friend of theirs.

Would victories so dearly won be suddenly snatched from their grasp? Would he demolish their churches, burn their holy books, and throw them to the wild beasts of the arena?

Fearing a resurgence of prosecution, they silently prayed for deliverance and watched with trepidation as Julian began to reverse the policies of his predecessors. But his persecution, if one could call it that, was more subtle. He recalled the banished "heretics," restored their churches, and left Christians to their own devices. By this means, he hoped the church would exhaust itself in infighting, allowing him to reduce its influence over the state.

JULIAN BEGINS HIS REFORMS

The throne that Julian inherited was more eastern than European. Over the previous century, the imperial office had gradually adopted the character and formalities of an Asian kingdom. Ostentatious clothes replaced the simple dress of the Roman nobility. Ceremonial courts, eunuchs, and a lavish retinue were de rigueur. Visitors to the emperor had to prostrate themselves as a sign of submission. Any remnants of the republican traditions were mainly confined to the old aristocracy of Italy.

Julian immediately began to reform the court, as he had done with the administration in Paris. When he asked for the services of a barber, a man dressed "like a receiver of the finances"[386] presented himself. He informed the emperor that in addition to a generous salary, he possessed 20 servants and 20 horses. The man was promptly sacked, together with a host of eunuchs, cooks, and cup-bearers who absorbed the revenues of the palace.

Julian's tastes in food and clothing were simple. He despised the pomp and flamboyance of his predecessors and tried to impart a spirit of hard work and frugality on his court.

It was in the religious sphere that the most significant change occurred. Notwithstanding his pious education, Julian had grown to despise Christians, or Galileans, as he called them. Their internal divisions and endless doctrinal squabbling were partly responsible for his attitude. More so was the murder of his father and other members of the royal household during earlier purges, which he blamed on the devout Christian Constantius.

On February 4, 362, he issued a proclamation granting all religions equality before the law. He then forced bishops to pay for any local temples they had destroyed.

Churches seized from the Donatists in Africa were returned to them. Elsewhere all other confiscated churches were returned to their "heretical" owners.

His views earned him the title "The Apostate." The philosopher in him opposed Christianity for its suppression of freedom of thought, but sensible of their reverence for martyrs, he avoided killing anyone.

To resolve the affliction of theological strife, he invited representatives from various Christian sects to air their disputes. While each welcomed the decree allowing the return of exiled clerics insofar as it applied to their sect, they regarded it as gross interference that this goodwill be applied to others. They ignored his pleas to live in peace, if not in concord with each other.

Julian had an ulterior motive for his toleration. Returning exiles added to the heat of dissension. While the Christian factions were engrossed in conflict with each other, they were less likely to unite against him. Their distraction allowed him to confiscate revenue from the church, including property bequeathed by the state. He also abolished their tax privileges, sarcastically observing that poverty would keep them virtuous, in accordance with their Scripture.

He bolstered the schools of philosophy and literature but forbade Christian teachers from teaching these subjects, fearing they used their knowledge of the classics to ridicule them.

He showed empathy for the Jews, who suffered more than perhaps any other group since the Christian ascendancy. He revoked the laws enacted to prosecute and avenge "their parricidal guilt in slaying their Lord."[387] They were permitted to return to Jerusalem, where, by order of the emperor, reconstruction of the temple commenced.

This project soon ran into problems, however. Strange balls of flame emanating from near the foundations which caused the death of some workers and brought the enterprise to a halt. Christians proclaimed this to be divine intervention. More likely explanations were an earthquake that struck Galilee or Christian sabotage.

SETTLING SCORES IN EGYPT

Meanwhile in Alexandria, when news of Constantius's death was proclaimed, the citizens felt emboldened to act. George of Cappadocia was imprisoned along with two of his ministers on charges of extortion and cruelty. But the impatient natives were in no mood to await a trial.

A mob broke down the prison doors and dragged the terrified bishop and his accomplices outside. They were savagely beaten to death, their bodies dragged through the streets. The remains of the former patriarch were placed on a camel and paraded publicly with those of his ministers. Finally, his corpse was taken to the shore and cremated, and the ashes were thrown into the sea.

Like many who suffered a violent end, the manner of his death rather than the character of his life gave George the distinction of martyrdom. To the Arians, he was a saint. As stories of his life became entwined with an earlier, possibly mythical George, reputed to have perished during the persecution of Diocletian, veneration grew beyond this sect.

A church at Lydda, Palestine, became the destination for pilgrims irrespective of creed or allegiance. Amid fables of generosity and kindness, the destruction of pagan idols, and various miracles attributed to George, the most notable was the slaying of the "wizard" Athanasius. Eventually, the wizard morphed into a dragon, and the twin saints, one real, the other obscure, merged as the legendary St. George, patron saint of England.

Athanasius was one of the beneficiaries of Julian's decree and returned amid much fanfare to his episcopal office in 362. He immediately set about reorganising his flock and purging the "theological errors" of his rivals. It was an easy task: George's policies had made Arianism unpopular. Its adherents subsequently kept a low profile, and their influence began to decline.

Athanasius also became the figurehead for a church frightened by the prospect of reinvigorated polytheism. Sanctioned acts of vandalism against pagan places of worship continued in defiance of the new regime. Christian mobs also attacked and destroyed temples in Antioch, Caesarea, and elsewhere.

Whether or not he had encouraged these acts, Athanasius became the object of the emperor's ire. Like his predecessors, Julian began to view the bishop with suspicion. In a letter to the prefect of Egypt, he urged that "the criminal," as he described him, be removed from office.[388] Athanasius was forced to flee to the refuge of his loyal monks yet again. This exile would be short.

SETTLING SCORES IN PERSIA

Having experienced the adrenaline rush of war in Europe, Julian quickly grew restless with his administrative duties. He began preparations for a campaign to avenge Persian encroaches during the reign of Constantius. Soon, the temple altars were drenched in the blood of sacrificial animals. Oracles were consulted, diviners sought out, and gods invoked. Julian ignored the grim omens foreseen by diviners or any advisor who told him the war was unnecessary.

In the spring of 363, he led the army across the Euphrates on a bridge of boats. His quick march took the Persians by surprise. Meeting little resistance, he headed towards the capital, Ctesiphon, besieging and destroying any towns that offered resistance on the way.

On reaching the capital, Julian deemed it too well defended for an outright assault. Although they had defeated the Persians at each encounter, the enemy, more familiar with the terrain, continued to harass his army, cutting off their food sources and disrupting their supply chain. Fearing isolation, Julian reluctantly ordered a withdrawal.

As they manoeuvred to disengage, a sudden attack caught the retreating force by surprise. Without time to don his armour, the emperor rashly led a charge against a Persian detachment when a spear pierced his ribs. He died some days later, rejoicing, as he put it, "to return to nature."[389] Thus ended a reign of only three years.

A rumour arose that his killer was one of his Christian soldiers. Deserters repeated the story to the Persian troops, who taunted the retreating Romans for killing their emperor. Ammianus, who participated in the campaign, does not give credence to the story. More likely, the spear came from one of the mounted Arab auxiliaries aligned to the Persian army. The rumour persisted nonetheless and was repeated later by the writer Sozomen.

Christians attributed Julian's demise to divine retribution, delivered by the warrior St. Mercurius, to whom Basil of Caesarea had been praying (presumably not for the good health of the emperor). When news of Julian's death reached Antioch, the three prominent Christian sects—Arians, Trinitarians, and Melitians—rejoiced and immediately resumed squabbling over whether the Son is the same substance as the Father.

Julian had forced them to live as equals with the reviled worshippers of idols and had deprived them of the right to persecute each other. Any chance that the various denominations could cohabit in peace perished with him, if any such chance had really existed. The one true religion need not coexist with any other false belief, "For what partnership can righteousness have with wickedness? Or what fellowship does light have with darkness?"[390] Christians remained divided, yet powerful enough to embroil their disputes with the business of the state. The reforms of Julian were reversed, and his advisors were dismissed in disgrace by a vengeful church.

But might a non-believer indifferent to their quarrels be preferable to a dogmatist bent on persecution? Assuming his successor was Christian, which faction would he favour, and which one would he oppress? Expectation and tension gripped the ranks of the faithful.

17

AN UNFORESEEN DISASTER

PREOCCUPIED AS THEY were with matters mystical, the Romans were ill prepared for the catastrophe that was about to unfold.

The Christology disputes concealed a more immediate threat to the empire. As emotions ran high and old tensions resumed, events beyond the Danube were conspiring to shatter their inward-focused preoccupations.

After signing a humiliating treaty that conceded territory to the Persians, Julian's successor, Jovian, went to Antioch. His Christianity was not in doubt. Pagan temples were again ordered shut; "philosophers laid aside their [distinctive] vestments and clothed themselves in ordinary attire."[391]

However, there was uncertainty as to which Christian faction Jovian belonged to. Uncertainty led to disquiet, and the roads to Antioch were busy as bishops and their followers hastened to offer homage and seek his favour. Soon, the city and palace were crowded with every manner of heretic, and the air was thick with the murky din of theological dispute.

Macedonians presented a petition asking him to expel all who said the Son is unlike the Father. Acacians, another sect, assured him of their orthodoxy. Arians warned him not to trust the mischievous Athanasius, and so it went on.

Athanasius arrived in person and was granted an audience. The new emperor's reverence for the patriarch quickly dispelled any uncertainty. The happy prelate returned to his beloved Alexandria after assuring Jovian that his devotion would be rewarded with a long and peaceful reign.

It proved a fatal prophecy. During his return journey to Constantinople, the emperor retired to his bedroom after a heavy meal of mushrooms and promptly expired. Maybe the chef was Arian. Ten days later, Valentinian was elected by the troops.

DIVIDED AGAIN

A tough soldier with a suspicious nature, Valentinian divided the empire again. He appointed his brother Valens to command the east while he took on the barbarian menace in the west.

Valentinian was well equipped for the task and managed to contain, if not overwhelm, the warlike Germans. In matters of faith, he was a Nicene Christian but reasonably tolerant. He opposed only the "fraud of magic" of the pagans[392] and the acquisitive excesses of Christian clergymen. But his irascible nature led to a reign of terror: "The expressions that issued the most readily from the mouth of the emperor of the west were, 'Strike off his head'; 'Burn him alive'; or 'Let him be beaten with clubs till he expires.' "[393]

His anger became his undoing. During a heated exchange with Germanic ambassadors over peace terms, he burst a blood vessel and died suddenly, leaving the west in the hands of his son Gratian.

In the east, Valens shared his brother's flaws without any of the redeeming qualities: "He was an immoderate covetor [sic] of great wealth ... too much inclined to cruelty; his behaviour was rude and rough; and he was little imbued with skill either in war or in the liberal arts, being void of accomplishments and illiterate, he willingly sought profit and advantage in the miseries of others."[394] Thus wrote Ammianus with the contempt of the soldier for an emperor who would soon lead them to military disaster.

An Arian by sentiment, Valens revoked Julian's decree that permitted exiled bishops to return. St. Athanasius, rather than wait for the inevitable visit of an armed troop, quietly slipped out of Alexandria. In exile once again, he hid in his father's tomb, according to Socrates. Valens, apprehensive of unrest in the city and disquiet among the patriarch's followers, made an exception to his universal decree.

Athanasius returned for the last time and spent his remaining years peacefully championing the Trinitarian cause. Despite being a frequent victim of persecution himself, he keenly advocated for the persecution of others. Confident of his convictions, he asserted that heretics "ought to be held in universal hatred for opposing the truth."[395] He died in 373.

Meanwhile, "heretic" Valens occupied himself persecuting Trinitarians and others he deemed nonconformist. According to Socrates and Sozomen, this included burning a boat containing "80 pious delegates of Nicomedia" and drowning some others.[396]

Polytheist teachers were arrested and tortured by a suspicious emperor. He worried their mystical divinations were a cover for a secret plot to overthrow him. He ordered the philosopher Simonides to be burned alive, and another called Maximus decapitated.

Fear of certain traditional rituals was not confined to Valens. Their association with treason and plots made magical diviners a target of emperors from the time of Constantine. Valens, however, combined paranoia with acquisitiveness. He found reasons to persecute imagined enemies as much from fear as from a desire for their property, according to his critics.

Having crushed a rebellion by a usurper called Procopius, Valens next crossed into Thrace to pursue a Gothic force that had belatedly arrived to support the rebels. He chased them across the river Danube before eventually signing a peace treaty to end hostilities.

That being settled, Valens resumed his campaign against heresy.

BARBARIANS AT THE GATE

However, the Gothic incursion was a precursor to a greater calamity. It might have been avoided if the emperor had devoted more attention to barbarians instead of heretics.

For more than a century, the Goths had launched regular incursions into Roman territory, returning with plunder and slaves. While many had peacefully settled and integrated within the empire, most remained beyond the borders and continued their intermittent raids.

In one of these forays, the tribesmen captured a family in Cappadocia. Their son Ulfilas was raised among the Goths and later sent to Constantinople, perhaps as an ambassador or hostage. After serving as a lector (reader) for the church, the bright young man was ordained by Eusebius of Nicomedia as a bishop of the Arian faith. Returning across the Danube, Ulfilas proceeded to convert the Goths to Christianity.

His mission caused a split among the tribesmen. Some converted to the "Roman religion." Others resisted, fearing it would undermine their warrior heritage and make them docile Roman subjects. As the two groups fought it out, they were disturbed by the arrival of fierce warriors from the eastern steppes. The Huns and their Asian allies drove the Goths from their homes near the Black Sea and forced them westward.

In desperation to escape these new marauders, Fritigern, leader of the Christian Gothic tribe the Tervingi, sent Ulfilas as an envoy to the Romans, seeking permission to cross the Danube and settle in Pannonia.

The emperor, who had some sympathy for his fellow Arians, was uneasy about this request. He granted permission on the condition that they surrender their arms and offer their high-born children as hostages.

In a massive operation, the Tervingi and other displaced clans were shipped across the Danube. In the confusion, bands of Huns and non-Christian

Goths followed, bringing the total number of refugees to several hundred thousand. In return for bribes, corrupt officials allowed the barbarians to keep their weapons. Considering the limited troops at their disposal, they could probably not enforce the terms anyway. To make matters worse, their arrival coincided with a local famine.

A CALAMITY UNFOLDS

Soon, matters got out of control. When local officials treacherously killed some of their chieftains, the barbarians ran amok. They were joined by disgruntled locals also suffering the effects of the shortages. Soon, their pillaging extended from the banks of the Danube to the villages and towns of Moesia and Thrace.

Alarmed, Valens hastened to Constantinople to assess the situation. After much vacillation, the jeers of the impatient citizens provoked him to move on. With an army of 25,000 veterans, he set up camp in Thrace near the city of Adrianople (modern Edirne, Turkey).

On a hot August day, he led his troops into an open field and arrayed them in battle formation. Opposite them was the Gothic encampment commanded by Fritigern. As the two sides negotiated, impatient Roman units launched an uncoordinated attack. They were quickly surrounded by the Gothic cavalry and forced into a tight pack. Unable to manoeuvre, they became easy targets for the mobile barbarians. Two-thirds of the army were wiped out. Valens perished in the slaughter, his body lost among the numerous casualties.

The battle of Adrianople was perhaps the single greatest defeat of the Roman army. Moesia, Pannonia, and Thrace were at the mercy of the rampant tribesmen with no force strong enough to rein them in. Polytheists naturally attributed the calamity to divine revenge for the closure of temples and neglect of the sacrifices.

Fortunately for the Romans, the walls of Adrianople and Constantinople were beyond their primitive weapons, so the east was safe. But the western part of the empire would now have to battle on two fronts: the Danube and the Rhine.

When news of the disaster reached the western emperor Gratian, he had to nominate a successor to stabilise the east. After much deliberation, he chose a distinguished general called Theodosius. Leaving the new ruler with a formidable task, Gratian focused on defending the Rhine.

Meanwhile, following their defeat in Adrianople, the eastern Romans took revenge on a softer target. In cities and towns, Gothic settlers were lured into the streets and massacred by the Roman forces.

A TENUOUS ALLIANCE

This did nothing to thwart rampaging tribesmen in the countryside. Theodosius, the new emperor, realised the defeat could not be avenged by massacring helpless migrants in the streets.

He improved the fortifications of the Balkan cities and used them as bases for raids on the Goths. Conscripting local farmers and miners, he ordered the commanders to engage only in minor skirmishes when they had a numerical advantage. These actions gradually wore down the enemy and improved the morale of his troops. After the death of Fritigern, the tribes split into isolated bands of brigands, allowing the Romans to pick them off.

Gradually, by a mixture of coercion and reassurance, the various Gothic clans and their allies signed separate peace treaties with Theodosius. They were allowed to settle in Thrace since they had practically conquered it anyway, and they were exempted from taxes. It was a tenuous alliance. The Goths were unlikely partners who might turn against their Roman masters at the first opportunity. Public safety rested on the competence of the new emperor.

And it wasn't just safety. The invaders, through their Arian faith, added a new dimension to religious factionalism. In opposing them, Nicene Christians faced the prospect of a religious war, a prospect that would vex the conscience of the most thoughtful believers. Killing for God was nothing new; after all, the scriptures had endorsed it. However, Jesus blessed the peacemakers and called them children of God.[397] Could violence be justified for a good cause?

Theodosius harboured no doubts. Having forcefully showcased his military prowess, the new emperor was ready to unveil his inflexible views on religious matters.

18

FREE WILL BITES THE DUST

ANY PROSPECT OF peaceful inter-Christian concord was quashed by the elevation of Theodosius to the eastern throne. There was room for only one winner in this contest of faith.

The new emperor soon found a kindred spirit in a western bishop who shared his dogmatic beliefs. Together, they sought to crush dissenters across the empire, regardless of their conviction. Sovereign governance would take a back seat to theology, and anyone who did not share their rigid perspective would forfeit their religious freedom.

Two years before he had subdued the first Gothic tribes, Theodosius found time for a triumphal entry to Constantinople. He placed his sectarian colours firmly on the mast by calling on the Arian patriarch Demophilus to subscribe to the Nicene Creed or leave. The bishop chose the latter option. His Arian flock were compelled to abandon the 100 or so churches they possessed within the city. Henceforth, they held their services outside its walls. Shortly afterward, the Macedonians joined them in forced exile. Both sects might have been disappointed at their expulsion, but they were hardly surprised.

Earlier that year at Thessalonica, Theodosius, with the western co-emperors Gratian and Valentinian II,[398] issued the Edict of Thessalonica. This affirmed "the one deity of the Father, the Son and the Holy Spirit, in equal majesty and in a holy Trinity." In other words, it established the Nicene Creed as the only true faith. The patriarchs of the eastern cities, which, except for Jerusalem and Alexandria, were entirely Arian, watched in helpless dismay.

A RELUCTANT BISHOP

Constantinople now had a new Trinitarian patriarch, the saintly Gregory Nazianzus. Gregory possessed a flair for theological discourse and an uncompromising faith, at least with pen in hand. Without his pen, he was a sensitive and timid man prone to bad health and ill suited to the tumultuous office he had acquired. A contemplative vocation was more appropriate to his nature, but an overbearing father and persuasive bishops determined otherwise. Transferred from an obscure diocese in Asia Minor called Sasima, "an utterly dreadful, pokey little hole; a paltry horse-stop on the main road ... with no water,"[399] as he described it, he reluctantly entered the teeming metropolis of Constantinople. At that time, it was still under the Arian patriarch.

His delicate nature was offended by "heretical depravity," as he termed it, and he advocated the suppression of those who made a "display of their disease"[400] by preaching doctrines contrary to the Nicene Creed. Gregory administered to the beleaguered Trinitarians from his home in the imperial capital, which he converted to a modest chapel called Anastasia.

His hostile sermons soon provoked a hostile response. During the Easter liturgy, a mob broke open the doors and, using sticks and stones, attacked the faithful within. The rabble consisted of "infuriated old women and young nuns, more terrible than Jezebels ... common beggars and monks like aged goats ... who lost even their pity through ferocity." "Our altars were insulted, our mysteries disturbed," he wrote to a friend.[401] Such was the violence that one bishop was killed in the affray.

With the entry of Theodosius, the Trinitarian party was triumphant again. Gregory accompanied the new emperor in solemn procession to the patriarchal chair, watched by the sullen-faced Arian Christians. The bishop had his wish. But the "depraved heretics" had been overcome by the might of the imperial sword, not the episcopal pen.

As soon as he became patriarch, Gregory was called upon to preside over what would become the First Council of Constantinople. The zealous Theodosius, anxious to impose the "one true faith" on his subjects, summoned 180 bishops to the capital. Their task was to ratify and impose the Nicene Creed.

The good emperor had taken the precaution of weighing the delegates on the side of the Trinitarian cause. Opposing groups were outgunned.

By the end of the council, the Nicene Creed had triumphed, not unexpectedly, and the emperor could reaffirm the *cunctos populos*: "We authorise the followers of this doctrine to assume the title of Catholic Christians; and as we judge that all others are extravagant madmen, we brand them with the infamous name of heretics and declare that their conventicles shall no longer usurp the respectable appellation of churches. Besides the condemnation of divine justice, they must expect to suffer the severe penalties, which our authority, guided by heavenly wisdom, shall think proper to inflict upon them."[402]

There was no doubt for those with ears to hear that it was open season on heretics. One does not argue with an emperor "guided by heavenly wisdom." For Gregory Nazianzus, however, the bickering was too much. When the council debated a vacant ecclesiastical seat at Antioch, his appeals to reason were met by "a cry like that of a flock of jackdaws" from the older members, while the younger ones "attacked [him] like a swarm of wasps."[403] Infighting within the Trinitarian camp was as fierce as that between them and non-Trinitarians.

Next, the "jackdaws" and "wasps" challenged his authority. After all, had not the Council of Nicaea decreed that a bishop could not leave his appointed see? This was the "pokey little hole" of Sasima that he had previously administered before his transfer to Constantinople.

Rather than argue with them, the weary Gregory resigned his position and retired to his native Cappadocia. There, he devoted his remaining years in literary service to his absolute faith, happily composing missives against local Apollinarist heretics. He is counted among the saints in western and eastern Christianity.

A POWERFUL BISHOP

Theodosius had a more formidable ally in the west. A few years before his coronation, a magistrate called Ambrose was elevated to the primacy of Milan. The two men, emperor and bishop, would together steer Christianity to a new ascendancy.

Ambrose was a shrewd manipulator and, like Theodosius, an uncompromising Trinitarian. When promoted to the episcopal see, he donated his lands and possessions to the poor. This clinched his popularity with the masses. He had animated the western emperor Gratian to renewed assaults on paganism. However, he soon came to loggerheads with the Arian Justina, stepmother to Gratian and mother of Valentinian II.

The conflict arose over the right of the Arians to use a church in Milan. Ambrose ordered that only Trinitarians were entitled to worship. The empress advocated a compromise that allowed the Arians to use one basilica, but the bishop would brook no compromise. "It is not lawful for you to have it," boomed the holy man. "What have you to do with an adulteress? For she is an adulteress who is not joined to Christ in lawful wedlock."[404] The term "adulteress" was a veiled insult aimed at Justina herself. She had become the second wife of Valentinian I after he divorced his first. The early church did not accept divorce.

Ambrose accused the empress of tyranny for allowing her followers to practise their religion. His sermons incited the populace so much that the streets became unsafe for Arians. He then intervened to rescue Arian clergymen from the violent mobs he himself had aroused.

When Justina asked him to calm those who were inflamed by his sermons, he denied that he had caused the unrest. Only God could appease the people's rage, he declared, professing concern at the scenes of blood and confusion likely to arise if the Arians were permitted to worship. With "fervent prayers," he beseeched that he "might not survive to behold the ruin of a flourishing city, and perhaps the desolation of all Italy."[405] The threat was subtle; the arrogance explicit.

Amid growing tensions, Ambrose "discovered" the remains of two hitherto unheard-of martyrs buried underneath the floor of a church. This unexpected stroke of luck bolstered his position. The skeletons of the long-deceased men were removed from the tomb "wet with blood" and put on display. Soon, miracles were reported: the blind could see, the deaf could hear, and the infirm were cured. "I cannot deny the favour which the Lord Jesus has granted to the time of my priesthood," exulted the proud bishop, who was not above accusing the heathens of trickery.[406] Quite clearly, God, all three of Him, supported the bishop.

Trinitarians lauded their magnanimous prelate. One word from him would have seen the overthrow of the empress and her young son, yet he refrained. But it was Justina herself who spared the Italians from the ravages of a civil conflict.

While Ambrose controlled the citizens, Justina commanded the Gothic auxiliaries whose swords she might have employed to defend their fellow Arians. This would have resulted in bloodshed and the uncertain outcome Ambrose "feared to behold." Instead, she chose the peaceful option and backed down. The church consequently gained a compelling victory over the temporal power.

The empress soon faced a challenge from another source. In a reign that had started so well, Gratian indulged in his private pastime of hunting and neglected the army, a policy fatal to both empire and emperor. In Gaul, he paid the ultimate price, dying at the hands of a rebel general, Magnus Maximus.

In 387, the usurper crossed the Alps and attacked Italy. Justina, fearful that her younger son Valentinian would suffer the fate of his brother, fled to the court of Theodosius and begged him for help. Touched by her pleas and charmed by the advances of her daughter, whom he later married, Theodosius led his army to confront Maximus. At Aquileia in northern Italy, with the support of Gothic auxiliaries, Theodosius was victorious. Maximus was slain, and the magnanimous victor restored the mother and son to the government of the west.

When Valentinian II was assassinated in another military coup, Theodosius was again forced to intervene in the west. He saw off the new usurper and became the absolute ruler of the empire. Two uncompromising Trinitarians, bishop and emperor, were now in control.

PERSECUTION INTENSIFIES

Theodosius issued proclamations to punish the bodies and save the souls of the misguided. Arians and other heretics were deprived of their churches and banned from public assemblies. In the east, Trinitarians were so few that they struggled to fill the many churches abandoned as a result. Magistrates were instructed to treat any enactment supporting Arians as fraud or forgery. They were disbarred from holding public office and forced by impoverishment to join the Trinitarian cause.

For others there was greater punishment. Manichaean heretics could only expect death. The same fate awaited Audians, who aligned Easter with the Jewish Passover, contrary to the Nicene Creed. In Gaul and the Iberian Peninsula, Priscillianists, who advocated asceticism and vegetarianism, suffered imprisonment or exile. Their founder, Priscillian, and his leading followers were arrested, tortured, and executed. This marked them as the first Christian martyrs sentenced to death by a Christian civil court. Paradoxically, it served to increase their number.

Martyrdom fell somewhat out of favour when these heretical "athletes of death" used it as a weapon against the established church. St. Augustine condemned it as suicide, notwithstanding that Jesus himself was a martyr.

The idolatrous sacrifices of polytheists became a treasonable act. Magistrates who failed to punish those engaged in this "abominable crime against the one true God"[407] were deemed equally guilty. Julian's reforms had sparked fear of a pagan revival, which increased Christian paranoia of old traditions.

By command of Theodosius, the armies of the east and west were ordered to shut the temples and to seize and destroy all idolatrous images and objects of worship. They confiscated property and handed it over to the church, the emperor, or the military. Instead of protecting the state's borders, the energies of both army and state were diverted against local shrines. This enraged a provincial population that cherished them. Their opposition modified the extent to which these orders were implemented.

HOLY MOBS

However, the decrees had the effect of inciting bands of Christian bigots. Clergymen who for decades had waited impatiently for the dismantling of pagan institutions now felt free to indulge their passion. In Gaul, St. Martin, bishop of Caesarodunum (modern Tours, France), launched attacks on temples and sacred trees that adorned these places of worship. As he travelled from village to town, demolishing and burning as he went, he was supported by a mob of fanatical hermits. He was also aided by the occasional "miracle." Describing one such event, his biographer Severus, who knew him personally, boasted that though "high priests and heathens" opposed him, "under the influence of the Lord they had been quiet."[408] More likely, they remained quiet in terror of their lives.

In Syria, another holy man, Marcellus of Apamea, led a troop of gladiators and black-robed monks throughout towns and villages on a similar mission. They destroyed the old sanctuaries as they went. Marcellus was eventually killed by some angry peasants defending their village shrine. Today, he is numbered among the Christian martyrs.

Maternus Cynegius, praetorian prefect of the east, had eagerly enforced Theodosius's decrees with Marcellus's help. His trail of destruction is reputed to have included the temple of Edessa, a lunar temple in Carrhae, the temple of Zeus Belos in Apamea, and the temple of Al-Lat in Palmyra. The latter monument would experience destruction again in the 21st century by the inheritors of another bigoted creed, ISIS.

The ancient stormtroopers of this devastation were the usual black-robed monks, "who [ate] more than elephants and, by the quantity of drink they consume[d], [wearied] those that [accompanied] their drinking with the singing of hymns ... These people, Sire, while the law yet [remained] in force, [hastened] to attack the temples with sticks and stones and bars of iron, and in some cases ... with hands and feet."[409]

A contemporary writer, Libanius, accused the drunken monks of using the destruction as a front for a lucrative business, selling artefacts and precious metals behind the façade of a holy mission. Greed rather than piety was their motivation.

In Cyprus, St. Epiphanius embarked on a personal struggle against all the prevailing heresies, comparing each in turn to a specific poisonous animal.[410] Gnostics were snakes, Origenists were toads, and so it went. The good bishop did not confine himself to debate; he was a man of action. With enthusiastic support from the faithful, he set about destroying all the remaining Hellenistic temples on the island. He claimed credit for exiling 70 noble ladies for their heresy. Theodosius applauded his efforts, declaring that those who would not obey his orders had no right to live in Cyprus. He didn't say where they should live instead.

On a similar mission, Theophilus, bishop of Alexandria, took control of a temple to Mithras and publicly ridiculed the rites and artefacts he found therein. The provocation had its effect: non-Christians and professors of philosophy retaliated. A bloody confrontation between pagans and Christians ensued with injury and loss of life on both sides. The pagans were forced to retreat to the temple of Serapis, the Serapeum, and barricade themselves within.

The great temple was one of the most magnificent structures of the empire. Positioned atop a rocky plateau, it overlooked the Mediterranean and was accessible by 100 marble steps. Towering above the city skyline, it dwarfed the churches of the faithful, and presented a challenge to their emergent status. Within its walls were lecture rooms of the philosophers and tomes preserved from the once-great Library of Alexandria. Although the Serapeum had suffered damage during interreligious clashes, its structure remained intact.

At the instigation of the bishop, Emperor Theodosius issued an order for the destruction of all heathen relics and buildings in the city. A Christian mob aided by rabid monks and soldiers was determined to carry out the instructions of the emperor and patriarch. With "screams and laughter," they tore down the giant effigy of Serapis and dragged sections of it through the streets. Statues, works of art, and manuscripts were pillaged and destroyed. Images of the gods were molten into pots and other utensils or transformed into artefacts to adorn the churches. Greed motivated many of the holy hoodlums. Polytheists looked on in dismay and fear.

Manuscripts containing ancient classics were destroyed. The philosophers salvaged a few; others would perish over time through neglect. With great effort and the toil of many, the building itself, with its stately halls and arches, was gradually demolished, leaving only the foundations. A new church dedicated to John the Baptist was erected upon this base.

Incidences of destruction were repeated throughout the empire: "In almost every province of the Roman world, an army of fanatics, without authority and without discipline, invaded the peaceful habitations; and the ruin of the fairest structures of antiquity still display the ravages of those barbarians who alone had time and inclination to execute such laborious destruction."[411]

Christians would later blame the invading barbarians for this destruction. However, the annals of the day clearly point the finger at the church. Early Christian clergy condemned themselves by their own pens, rejoicing at the carnage wrought on centuries of craftmanship. However, Gibbon might have given too much credence to their boasts that pagan practices had been utterly destroyed along with their shrines. Many of the "conversions" were fake. In a letter to Theodosius, Libanius cautioned that claims of pagans converting were not true. He warned that his advisors "speak of conversions apparent not real … Their converts have not really been changed, they only say they have."[412] Traditional rituals stubbornly persisted despite the persecution.

Apart from the bursts of demolition caused by the more fanatical brethren, a less dramatic but lethal corrosion endured. In most cases, this involved removing an altar, performing a cleansing rite to deconsecrate the temple, and confiscating, defacing, or chiselling a sign of the cross on the statue of the local deity. Many Christians genuinely believed heathen gods were evil spirits who could revenge themselves on their attackers. Needless to say, caution was advised. Pagans, for their part, often returned the altars and resumed their ceremonies after the Christian mob had departed and things settled down.

"DRINKING POISON WITH HONEY"[413]

As in Alexandria, literature was not immune from attack. Manuscript burning, a common practice among tyrants, continued during this time, as it had during Constantine's reign. It mainly focused on works directly attacking Christianity itself. Among the many documents put to the flames was a work by the philosopher Porphyry called *Adversus Christianos* (*Against the Christians*). It consisted of 15 books written a century and a half earlier, which had caused much angst among Christian theologians.

Evidently familiar with the Scriptures, Porphyry focused on the book of Daniel. He argued that the so-called prophecies contained in the second part of the book had been written in the mid-second century BC and not the sixth century BC, when the story is set. In other words, it had been written after the fact but using the future tense.

He had a point: Daniel does not appear in the Hebrew canon of the prophets and other references to Old Testament Scriptures before 180 BC. Thus, argued Porphyry, the book was a fraud. Since Christians claimed that the life of Jesus was a fulfilment of these prophecies, this claim, too, must be a fraud. The passage in Matthew, "So when you see standing in the holy place 'the abomination that causes desolation,' spoken of through the prophet Daniel,"[414] endorsed a fake story, reasoned the philosopher. If Daniel is a forgery, then the New Testament reference is also a forgery. If this pillar of faith was shaken, the philosopher argued, then the whole edifice of the faith must crash with it. Clearly, his books had to burn.

Like the writings of that other critic Celsus, we know of Porphyry's words only from the retorts of men such as Eusebius, Augustine, and Jerome. Other works by Porphyry—a commentary on Aristotle, for example—were not destroyed but studied by Christian scholars into the Middle Ages.

Several monasteries maintained the old tradition of copying Greek and Roman literary classics. However, these were replaced by Christian scriptures and ever-growing volumes of theological treatises. Old classics left unopened on the shelves gradually fell into decay. Some were overwritten.

Because parchment was prohibitively expensive, it was easier to wash away or scrape the old ink and write a religious text over it. This consigned many classical works to obscurity. Fortunately, the destruction was not universal. Thanks to the more scholarly monks, certain texts were preserved or reproduced. However, far more were destroyed than preserved, and only a fraction of the ancient literature survived.

Christian horror at the classical scribes is exemplified by the likes of St. Jerome, despite his evident learning. He warned the faithful not to pollute themselves by reading such works. St. Basil also considered them dangerous and liable to contaminate the unwary, akin to drinking poison with honey.[415] He urged Christians to steer away from such fables.

Christian thugs scoured the houses of educated pagans for their "evil" manuscripts. Many intellectuals were compelled to destroy their books publicly. If not, they were forced to watch them being confiscated. "Throughout the eastern provinces, whole libraries were burnt by their owners for fear of a similar fate; such was the terror that seized all hearts."[416] Among the writings lost to posterity were scientific treatises by Democritus, an early pioneer of atomic theory.

"All people now having rejected the antics of the philosophers, gloat over the teachings of the fishermen [gospels]. Those elaborately decorated fables [classics] have been utterly banned," gloated Theodoret of Cyrrhus.[417]

Jews were not immune from the ravages of Christian fanaticism. Like a child who turns on its parent, Christians reserved their greatest vehemence for the religion from whose womb their Saviour and creed had emerged. In addition to laws enacted by Constantine on intermarriage and slave ownership, Jews had to endure insidious aggravation. Churches were built in the middle of Jewish communities as a provocation, and attacks on Jews and their property became more frequent.

Theodosius treated Jews with the same discriminatory laws he employed against heretics. They were only admissible as witnesses when neither plaintiff nor defendant was Catholic, and they were subject to the same random violence from the Christian mobs as all dissenters.

TEMPORAL JUSTICE SIDELINED

Two incidents involving arbitrary justice illustrate the character and relationship of the two principal players in this period of Roman history.

In the Greek town of Thessalonica, a charioteer raped a young boy. The culprit was apprehended and arrested by the town's Gothic garrison. The guilty man was a local hero, and on the day of some important games, his supporters demanded his release so he could take part. When the captain of the garrison refused their request, a riot ensued. The mob lynched the commander and some of his men and paraded their bodies through the streets.

Theodosius, in Milan at the time, flew into a rage and ordered retribution. He dispatched a company of Gothic auxiliaries to carry out his commands. Later, when his anger subsided, he sent a messenger to rescind his orders. The messenger arrived too late.

Following the original instructions of the emperor, and no doubt anxious to avenge their fellow warriors, the troops enticed the inhabitants to the circus under the pretence of a free spectacle. At the signal to commence the games, they launched their attack, massacring 7,000 spectators.

According to separate accounts, Ambrose either wrote to the emperor or, less likely, stood at the door of the cathedral "like an ambassador from heaven," refusing him entry unless he repented of his crime. Theodosius was excommunicated and denied the Eucharist.

The emperor entered a state of contrition, exchanged the purple robes of his office for a penitent's dress, and regularly visited the church to beg forgiveness. After seven months of these very public supplications, the bishop condescended to forgive him on behalf of God. The excommunication was retracted, and the Eucharist administered.

The subservience of a sovereign to a higher moral authority might appear virtuous, a restraint on the extremes of despotism. However, when the moral power is more despotic than the temporal power, one is left with the tyranny of a theocracy. Despite the severity of his laws against heretics and his intemperate act of violence, Theodosius had shown, at times, a generous and tolerant spirit. Ambrose did not share his impartiality, as the second incident will demonstrate.

In Callinicum on the Euphrates (modern al-Raqqah, Syria), the citizens burned a Jewish synagogue. They were incited by the sermons of their rabble-rousing bishop, the enthusiasm of local monks, and the writings of John Chrysostom. Continuing their rampage, the monks also attacked and burned a church of the Valentinians, a heretical Christian sect. The provincial magistrate ordered the bishop to rebuild the synagogue or repay the damage. The emperor endorsed this reasonable proposal.

Ambrose intervened. In a letter to Theodosius, he warned that tolerating the Jews was equivalent to persecuting the Christians. "Will you give this triumph over the Church of God to the Jews?" he asked, describing the synagogue as "a home of unbelief, a house of impiety, a receptacle of folly, which God Himself has condemned."[418] Privately, he tried to manipulate Theodosius. Using the pretext of love and concern for the emperor, he warned that Theodosius's subjects might suspect he was secretly a Jew if he persisted.

When that failed, Ambrose admonished him from the pulpit, even as the emperor sat among the congregation. Ambrose would not allow him to partake in the service unless he promised to rescind the magisterial order. Theodosius relented, allowing secular justice to yield to religious bigotry.

A SOMBRE LEGACY

Theodosius would be the last emperor to govern east and west. As he lay on his deathbed, his final breath voiced the name of his beloved bishop. His legacy was a state subservient to the church's power and two sons who would govern the west and east separately and ineptly.

In 397, two years after Theodosius's death, Ambrose, too, parted this world and achieved sainthood. He left a powerful church that was predominantly Catholic and despotic.

These two men had effectively ensured the triumph of one interpretation of Christianity. They not only consolidated the power of the church but, in the process, made the state compliant to its whims. Indirectly, this paved the way for attacks on Jews, polytheists, and any other dissident faiths, making Rome a theocracy of sorts, a concept that still enjoys some popularity and fosters impassioned opposition.

A confident Christianity would now find its most influential advocate.

19

GOD'S PHILOSOPHER

"**OH LORD, MAKE** me chaste and celibate, but not yet!"[419] implored the wayward youth.

This heartfelt plea of St. Augustine will resonate with many young individuals caught between worldly temptations and their consciences. When this restive African finally matured, he provided answers to questions the church had not yet thought to ask. He formulated a philosophy that would find consensus among diverse sects for centuries. Even today, his teachings continue to hold significance for believers. For traditional Roman polytheists, he became the "progressive" tormentor of their society.

He was an apostle of Ambrose and came to share his mentor's esteem for the celibate life—but not yet! Augustine had come to Milan to take up the post of professor at a local school, where he came under the bishop's influence.

Born in 354 in Thagaste (modern Souk Ahras, Algeria), Augustine's mother was a Christian. As in many Roman households, she managed to convert her polytheist husband. His parents sent him to Carthage, where he devoted himself to debauchery and alcohol. He engaged in petty theft with some of his friends and formed a relationship with a woman who bore him a child, "the son of my sin," as he later termed it. Officially, the church condemned this kind of concubinage, but it was tolerated in practice.

While in Carthage, Augustine embraced the Manichaean faith and devoted himself wholeheartedly to its cause. He remained with them for nine years and was admitted into the lower ranks, the Hearers. However, he became disillusioned by "irreconcilable inconsistencies" in its doctrine and left. His departure was timely. Shortly afterward, Theodosius began a persecution of the sect, decreeing the death penalty for the Elect, much as Diocletian had done more than half a century earlier.

A new path opened in Augustine's life when, after reading Cicero, he turned to philosophy. Inspired by Plato, he opened a school of rhetoric in Rome and later took up a professorship in Milan. Here, he became fascinated by the sermons of St. Ambrose; "that man of God [who] received me as a father would,"[420] he later said. At the age of 33, he submitted to baptism and rejoined the Catholic Church, much to the delight of his mother, Monica, who had been following his intellectual meanderings with dismay.

CHASTE AND CELIBATE

Also at the urging of Monica, Augustine sent his mistress of 14 years back to Carthage. This cleared the path for a formal marriage with a more socially acceptable spouse. Having already abandoned his lover to save his soul, he finally abandoned sexual passions entirely. He was no doubt influenced by Ambrose and perhaps his earlier sally with Manichaeism. Henceforth he devoted himself to celibacy.

He was still Platonist—or, to be exact, Neoplatonist. Whenever a contradiction existed between faith and learning, he subordinated his philosophy to religion and his reason to superstition. Above all, he remained faithful to Jesus Christ, that great authority from whence all truth emanates.

Unlike St. Ambrose, he was not a devious manipulator, but rather an honest searcher for truth. This is reflected in his conduct and his writings. After reading *The Life of St. Anthony*, he became inspired by Egyptian monks, those Fathers of the Desert who had "stormed the gates of heaven," as he saw it. Retiring to his hometown of Thagaste, he sold all his possessions and, along with some friends, embarked on a communal life. He was ordained to the priesthood, set up a monastery, and was eventually persuaded to take up a bishopric in the city of Hippo.

In St. Augustine, Christianity found perhaps its greatest apologist. His genius and prolific writings were primarily aimed at the principal heresies of his day. They formulated the ideas that have governed Christian theological thought to the present. Later reformers such as Luther and Calvin were admirers, despite rejecting some of his ideas. A variety of significant theological concepts were either introduced or defined by Augustine, such as the notion of venial and mortal sins, each meriting separate levels of punishment in the afterlife. He explored the concepts of original sin, free will, the just war, immortality of the soul, predestination, and the grace of God.

Augustine rejected the Gnostic hypothesis of good and evil locked in an eternal conflict. For him, this idea presupposed a less than omnipotent God. Instead, he built on the Platonic idea of evil as the absence of good. The material world itself was not malevolent, but materialism devoid of the spiritual was. Unfettered ambition, greed, lust, and indifference to the common well-being were sinful manifestations of excessive self-love. This was partly the theme of his *Confessions*, an autobiography of 13 volumes.

TRAMPLING EVIL UNDERFOOT

Using the power of his intellect, he launched a fusillade against heretics and polytheists, writing several volumes on the subject. Having rejected the Manichaeans, he proceeded to attack them, exposing contradictions in their theology. He criticised the lax morals and double standards of their hierarchy, criticisms that could be applied with equal measure against his own church.

He scorned Donatists for their exclusivity in denying the grace of God to humankind. This denial flouted the command to bear witness to all nations "unto the uttermost parts of the earth."

This criticism could also be double edged. Since the Gospel had not spread to all parts of the earth and remains unheard by many to this day, the command could never be fulfilled. Those who did not have the opportunity to accept or deny God's grace because they lived in the wrong time or place are condemned to eternal damnation by his theology.

His ideas put him on a collision course with another contemporary, Pelagius. Pelagius emphasised human free will as the decisive element in choosing good or evil actions. Augustine believed free will alone was insufficient; God's help was also required. Redemption was not possible without His grace.

To Pelagius, reliance on God's grace rather than one's personal efforts gave Christians an excuse for laxity. He denied the concept of original sin and the need for infant baptism, arguing that sin was the product of bad example and habit. Nurture rather than nature, in other words. For Pelagius, Adam's fall did not affect the human condition. The faithful must merit heaven by their own efforts.

Not so, Augustine retorted. God intervenes, but man can choose to accept or reject His grace. Since God, who knows all things, must also know who will accept and who will deny it—in other words, who will be saved and who will be damned—this broaches the idea of predestination. This concept compelled Augustine to explain how those predestined for salvation (the elect) and those predestined for damnation are still responsible for their fates.

The idea of predestination would be taken a step further in the 16th century by the Protestant reformer Calvin. He would form the basic creed of Presbyterianism and further diminish the role of free will since the fall of Adam.

Baptism was essential to remove original sin. Those who died without receiving it were de facto predestined to damnation. This presents a disquieting concept. A sinner such as Augustine, who engaged in theft, fornication, and heresy before following the righteous path by God's grace, merits eternal salvation. On the other hand, newborn infants who die before baptism and those who never hear the Gospel are denied salvation.

To that dilemma, Augustine might respond as he did when contemplating why God allowed the barbarian invaders to rape virtuous Christian women: "unsearchable are His judgments, and His ways past finding out."[421] This did not persuade him to follow the example of Plato, or indeed Buddha and Confucius, who refrained from speculating on the unknown—nor, for that matter, professing to understand its mysteries and pronouncing eternal punishment on those who disagreed.

Augustine did allow that some evil acts, called venial sins, were less severe than others, called mortal sins. Venial sins would merit punishment but not eternal suffering. He then went on to attack Pelagius for not permitting this distinction: "If Pelagius had actually said that all sinners whatever without exception would be punished in an eternity of everlasting fire, then whosoever had approved of this judgment would, to begin with, have brought the sentence down on his own head. For he that shows no mercy shall receive no mercy."[422]

Perhaps Augustine might also bring the same sentence of eternal damnation on his own head that he reserved for those who died blameless without baptism.

Whatever their differences, the two rivals united in condemning Origen. Origen taught that punishment was not eternal. All sinners would eventually be purged of their sins and enter heaven. Augustine didn't agree, and neither did many of his fellow theologians. Due to their efforts, transcripts by the once-great Church Father were thoroughly scrutinised. Eventually, Origen was posthumously counted among the heretics, and many of his books were consigned to the flames. The true path to righteousness had narrowed.

HARSH COUNCILS

In Carthage, Augustine and the African bishops convened many synods and conferences to condemn, variously, Donatists, Pelagius, and pagans. They pronounced severe measures against Donatists at the Council of 411, underlying previous imperial decrees of 405. Pelagius was censured in the Council of 418, and the pagans in 419, together with another blast at the Donatists.

The latter council implored the emperor to remove the remaining idols of the polytheists and destroy their places of worship. They also asked him to ban theatrical spectacles and other plays and forbid heathen feasts. These latter events included "wicked leapings throughout the fields," which apparently compromised the honour and modesty of sensitive women.

The influence of Augustine, who regarded the theatre as sinful and depraved, can be seen in these pronouncements. The same council also forbade actors, heretics, Jews, heathens, slaves, or freedmen from bringing accusations in any criminal proceedings.

Thousands of Donatist clergy were removed from their churches, dispossessed, and banished to neighbouring islands. Their congregations were forbidden to worship and deprived of citizenship. Severe financial penalties were exacted for anyone attempting to convene or attend a religious service of the banned sect. Beatings were administered to force them to renounce their beliefs. In some cases, even the death sentence was applied.

Although initially opposed to coercion, Augustine later wholeheartedly approved of these measures and lent his considerable eloquence in their defence: "For if anyone saw his enemy running headlong to destroy himself when he had become delirious through a dangerous fever, would he not in that case be much more truly rendering evil for evil if he permitted him to run on thus than if he took measures to have him seized and bound? ... Better to administer to him the sharp medicine of tribulation."[423]

"Love your enemy," says the Lord, and what better way to show your love than by beating the daylights out of him until he shares your vision? A crude summary of his paradox, perhaps. No doubt the bishop genuinely believed such measures were essential to save the soul of a sinner.

The punishments might be understandable if reserved for the most violent Donatists, the *circumcelliones*. The brutality of these fanatics had increased in response to the repressive measures against them, or so they claimed. They savagely attacked Augustine's colleagues, whom he had sent to mediate and poured a mixture of lime and vinegar into the eyes of captured clergymen. Their victims, "blind to the truth," were literally blinded by this action.

The punishment Augustine advocated was not merely a response to the law-breaking *circumcelliones*. It was also an attempt at forceful conversion. Violence was extended to peaceful Donatists who had already split with the violent extremists. Augustine was convinced that many secretly wanted to convert but feared offending their fellow believers: "How many, believing that it mattered not to which party a Christian might belong, remained in the schism of Donatus only because they had been born in it … it is our duty to inflict annoyance upon them, in order to prevent them from perishing under the disease of lethargic habit, as under a fatal sleep!"[424]

He justified this by drawing a comparison with the violent conversion of St. Paul, who, blinded by a vision, remained in that state until converted: "The shepherd brings wandering sheep back to the flock with his rod."

Enforcing measures against them proved difficult. Many *circumcelliones* were seasonal farm workers. The powerful landowners who depended on their labour were motivated to protect them. This annoyed the good bishop, who roundly criticised the landed gentry in his sermons.

Steadfast in this belief, he championed the right of the virtuous to inflict punishment on the wicked, who had no such rights: "They who have waged war in obedience to the divine command, or in conformity with His laws, have by no means violated the commandment, 'Thou shalt not kill' "[425] Abraham, who had consented to sacrifice his only son, and Jephthah, who had sacrificed his daughter, were deemed guiltless. They were applauded for their piety because they had obeyed the will of God.

This was a short step to Augustine's concept of the just war (*bellium iustum*). It envisioned a defensive action, fought for the benefit of the adversary, without any ill will towards them. By waging such wars, the righteous would not violate the commandment "Thou shalt not kill." This exemption would be the exclusive prerogative of the faithful.

Following riots in Calama between pagans and Christians, Augustine refused to intervene to save the polytheists from punishment because they had not converted. Although they sought forgiveness, he considered remorse without submission to God as insincere. Only those who endorsed the Christian religion could lead a genuinely virtuous life or be truly sorry for their actions.

Augustine debased philosophy by subjugating reason to superstition and treating as "spiritual facts" what were no more than speculations. He allowed that his views, though thoughtfully formulated and eloquently recorded, could be forcefully applied. While the youthful student searched for the truth and eventually found it after many erroneous paths, the mature bishop would not permit others to take this journey without a similar conclusion. Believing himself to have superior insight, he felt compelled to impose it on others. If all failed, then force would bring them around. This was hardly a humble search for the truth, although Augustine might have believed it was.

He fast-tracked the Christian church in a direction it was already heading, a version of Plato's *Republic*. In this adaptation of the ancient classic, the Catholic Church becomes the autocracy governed by celibate philosophers (the clergy) guiding lesser mortals. Augustine had left Manichaeism, but Manichaeism never entirely left him.

In keeping with the ethos of his day, the lesser mortals included women, who were socially inferior to men and thus must wear veils. Men, on the other hand, created in God's image, as mentioned in 1 Corinthians 11:7, had no reason to conceal themselves.

Nonetheless, Augustine's allure to Christians and even those without belief is understandable. His admission, "I do not know to what temptation I will surrender next,"[426] strikes a chord with those seeking to lead a moral life. Evil exists because we choose to allow it by our actions and words, not because of some external demonic force.

Beneath this lay a restrictive doctrine that reserved salvation to those who followed his guidance. All others were excluded. No matter how virtuous and sincere one might be, beyond his narrow ideology, redemption was unattainable.

While Augustine pondered the hazards to the soul, hazards of a more tangible nature were starting to exert their influence.

20

JEALOUSY AND MISTRUST

ROME'S INTERNAL MALADY was a prerequisite for its external destruction.

Christians now saw themselves as a righteous elite awakened ("woke" in modern parlance) to the sins of their Roman forebears. They were contemptuous of its ancient culture and perceived wrongdoings. Distracted by their pious deliberations, they left warfare largely in the hands of migrant barbarian auxiliaries who despised their weakness. Eventually, Rome could neither control its barbarians nor withstand the relenting hordes that daily poured across its borders. Its religious preoccupations had left it exposed.

GOTHS RETURN TO THE WARPATH

The reign of Theodosius had merely brought a respite from Gothic aggression. His sons—Honorius, emperor in the west, and Arcadius in the east—were both young and vulnerable. Sensing this and feeling somewhat shortchanged by the administration, the tribesmen revolted. Their grievance was the inadequacy of the annual subsidy the Romans paid them to remain peaceful and defend the empire. Unable to surmount the battlements of Constantinople, they descended on the defenceless country of Greece, advancing through the pass of Thermopylae, where, in a long-forgotten century, Leonidas and 300 Spartans had held off the might of the Persian army.

The Goths encountered a less formidable race of Greeks, who failed to repel them. Polytheists hoped the goddess Minerva and the ghost of Achilles would defend the walls of Athens. Christians prayed for the intercession of the saints and martyrs.

Redemption came in a worldlier form. Flavius Stilicho, *magister militum* of the west, sailed from Italy with an army to their defence. The son of a barbarian cavalry officer and a Roman provincial woman, this veteran warrior had earned the confidence of western Emperor Honorius. The Goths, having plundered all they needed, decided not to fight a more formidable opponent. They managed to escape encirclement and retire northward.

It is a measure of the Roman weakness that Alaric, their leader, was rewarded with the title of *magister militum* of eastern Illyricum by the emperor Arcadius to buy his peace.

The Romans continued to rely on the protection of these mercenaries but failed to give them what they most wanted: a secure homeland within the empire. They feared a homeland might become a rival state, complete with an alien faith. Subsequent events would show that this fear was not entirely unjustified. When Constantinople later deprived Alaric of his new title and the subsidy that went with it, he had no further reason to remain peaceful.

He led his tribesmen across the Alps to invade Italy. Honorius fled Milan with his train of clerics and eunuchs, leaving his general to face the horde. Stilicho was obliged to recall troops from the banks of the Rhine and the borders of Caledonia (modern Scotland) to rush to the peninsula's defence. He repulsed the invaders but did not destroy them. Alaric retreated with his army still intact and still menacing.

Nonetheless, the citizens of Rome could finally celebrate a victory that had not resulted from civil conflict. In the triumphal games that followed, they witnessed their last gladiatorial contest in the capital.

While celebrations continued in Rome, Alaric lurked beyond the Alps, gathering his forces for a fresh assault. Events elsewhere determined the next chapter in the ongoing wars with the barbarians.

AND STILL THEY COME

Severe cooling caused by climate change had forced the Huns to move their families and herds westward in search of fresh pastures. This had contributed to the Gothic incursion in the Balkans that culminated in the battle of Adrianople.

Amid worsening weather conditions, further incursions were inevitable. Wandering tribes displaced each other, struggling for meagre pastures. With virtually no legions to oppose them, tribes of Vandals, Alani, and Suevi poured into Gaul. Following close behind were the Franks, Burgundians, and Alemanni. A massive migration moved southward augmented by wayward Gothic units.

For historical convenience, the Goths are henceforth divided into two groups. The new arrivals are designated Ostrogoths (eastern Goths), and tribespeople under Alaric are called Visigoths (western Goths).

When the Ostrogoths crossed the Alps, Honorius again fled for safety, this time to the marshes of Ravenna. Stilicho, leading an army composed of foreign auxiliaries and slaves, managed to repel them at Florence. The semi-barbarian commander had once again saved his homeland.

THE PURSUIT OF HERETICS

While leaving the defence of his earthly domains in the hands of his general, Honorius occupied himself with the protection of the spiritual realm. Fifteen synods and church councils were held, averaging more than one for every two years of his reign. Each required substantial expenditure, energy, and resources. Severe decrees were issued against Manichaeans, Montanists, Priscillianists, Pelagians, Novatians, and Donatists. Otherwise loyal citizens of the empire were harassed and persecuted as barbarians rampaged within its borders.

Honorius dispatched countless letters on theological and ecclesiastic administrative matters, sometimes even outdoing the pope in a single-minded mission to keep the church free of errors.

The papal office became a rather grand institution, taking on the trappings of secular majesty. During the reign of Gratian, the title Pontifex Maximus (chief high priest), initially established during the Republic and subsequently adopted by emperors, was transferred to Pope Damasus. Henceforth all popes would hold the title Pontifex Maximus, or pontiff, underlining the stateliness to the office.

Ecclesiastics and other clergy sought to imitate this opulence in their own way with the help of gifts, legacies, and the reluctant consent of widows and orphans.

This provoked a reaction from Jerome, a man somewhat in the mould of Augustine. Like St. Augustine, a dissolute past troubled his conscience and visions of dancing girls haunted his dreams. He sought escape in the catacombs of Rome, wandering the dark passages between walls lined with corpses. There he endured its horrors as a penance and distraction. "The very silence breathed a terror on my soul," he remarked, quoting Virgil.

Like Augustine and Ambrose, he placed a high value on virginity, devoting an entire book, *Adversus Helvidium*, to attacking the "heretic" Helvidius for merely suggesting that Mary bore children after the virginal birth of Jesus.

Like St. Paul, he saw marriage as a lesser choice for those who could not control their passions. Only the celibate could devote themselves fully to a churchly vocation. Ambrose, Augustine, and Jerome helped transform this concept into Christian practice.

Despite this, Jerome retained a following among noble women who inhabited the exclusive villas of Rome's Aventine Hill. Intrigued by his hermitic lifestyle, these affluent ladies dressed themselves in rags, abandoned the worldly pleasures of their neighbours, and even refused to bathe. When one young devotee died due to extreme deprivations, Jerome admonished the mother for crying at her funeral.

Jerome's hostility to the rich and his caustic pen earned him the enmity of the Roman hierarchy. He was compelled to leave after the death of Damasus amid rumours of an improper affair with one of his female protégées.

Settling in Palestine, he took up residence in a cave that the ever-resourceful locals affirmed to be the birthplace of Jesus. He was shortly joined by his former lady admirers. Their considerable wealth helped him establish monasteries in the region.

Despite his unease with their sexuality, he enjoyed their company. His writings display a revulsion for female body parts while simultaneously employing erotic allusions to them. This bizarre obsession with sexual detail is repeated in the works of ascetic monks, along with descriptive paragraphs on food—both perhaps the consequence of self-imposed abstinence.

Like Augustine, Jerome wrote a manuscript against the followers of Pelagius for their rejection of original sin. He provoked them so much with his hostile *Dialogi contra Pelagianos* that they retaliated violently, setting fire to monasteries and attacking a convent. Jerome survived by hiding in a fortress. A less fortunate deacon died in the affray.

When he was not provoking "heretics," Jerome wrote several texts on history. He is chiefly remembered for his translation of the Hebrew scriptures into Latin.

Previously, Christians relied primarily on the Greek versions, the Septuagint, or translations of it. Jerome decided a translation from the original was more appropriate. He was well prepared for the task. Already an accomplished linguist, he had studied Hebrew to distract his mind from erotic fantasies. The resulting work became the basis for the Vulgate, or Latin Bible, the official version of the Western church until it was replaced by the King James and other translations.

Some passages underline his peculiar prudishness. In Genesis 3:16 of the Hebrew version, God tells Eve after the fall, "Your desire will be for your husband." To remove the sexual innuendo, Jerome translated it as, "You will be under the power of your husband" (*sub postate viri*). These alterations were retained when the Vulgate underwent later translations.

ROME THREATENED

With Honorius and his bishops occupied in matters of faith, the legions in Britain, who had not been paid, decided to mutiny. They elected a soldier, Flavius Constantinus, as their leader, and he promptly led them into Gaul. With no army to defend it, Pictish, Irish, and Saxon pirates raided the island unmolested. Romanised inhabitants buried their gold and waited for the troops to return. They never did. Imperial rule on the island had come to an end.

When the rebels took control of Gaul, Stilicho realised he needed Alaric on his side to overcome them. The Visigoth commander would support Rome against the usurper—but at a price in coin or territory. Otherwise, he would invade Italy once again. In 408, Stilicho went to Rome and persuaded the Senate to pay 4,000 pounds of gold to buy his services.

Many senators consented only out of fear of Stilicho, while others openly objected. Senator Lampadius declared, "This is not a peace, but a bond of servitude."[427] Secretly, they murmured that their general was in league with the barbarian.

The insinuations were repeated to the emperor by his chancellor, Olympius. Fearful that the Arian Stilicho, with the help of Arian Visigoths, might usurp his throne, Honorius plotted against him. A plan was hatched. At Ticinum (modern Pavia, Italy), the troops mutinied, probably inspired by Olympius, and killed officers loyal to Stilicho. The general himself escaped to Ravenna. There, he unwisely permitted himself to be taken into custody and was executed by order of the emperor.

Olympius had him posthumously slandered, *damnatio memoriae*. Stilicho's victories were attributed alternatively to God, miracles, or the intercession of the clergy. According to this narrative, his true purpose was to seize the throne for his son and restore polytheism or the heretical Arian faith. Stilicho's friends and family, including his young son, were mercilessly pursued and brutally tortured to exact confessions of a plot that might never have existed. With no credible confession forthcoming, they were executed without trial.

Olympius was now effectively in control. Under his influence, Honorius excluded from public office anyone who did not subscribe to the Catholic faith. Arians and pagans were prevented from leading the armies of the crumbling empire.

Alaric looked on in astonishment as the Romans first assassinated the general who had twice defeated him and then proceeded to alienate 30,000 of the finest troops who had served under his banner by massacring their Arian families. He again crossed the Alps, and this time, with neither army nor commander of note to oppose him, he plundered his way to the gates of Rome.

DIVIDED CITY

Unlike the citizens who defended their city during the Republic, the population within did not seem willing to fight. Centuries of imperial control and reliance on slavery had weakened their social coherence. At the top was an ineffectual aristocratic elite. Heavy taxation had reduced their wealth, and the Catholic hierarchy had undermined their influence.

The hierarchy itself sought to save the eternal souls of their flock in preference to their mortal bodies. For this service, they exacted a generous subsidy.

Below them were productive freemen, entrepreneurs who provided goods and services to the elite. Next in the pecking order were commoners who lived off a welfare system that gave them a weekly ration of free bread, meat, oil, and corn. At the bottom of this social ladder were the slaves. Like the freemen, they were productive people whose status had deteriorated over the centuries.

They were frequently beaten and abused, their lives considered worthless by haughty masters.

The nouveau Christian elite despised these disaffected people, who formed the early converts to their faith. Freedmen and slaves, including those with the "stain of infamy," like actors, singers, heathens, heretics, and Jews, were advised to accept their fate and refrain from litigation against their betters.[428] In the words of a patriarch, "The slave should be resigned to his lot … in obeying his master, he is obeying God."[429]

Ammianus, who had visited the city a generation earlier, described a frivolous nobility "ignorant that their ancestors, who won greatness for Rome, were not eminent in riches; but through many, a direful war overpowered their foes by valour." The poor he described as "idle plebeians … who from sunrise till evening, through sunshine or rain, stay gaping and examining the charioteers and their horses." Philosophers were replaced by "actresses, singers and teachers of silly arts." The cultivation of liberal studies had been suppressed by the Christian hierarchy, and "libraries [were] shut up like tombs."[430]

THE SIEGE BEGINS

This was the state of Rome in autumn 408, when the army of Alaric encamped outside its walls. They planned to starve the city into submission.

Reduced to a state of desperation, the Senate sent a delegation to discuss terms. When they warned Alaric that the citizens outnumbered his troops, he scornfully responded, "Come out to us then, the thicker the hay, the easier mowed."

The delegation meekly submitted to his terms and the Goths retreated to Tuscany. However, infighting in the court, coupled with the religious fanaticism of Olympius, frustrated their efforts to comply with his demands.

Accusing the Romans of bad faith, Alaric marched south for a final siege in AD 410. On this occasion, the Goths had conspired with slaves inside who were sympathetic to their cause. The gates were secretly opened. More than a millennium after the foundation of the city and eight centuries since it was sacked by the Gauls, Rome was invaded by barbarians. Resistance was brutally suppressed. Slaves exacted revenge on their former masters. The city was pillaged of its treasures, and many of the noble families were reduced to the status of beggars. Their homes were destroyed, and their fortunes stolen.

Pelagius, who was there at the time, wrote of the event in a letter to a friend: "The slave and the man of quality were in similar circumstances, and everywhere the terror of death and slaughter was the same, unless we may say the fright made the greatest impression on those who had the greatest interest in living."[431]

Refugees poured out of the city seeking sanctuary in the provinces of Africa and the east. Their plight was not always met with sympathy. In Africa, the governor Heraclianus sold many helpless wretches into slavery.

For Alaric, it was not the victory he wanted. He might have gained some grim satisfaction from reading the inscription on a triumphal arch celebrating his earlier defeat by Stilicho. It prematurely proclaimed the annihilation of him and his troops. But he had wanted a home for his people and a role for himself in the military establishment. That was no longer possible.

The Goths evacuated the city after six days and proceeded to plunder the towns and countryside of southern Italy. Food was probably the prime object. They attempted to invade Sicily but were repulsed by a storm. Soon afterward, Alaric fell ill and died.

Though severely wounded, the empire remained intact. However, its citizens lacked a clear incentive to defend it. Religious infighting, weak leadership, corruption, inequality, and a loss of identity all contributed to undermine morale. Barbarian bonds of kinship and need for self-preservation eclipsed Roman faith in God and allegiance to the state.

Could the ministers of faith propose a cure, or were their ideals inadequate for the impending challenge? Could the temporal leaders unite their subjects under a common cause that transcended faith, class, and prejudice? The responses to these questions would determine the very survival of the empire.

21

A TRAGEDY UNFOLDS

THE ROMANS WERE deeply shocked by the capture and plunder of their ancient capital. As the Gothic invaders abandoned the city, more enemies gathered on the horizon. The empire needed to recover quickly and prepare to meet the challenge. There was no time to waste.

Like an ailing patient requiring urgent treatment, the empire awaited a remedy. However, the doctors of the church and their compliant statesmen, obsessed with the spiritual welfare of their patient, were oblivious to its physical needs. The symptoms were unclear, the diagnosis uncertain, the cure a matter of debate. Instead of firm action, her leaders fatally procrastinated.

Polytheists attributed the sack of Rome to the Christian violation of the Vestal Virgins temple, the removal of the Altar of Victory, and the failure to offer sacrifices to the gods. Christians questioned why their god had permitted this disaster just when the empire embraced the true faith. How, they asked, had a city that had survived for centuries under pagan rule collapsed a few generations after it became Christian?

Some, like the priest Orosius, who visited the city after the event, downplayed its significance.[432] The fire started by Nero had caused greater destruction, he reasoned. Another priest, Salvian from Gaul, writing much later, saw it as a punishment for their sins.

The Christian historian Sozomen continued in the same vein: "All persons of good sense [meaning Christians] were aware that the calamities which this siege entailed upon the Romans were indications of divine wrath sent to chastise them for their luxury, their debauchery, and their various acts of injustice towards each other as well as towards strangers."[433]

For St. Jerome, it was a calamitous event, a day of doom. As fugitives from Rome gathered like beggars at his home in Bethlehem, it seemed as if the world were coming to an end. Pelagius, Jerome's bête noire, likened it to judgement day.

St. Augustine went on the attack: "The worshippers of false gods and of many gods, to whom we colloquially refer as pagans, tried to blame this on the Christian religion and began to blaspheme the true God with more bitterness and more severity than usual."[434]

In his sermons, he attributed the limited destruction to the providence of God. The root cause was Roman lust for dominance and conflict. The terrible event and the recriminations of non-Christians became the inspiration for one of his greatest works, *De Civitate Dei contra Paganos*, more commonly known as *The City of God*.

As for the emperor, when he heard Rome had perished, he was said to have cried out, "And yet it has just eaten from my hands!"[435] He was referring to a rooster (for he was fond of keeping poultry) that he had named "Rome," and he was relieved when informed that it was the city and not his favourite chicken that had succumbed. The story is almost certainly an invention to parody an inept leader whose reign had witnessed the sack of Rome and the loss of Britain.

RESPONSE OF THE EMPEROR

However, soon afterward, Honorius was aroused to action. At his command, the cities resounded with the trample of horses' hooves and the rustle of silk. Plans were drawn up, provisions gathered, pens and mitres made ready. Bishops were once again on the march. A new synod was convened!

The purpose on this occasion was a dispute over the papacy. Following the death of Pope Zosimus, members of the lower clergy, mainly deacons, seized the Lateran Basilica and elected one of their own, Eulalius, as pope. When the higher clergy tried to intervene, they were violently repulsed by the mob, so they assembled elsewhere and elected one of their own, Boniface. The underlying cause was a conflict between the privileged and poorer classes in Rome.

The synod at Ravenna, 419, failed to resolve the issue, so it was deferred to a general council. The upshot was the appointment of Pope Boniface I.

Boniface proceeded to renew legislation of an earlier pontiff, Pope Soter, that prohibited women from touching the sacred linens or burning incense at mass and other ceremonies. He enforced existing laws forbidding slaves to become clerics, reminding them of their secondary status. If Jesus said the poor must always be with us, then they should at least maintain a respectable distance.

Amid all this, Honorius managed to make a treaty with the Visigoths following the death of Alaric. At his command, they invaded Gaul, now overrun with barbarians and rebels, and restored a semblance of order for a while. Then came another incursion.

AFRICA DEVASTATED

Among the German tribes that had entered Gaul were the Vandals, whose passion for looting and pillaging has immortalised their name. They crossed the Pyrenees into Hispania, pursued by Visigothic *foederati*, who assaulted them on behalf of the empire. Totalling between 20,000 and 80,000 men, women, and children, the invaders soon acquired the use of ships that they used to escape to the coast of North Africa in 429.

Their crafty leader, Gaiseric, quickly grasped the politics of the new territory. Thanks to St. Augustine, the Donatists were undergoing their most severe persecution since Constantine. The armed *circumcelliones* continued their resistance, while the list of martyrs grew on both sides. For these oppressed die-hards, the arrival of the Vandals signalled payback time.

Gaiseric, himself a heretic, albeit an Arian, delivered them from the cruelty of Catholic dominion. Fanatics rushed to his standard seeking retribution against their former persecutors, clergy and laypeople alike. Together, they swooped on the villages and towns, crushing all resistance. Clerics who managed to escape death were stripped of their possessions and forced to beg in the streets. Vengeful Catholic scribes later blamed the Vandals for destroying churches and other buildings. In fact, much of the destruction was committed by Donatist mobs.

By the spring of 430, the invaders were at the walls of Hippo Regius. Residing within, the ageing St. Augustine recited the Psalms of David together with fugitive bishops who had sought refuge there. No doubt he pondered the vagaries of fortune that saw heretics first sack Rome and then besiege his city. As he perceived "the awful judgment of God laid bare before [their] eyes,"[436] it must have seemed unlikely that the doctrine he had formulated would ultimately prevail. He died, probably from illness or the deprivations of the siege, before the Vandals finally breached the defences and put the city to the torch.

A treaty between the Vandals and Rome brought hostilities to an end. But after four years of peace, when the Romans were preoccupied with more barbarian incursions, Gaiseric resumed his attacks. In 439, he conquered Carthage, 500 years after Rome had taken it from Hannibal in the Punic Wars. Factionalism within the Christian community had contributed to the loss, and its capture deprived the Romans of a valuable source of tax and foodstuffs.

The Vandals treated the Catholics much as the Catholics had treated the Donatists. The Arians took control of the churches within the city and forced them to worship outside. Those among the clergy who could not endure persecution chose exile instead. The Catholic religion underwent a period of decline as the faithful emigrated or converted to Arianism.

ITALY THREATENED

From the north, the Huns advanced again under the charismatic leader Attila. This time, Rome turned to another formidable general, Flavius Aetius. Flavius had been a hostage of the Huns in his youth and knew their manners and tactics.

Supported by Visigoths, he managed to defeat them at Chalons, in northern Gaul. Attila was forced to retreat, and Aetius could claim the last great victory that the Western Roman Empire would ever win.

For the Huns, the setback was temporary. After regrouping his followers, Attila returned the following year to ravage northern Italy. This time, Aetius, with diminished resources and without allies, was unable to repel them.

As they rested their hardy ponies near Lake Garda, the motley band of Huns and Goths in rugged animal skins were met by a delegation of silk-clad ambassadors from the Eternal City. Among them was the new pope, Leo I.

According to the Christian writer Prosper of Aquitaine, Attila was so impressed with the pontiff that he ordered his army to abandon warfare and pursue the path of peace. He departed Italy and headed back across the Danube. Prosper was not present at the negotiations, but the story held currency throughout Christendom.

A famine in Italy, the ravages of pestilence, rumours of a relief force from the eastern empire, and a hefty ransom all contributed to his decision to withdraw. If Attila had promised peace, he didn't keep it but immediately resumed his raids.

AUTHORITATIVE CHURCH, DIMINISHING STATE

Leo himself resumed hostilities against heretics as soon as he returned to Rome. He burned the books of Manichaean refugees from Vandal Africa, expelled the Pelagians from the community, conducted a witch hunt of Priscillianists in Hispania, and terrorised anyone whose pronouncements were deemed unorthodox.

He was helped in this by the new emperor Valentinian III, son of Honorius, who inherited the Theodosian family's deference to hierarchical authority. In a decree of 455, the emperor made it a treasonable offence to challenge any ruling of the papacy. Thus, the holy pronouncements of the pontiff were upheld in the secular courts of the empire. Successive decrees against polytheists and heretics came to define a slender path of permissible thought. To venture beyond this narrow trail invited risk. The intellectual freedom that characterised classical Rome was in retreat.

Both emperor and pope promoted the idea that the See of Rome was the successor to St. Peter, holding primacy over all other Christian cities. The autocracy of the pope increased in inverse proportion to the political decline of the state. This would create a problem for the future as real power shifted from Rome to Constantinople.

Meanwhile, Leo continued his predecessors' position of excluding slaves and others of low birth from ordination. This added to the elitism of the hierarchy: "Slaves and serfs [*coloni*] are not to be ordained … as if sorry slaves were fit for that honour … the sacred ministry is polluted by such poor partners in it, and the rights of masters are infringed so far as unlawful possession is rashly taken of them."[437]

With the Huns out of the picture, the jealous Valentinian had no further use for Aetius, whom he suspected of coveting the throne. The general was lured to a private audience, where the treacherous daggers of eunuchs, courtiers, and the emperor himself terminated his life. History had repeated itself, the son imitating the father's sins by killing the general who had served him and his empire so well.

Valentinian paid the ultimate price for his action. Some former soldiers of Aetius stabbed the worthless monarch at the instigation of a senator called Petronius Maximus. It was alleged that Valentinian had raped the senator's wife. Petronius became the new emperor, but as events would soon show, he was well out of his depth.

THE FATAL BLOW

Gaiseric watched these events from his stronghold in Carthage. He had made the ancient city his base from which he sent ships to plunder the islands and coastal regions of Europe. A peace treaty with Valentinian exempted Rome itself from attack. One of its conditions was the marriage of Eudocia, Valentinian's daughter, to Huneric, son of Gaiseric. The emperor's death provided Gaiseric with a pretext to break the treaty. It helped his case that either Eudocia or her mother sent him an invitation to come to their assistance.

Within three months of the assassination and without the one general who could save them, the Romans awoke to the sight of a Vandal fleet at Ostia, the city's harbour. Disembarking from their ships, the warriors rushed towards the city gates with weapons drawn. They might have expected a legion of the finest troops in full armour to block their passage. Instead, they were met by a communion of bishops in soft tunics and flowing beards. At the forefront stood Pope Leo I, imploring them to desist.

Unlike his previous encounter with Attila, the meeting with Gaiseric did not produce the required retreat. The Vandal king made the necessary promises and promptly broke them. Christian historians credit Leo with persuading him to moderate his treatment of the city and its inhabitants, if not to spare it. There is little evidence that he complied.

During 14 days of robbery and destruction, the Vandals deprived the city of its treasures. This included the valuables taken from the temple of Jerusalem by the victorious Titus 400 years earlier. What remained of its wealth and artefacts was loaded onto ships and transported to Carthage, along with numerous captives.

Rome never fully recovered from this pillage. After the death of Valentinian III, a series of eight emperors followed in quick succession over a period of 21 years. The last one, Romulus Augustus, was banished to a villa near Naples and received an annual stipend courtesy of the Gothic ruler of Italy, Odoacer. Odoacer was an Arian, but he permitted Catholics freedom of worship. Italy, depopulated and impoverished, was finally at peace, at least for now.

With the trade routes to Africa and the east no longer accessible, Europeans came to rely on local products, cruder perhaps but functional. They experienced what the British historian Chris Wickham called "radical material simplification";[438] in other words, a massive drop in living standards.

Salvian, who saw the hand of God in these calamities, declared, "What hope can there be for the Roman state when the barbarians are more chaste and purer than the Romans."[439] As an example, he pointed out that it was the savages and not the Christian Romans who finally put an end to the gladiatorial contests and other circus games. These same barbarians were now the rulers of a fragmented Europe.

Impoverished provincials, many of whom still clung to the old pagan traditions, had long since lost the will to fight for an empire where the rich had become remote, taxation more oppressive, and the combined autocracy of an alien faith and government unable to protect them. Polytheism endured, despite the many decrees of Christian emperors and the rampages of monks. However, the localised nature of their traditions made them incapable of resisting the sustained opposition of a dogmatic opponent.

As we have seen, the customs and festivals of polytheism were incorporated into the Christian calendar with little alteration other than terminology. Local deities were replaced by local saints, some as mythical as the gods they replaced. Even pagan shrines morphed into Christian places of pilgrimage.

Pagans became Christian, and Christians assimilated paganism. Tombstones of the departed sometimes depicted the cross alongside symbols of the ancient rites. The process of assimilation continued for centuries, and not always peacefully.

As the central power declined, young aristocrats who traditionally sought advancement in public office chose a religious vocation instead. Thus, bishops, who were often interrelated, survived as a noble class under the jurisdiction of barbarian overlords and the spiritual dictates of an imperial pontiff. In this capacity, they acted as mediators between the people and their rulers. The new chieftains, anxious to assume a Roman demeanour and fearful of dead saints, embraced Christianity and showed deference to the spiritual fathers who still spoke the Latin tongue.

Rome's failure to quell religious strife in Africa left it exposed, allowing the Vandals to use it as a base for their deadly attacks. Shortly afterward, the Western Roman Empire ceased to exist as a political entity.

Only the Christian religion endured. It survived because it adapted. It provided spiritual leadership at a time of uncertainty and offered a sense of stability amid violent upheaval.

Thus, regardless of its role in the downfall of the empire, the church emerged the clear winner in its aftermath. It would henceforth guide the conscience of Europe, and the people would be subject to its benevolence or its tyranny.

Meanwhile, the political and administrative centre of gravity was now firmly in the east. Therefore, to the east we must look for the next chapter in our story.

PART FOUR

CITY OF GOD

"The kingdom of the world now belongs to our Lord and to his Anointed, and he will reign forever and ever."

—Revelation 11:15

22

THE BISHOP WITH THE GOLDEN MOUTH

JOHN CHRYSOSTOM HAD an extensive inventory of things he hated. The list was longer than his great flowing beard. It included Jews, homosexuals, pagans, heretics, horse racing, games, and the theatre. And that was just for starters. He didn't particularly like women either.

So long as his prejudices were confined to his remote monastery near Antioch, it did not matter too much. That all changed when he received an invitation from the emperor to become Patriarch of Constantinople.

The emperor would soon learn that this single-minded bigot enjoyed the love of the people. Without his support, governing them would be near impossible. Henceforth, the fate of church and state were inexorably linked. The edicts of one must reflect the prejudices of the other.

THE EAST STANDS ALONE

Constantinople, protected by its walls and enriched by the vast hinterlands of Asia Minor and Egypt, watched from relative security the gradual destruction of its sister capital on the Tiber.

Although its Balkan provinces were plundered and impoverished by the same barbarians that ravaged Rome, the eastern empire remained intact, if somewhat wounded. Its citizens considered themselves Roman, although the predominant language was Greek rather than Latin. They looked at the fall of the west as a temporary setback and considered it their destiny to reverse this condition someday.

On the eastern frontier, across the river Tigris, lurked the old enemy, Persia. Rivalry between the two powers ensured an ever-present tension. This alternated between periods of open conflict and uneasy peace. Neither side was willing to engage in an all-out war that might end with the destruction of one and the economic ruin of both.

In this comparative tranquillity, Christianity thrived. Rulers challenged its power at their peril and struggled to adjudicate the growing ferocity of rival bishops. For their diverse subjects, faith was not a private matter. Abstract interpretations of Christ's nature were as much a badge of identity as their language, dress code, and customs.

Aided by a series of amenable rulers, the church assumed the role of joint government in practice, if not in name. The lifestyle of the higher clerics imitated that of the temporal rulers in its ostentation. Gone were the simple white togas of the Roman senatorial class and the white linen tunics of the early bishops. Their wealth made them inaccessible to the common subjects, whom they kept in miserable subjugation by the terror of superstition.

The happy state of these holy men was interrupted briefly by the zeal of a reformer, John Chrysostom.

As a youth, John had abandoned a promising career in law in favour of baptism and the tranquil life of a monastery. There, nestled in the mountains of his native Antioch, he devoted himself to reading the sacred Scriptures in its stark chambers. When the rigorous austerity affected his health, he returned to the city and was ordained to the priesthood. Soon, the power of his pen and the eloquence of his sermons earned him a reputation and the name Chrysostom, "golden mouth."

Crowds flocked to hear his words, filling the churches where he spoke to capacity. His orations were frequently interrupted by the sound of clapping hands and cheering voices.

Preaching without a script, he denounced pagans for their amusements, theatrical plays, horse races, and excessive revelry during public holidays. He lamented that Christians knew the names of thoroughbred stallions better than those of the saints.

Homosexuals did not escape either. Same-sex liaisons were worse than murder,[440] he declared, implying that those who partook were beyond salvation. Heterosexuals were no better if they used contraceptives: "Why do you sow where the field is eager to destroy the fruit? Where there are medicines of sterility? Where there is murder before birth?"[441] he enquired.

In eight homilies entitled *Adversus Judaeos*, he compared the Jews to animals who harboured Satan in their souls and synagogues. They were the killers of the Saviour, and the bloodlust had not left them, he warned, darkly hinting that they might kill again.[442]

The burning of the synagogue in Callinicum, Syria (see chapter 18), was inspired by his words, as were other mob attacks on Jewish communities for various imaginary crimes.

Partly thanks to Chrysostom, Jews and homosexuals joined the list of those whose persecution was sanctioned by the church.

CARNAGE IN CONSTANTINOPLE

Chrysostom's reputation spread beyond Antioch. When a dispute arose between rival factions over the vacant episcopal See of Constantinople, the emperor opted for an outsider. He hoped this would be preferable to one of the squabbling locals. So, in 397, he summoned Chrysostom to take the post.

The royal family would regret elevating this ascetic to a powerful position in a city where luxury and display were the hallmarks of the elite.

On arrival in Constantinople, Chrysostom was dismayed to find it still retained a community of Arians, mostly Goths. Since the time of Theodosius, they were forced to worship beyond the city walls. It was their custom to form a procession and sing hymns as they slowly strolled to their churches on the outside. Unable to tolerate even this harmless ceremony, Chrysostom organised a counter-procession of hymn-singing Trinitarians. The inevitable conflict followed.

Tensions increased when Gainas, a Gothic commander who had served Theodosius, petitioned for a church within the city itself. Chrysostom bitterly opposed the request but was overruled by Emperor Arcadius.

The new patriarch found an ally in the Empress Aelia Eudoxia, who was hostile to the Goths. She urged the citizens to attack the heretics. To escape slaughter, many Arians sought refuge in the church. Trinitarians attacked the building and burned it to the ground. The congregation, trapped inside the locked doors, perished. Others were assaulted in the streets, and the total carnage came to 7,000 dead. Gainas was later killed while attempting an insurrection against the regime.

Having dealt with heretics, Chrysostom used his office to divert the ample church revenues to the building of hospitals. This and other demonstrations of charity earned him the support and love of the poor. From his pulpit, he thundered against the vices of the city. He condemned domestic females of the clergy, who, under the guise of being servants or sisters, performed a more worldly service. Ill-disciplined monks who aimlessly roamed the streets were confined to their monasteries by his strict injunction. He took measures against simony and bribery in the priesthood. By his order, 13 bishops of the Asiatic provinces were deposed for having purchased their offices.

To confront this multitude of vices threatening the faithful, Chrysostom encouraged Christians to spy on each other, enter each other's homes, expose sinners, and thereby save their souls.[443] Anyone who visited the "place of the devil" (as he described the theatre) or indulged in festivities, the baths, or homosexuality was liable to public denouncement.

However, lack of tact hindered his reforming goals. His manner was stern and haughty; his golden tongue had an abrasive edge that was offensive to many and ultimately harmful to himself. While his public preaching "was powerful in reforming the morals of his auditors, in private conversation, he was frequently thought haughty and assuming."[444]

Preferring to eat alone, he regularly declined invitations to dinner, citing a delicate stomach and a distaste for wine. Since he listed laughter, banter, the theatre, games, and beautiful women among the "terrible snares" to corrupt the faithful, he was hardly a fun guest. To his peers, he displayed a cold and gloomy demeanour, impatient with their pleas, intolerant of dissent.

His preaching against the corruption and greed in the imperial city was relentless. The arrows of his invective soon found their mark. This included the emperor's family, attendant eunuchs, various bishops, and an assortment of higher clerics.

TENSION WITH THE EMPRESS

Although the common people loved Chrysostom, his enemies among the clergy grew. He might have escaped their revenge if he had not united them with another powerful force: Empress Eudoxia. Chrysostom seemed to have an aversion to women and a prudish distaste for sexual relationships. He went further than St. Ambrose in extolling the virtues of virginity, "not because marriage is an evil; but because virginity is superior."[445]

"Being of a fiery temperament and a ready utterance, he later pronounced a public invective against women in general."[446] In a sermon on the vices of women, he denounced their luxury and extravagance. The empress felt with some justification that the attacks were directed at her and the ladies of the court, whose ostentatious dress provoked his ire. Gone was the unity they had enjoyed against the Arians. She resolved to retaliate.

DISCORD IN EGYPT

At that crucial moment, the Patriarch of Alexandria, Theophilus,[447] disembarked at the port of Constantinople. He was there to answer charges concerning a theological dispute with some monks in his dominion. This was no petty quarrel.

The disagreement centred on the writings of Origen. The monks, or at least most of them, believed that God was anthropomorphic, possessing a human form complete with eyes, nose, arms, legs, and so forth. Theophilus upheld the views of Origen that God was incorporeal or alien to any human form. The fact that neither Theophilus nor the monks had actually seen God didn't stop them having firm views on the subject.

When the patriarch declared those who believed otherwise were guilty of blasphemy, the monks were mightily offended. Soon, an angry mob of ragged beards and dirty tunics could be seen trampling the roads to Alexandria with murder in their hearts. Having incited the citizens, who were readily prone to incitement, they readied themselves for a fight.

When faced with the bloodthirsty mob, the wily Theophilus managed to quell their anger with soft words: "When I look upon you, it is as if I behold the face of God."[448] He might have meant they looked inhuman, but the simple monks did not detect any double meaning if one was intended. Peace was restored for the moment, but the patriarch seemed to thrive on conflict.

Later, he planted the seed of discord by revealing discussions he recently had with certain monks who endorsed the Origenist concept of an incorporeal God. Having reinvented himself as an anti-Origenist, Theophilus pretended to be shocked by such views. The crude monks, unskilled in the arts of subtle debate, preferred to settle matters with insults and blows. They immediately began fighting among themselves over the issue.

Not content with being a passive observer, Theophilus, with the governor's approval, gathered troops and a "mob of ruffians and slaves," whom he primed with liquor. In the dead of night, they crept into the monasteries and assaulted the sleeping monks. Setting fire to their cells and other meagre possessions, they tortured captives and even caused the death of a boy who was caught in the conflagration.[449]

The pro-Origenist monks fled to Constantinople to make a formal complaint about their treatment at the hands of the bishop. They presented their case to Chrysostom and later to the empress herself. At her urging, the emperor summoned Theophilus to answer the charges.

The Alexandrian bishop was a bitter rival of Chrysostom and had only supported his elevation to the patriarchy of Constantinople under duress. Before departing for the capital, he carefully laid the groundwork for the coming confrontation. Knowing that the patriarch had many rivals among the hierarchy, he wrote to them requesting support. In his correspondence, he subtly hinted that Chrysostom had pro-Origenist sentiments.

SYNOD OF THE OAK

Thus, when Theophilus arrived in Constantinople, it was not as a supplicant but as a challenger. The power of Alexandria that allowed Athanasius to defy imperial orders had equally emboldened Theophilus. There was more than theology at play. This dispute had a political dimension.

The Council of Nicaea had granted primacy to the sees of Alexandria, Antioch, and Rome over lesser dioceses, including the new imperial capital. As Constantinople grew in prestige, Alexandria, formerly the second city of the empire, saw its importance diminish. A power struggle between the two cities underlined the conflict. Theophilus wished to reassert Egyptian authority.

He had a party of 29 bishops with him, which he supplemented with armed mariners from his native Alexandria. He quickly became the focal point of opposition to the patriarch. Disaffected monks, jealous bishops, irate courtiers, and the empress herself all rallied to his side.

At a place known as The Oak in the suburb of Chalcedon on the Asiatic side of the Bosphorus, Theophilus convened a synod. Technically, this was illegal. The diocese was outside his jurisdiction and beyond his authority, but that did not bother the assembled delegates. He read a list of 46 charges against the patriarch, most of them groundless except for the charge of comparing the empress to Jezebel. The accused had become the accuser, and the patriarch was commanded to answer the charges.

Chrysostom refused to respond to the summons. Apart from its illegality, the assembly was partisan, and his accusers would be both witnesses and judges. He was promptly condemned in absentia. The verdict had imperial approval, and an order was issued for his arrest. To avoid bloodshed, he consented to a sentence of exile.

EXILE AND RETURN

Before his departure, he ran into St. Epiphanius, who had taken time off from persecuting heretics in Cyprus to support Theophilus. The two men had a brief exchange of pleasantries. "I hope you will not die a bishop," said Epiphanius, to which Chrysostom replied, "I hope you will never return to your bishopric."[450] The hopes of both men were realised. Epiphanius died on the voyage home, and Chrysostom, as we shall see, would not remain a bishop for long.

His sudden departure did not prevent bloodshed. As might be expected, the common people reacted violently. A mob killed some of the monks and the Egyptian mariners who had supported Theophilus. Realising he might see the face of God sooner than planned, the Alexandrian bishop fled to the harbour and scurried aboard the first departing ship. The emperor was obliged to recall the banished patriarch to quell the unrest.

Chrysostom returned to widespread acclaim. Enthralled by the rush of cheering crowds, he failed to take the precaution of having his sentence revoked by a formal synod. He quickly resumed his old confrontational style, preaching against corruption and the vices of women.

In an act of ill-advised vanity, the empress allowed a silver statue of herself to be placed on a porphyry column near the Great Church (*Magna Ecclesia*). It provoked the intemperate wrath of the patriarch, especially as its installation was accompanied by celebrations—dancing in the streets and games in the circus, the very spectacles that so easily darkened his gloomy countenance. There was a slight pagan flavour to it all. "These proceedings bring dishonour on the church," he declared, ridiculing those who took part.

For the empress, the public condemnation reopened an old wound. She convened another synod to deal with the troublesome cleric. His reaction incited Eudoxia ever further. From the pulpit, he delivered another fiery sermon comparing his fate to that of John the Baptist. "Again Herodias raves," he thundered, a trifle overdramatic; "again she is troubled; she dances again; and again, desires to receive John's head on a charger."[451]

FINAL EXILE

This was the final straw. Exploiting the fact that the original sentence had not been officially rescinded, the synod banished Chrysostom without debate. On Easter eve, imperial troops stormed the baptistery and violently dispersed the angry congregation. Describing the event in a letter to the pope later, Chrysostom wrote, "The baptismal pools were filled with blood, and the sacred water reddened by it."[452]

Following his second exile, his supporters rioted, again setting fire to buildings and churches. The authorities used this as a pretext to crush them. The most prominent were hunted down, imprisoned, tortured, and executed. Others were simply stripped of their possessions. Ladies had their jewellery torn from them in the streets by the imperial guard. Many supporters simply fled.

Chrysostom's new abode was a desolate town in remote Armenia. It suited his temperament, and the venerable old man thrived. He received funds from well-wishers and used them to free captives kidnapped by lawless bandits and to finance monks engaged in destroying pagan shrines. He remained in the public consciousness through diligent correspondence and persistent attacks against heretics. His absence helped erase memories of his faults and enhanced recollections of his qualities. Finally, perhaps to silence him, he was removed from his place of exile and forced on a long march to the Caucasus.

He expired on the journey.

St. John Chrysostom had been a champion of the poor and a strong critic of corruption and extravagance. Yet his reforming zeal failed to end the simony and malpractice that permeated the church. His polemics against women would have found favour with that bleak 16th-century Scottish reformer John Knox. His religion was a sombre affair, morally austere, devoid of joy, and characterised by prejudice. Pagans, heretics, Jews, and homosexuals all trembled at his invective.

Death did not diminish the legend. His saintly name endured longer than that of any racehorse. Thirty years after his death, his body was exhumed and transported to Constantinople. As the funeral entourage approached the city, the new emperor Theodosius II went forth to meet it. On reaching the coffin, he fell in supplication and begged forgiveness from the lifeless remains for the sins of his parents, Eudoxia and Arcadius. Then, with lavish ceremony, the corpse was moved to the city and buried in the Church of the Apostles.

The posthumous reverence accorded to the bishop was an acknowledgement by the regime of the influence the church wielded over the people. Emperors would henceforth be mindful of preachers who could arouse the religious passions of the mob. No aspirant to power could succeed without the endorsement of charismatic clerics and their followers.

After his death, the conflict between the two great episcopal sees of Alexandria and Constantinople intensified. In this struggle, the imperial family became bit players rather than masters of events. The quarrel would help seal the fate of Egypt and its place within the empire.

23

ELIMINATE THE HERETICS

NESTORIUS, PATRIARCH OF Constantinople, having resolved to purge the world of heretics, awoke one day to the dreadful realisation that he was one of them himself.

In the fervour of theological discourse, a fine line existed between pronouncements considered dogmatically correct or offensive. An incautious word or phrase could destroy the reputation of its speaker while providing an opportunity for his enemy. One man's destruction became a triumph for another. The integrity of either was of little consequence.

THE EMPEROR, HIS HOLY FAMILY, AND HIS FAITH

Named after his famous grandfather, Theodosius II became emperor in AD 408. Just as his father, Arcadius, had been overshadowed by the Empress Eudoxia, Theodosius, too, was eclipsed by the power of a woman, his elder sister Pulcheria. The Senate granted this pious lady the title Augusta when the seven-year-old Theodosius II assumed the throne.

She took a vow of virginity, relinquished jewellery and fine clothes, gave alms to the poor, recited daily prayers, and fasted twice a week. During her stern regency, she prohibited the building of new synagogues and ordered the destruction of many existing ones. This effectively revoked the status of *religio licita* that had been granted to Jews under Roman law since pre-Christian times. A decree banning pagans from holding public office or partaking in military service intensified the persecution of earlier times. Chrysostom would have approved. In fact, it was due partly to her influence that his remains were returned to Constantinople.

Pulcheria exerted obsessive control over her younger brother. Under her influence, the young Theodosius embraced the superstition of his time. He fasted, prayed, sang psalms, and blindly accepted the miracles and dogma essential to the true faith. When he reached maturity, his elder sister still retained her influence.

Theodosius's wife, Eudocia, was no less devout, although she probably converted to Christianity only after her betrothal. Her father was a lecturer in that great bastion of philosophy, the Academy of Athens. Eudocia may have influenced Theodosius to commission a similar academy in Constantinople in 425 dedicated to the classics, medicine, maths, and astronomy. It ensured some continuity of ancient scholarship.

To assert her Christian credentials, Eudocia visited the Holy Land, where the ever-resourceful Palestinians rewarded her with of the chains of St. Peter, the right arm of St. Stephen, and a portrait of the Blessed Virgin painted by no less an artist than St. Luke himself. All of these she triumphantly transported back to Constantinople.

By this time, thanks to the ongoing threat from the Huns, a more formidable defence was under construction around the city's perimeter. The Theodosian wall, as it became known, would serve the imperial capital well in the coming centuries.

When he was not building walls, matters of a more abstract nature occupied the mind of the emperor. Disputes concerning the Trinity and the persecution of Arians were replaced by a new controversy: the incarnation of Jesus.

Eastern philosophy struggled with the concept of an all-perfect creator in a human, and thus imperfect, form. If he could suffer pain, temptation, and ignorance and exercise all the bodily functions of a man, then some believed he would cease to be God.

Three different scenarios emerged. First, Jesus was not God, but a prophet. Second, Jesus never actually became a man but had the form—though not the substance—of one. This entity passed through the womb of Mary like "a beam of light through Glass," allowing her to maintain the "seal of virginity." A third view was that Jesus was a mortal man of superior goodness. The spirit of God had entered his body at birth and departed on his death.

All three scenarios challenged the Orthodox Trinitarian view that Jesus, the second person of the Trinity equal and of one substance with God, confined for a time in the womb of Mary, born of the flesh, had lived on Earth, experienced pain and ignorance, and in his human form, expired in anguish on the cross.

Why should such abstract matters concern the simple believer, one might ask?

The diverse communities of the empire chose to identify themselves by their interpretation of the scriptures. Populist clerics shamelessly encouraged them to regard the slightest deviation as an assault on their community. These opportunists ruthlessly pursued any rival with an alternative view. By this means, they enhanced their own influence and authority. It proved a formidable challenge to the regime in Constantinople and an opportunity for any aspirant to power in Syria or Egypt. Such a man now sought control in Alexandria.

EGYPT'S MILITANT PATRIARCH

During his mission to Constantinople to confront Chrysostom, Theophilus of Alexandria had been accompanied by his nephew Cyril. The pair had fled together when the events turned sour.

Cyril embraced the routine of the desert monks in the monastery where he was educated. He fasted and prayed, sharing their frugal meals and their distaste for Origen while patiently awaiting his uncle's demise. When the moment arrived, Cyril assumed the role of patriarch. It was not a gentle transition. A street clash between his supporters and those of a rival determined the outcome. Thus were matters resolved in Alexandria.

By this time, the patriarchy of Alexandria had become more powerful than the temporal offices of the governor or civil magistrate. Cyril, who possessed all the duplicity of his uncle, lost no time in using that power. He first confronted the Novatians, who, like the Donatists, denied absolution for mortal sins. (See chapter 15) Unlike the Donatists, they did not fight back. They watched helplessly as their churches were closed and their sacramental vessels confiscated.

His next target was the Jews of Alexandria. This community had resided in the city since its inception by Alexander the Great. They had long enjoyed the protection of the heathen Romans and were ill prepared for an assault by its Christian rulers.

Jewish festivals involved theatrical pageants, dancing, and joviality. This attracted Christian participation and upset the hierarchy. When agents of the patriarch tried to ban the proceedings, the Jews retaliated and killed some Christians.

Rather than prosecuting the guilty through judicial process, the holy bishop preferred to punish the whole race.

Early one morning, Cyril marched into their quarters at the head of a hostile crowd. With a fearful clamour, they ravaged through the narrow streets, burning synagogues, demolishing houses, looting stores, and killing any who resisted. The wretched Jews, men and women, old and young, were then driven into the unforgiving desert to seek refuge in distant towns and cities. Alexandria was thus deprived of an ancient and productive community.

Orestes, the prefect of Egypt, who resented the power of the patriarch, sent a letter of protest to the emperor. This had the effect of drawing to himself the wrath of a vengeful Cyril without any positive outcome for the injured parties. A troop of 500 monks left their monastic seclusion in the nearby hills and entered the city to defend their bishop.

As Orestes rode through the streets, he was confronted by these screaming fanatics accusing him of idolatry. While he was vehemently affirming his Christian credentials, a well-aimed stone struck his head. Prompt intervention by his guards and some loyal citizens prevented a public lynching. An angry Orestes avenged the outrage by ordering the torture and execution of the stone-throwing monk, Ammonius.

CYRIL'S REVENGE

It was now the turn of the great patriarch himself to feel provoked. Defiantly, Cyril had the body of Ammonius exhumed and carried in sombre procession to the Great Church. There, in a solemn ceremony, the would-be assassin was given the dignity of a martyr's funeral. Few of the Christian inhabitants felt the thug deserved the honour. Many were troubled by the growing rift between patriarch and prefect.

Cyril now had a score to settle with Orestes, and he chose a certain virgin called Hypatia as the scapegoat. The daughter of a renowned scholar, Hypatia was a learned woman and skilled mathematician who lectured in the academies of Athens and Alexandria. In Cyril's eyes, the qualities of intelligence and beauty magnified the evil of her idolatry. So, too, did her ungodly lectures on rational thought. Her friendship with Orestes inspired the rumour that she prevented a reconciliation between the two men.

During the season of Lent, while she was returning from an interview with Orestes, a Christian mob ambushed Hypatia. They dragged her from her chariot into a nearby church. There, the monks stripped her naked and flayed the flesh from her body using sharp oyster shells and fragments of pottery. The slow, painful torture ended when they took her body—or what remained of it—to a place called Cinaron and cast it into the flames. Cyril's complicity in this barbaric act was never attested, however. A judicial enquiry was rescinded by generous donations and timely bribes. Alexandria had become a hostile environment for scholars, henceforth they would live in fear of their lives.

CONSTANTINOPLE'S UNWELCOME PATRIARCH

Resentment towards Constantinople was never far below the surface. Cyril soon had the opportunity to reopen the conflict with the imperial capital and its new patriarch. Nestorius was a priest who resided in the monastery of Euprepius outside Antioch when the emperor invited him to succeed to the patriarchy in 428. The popular memory of John Chrysostom might have influenced the decision. Like John, Nestorius was an eloquent orator, a rigid moralist, and an outsider.

On assuming office, the new patriarch immediately declared himself a vigorous persecutor of heresy. He might have displayed a little too much enthusiasm. "Give me, my prince, the earth purged of heretics, and I will give you heaven as a recompense."[453]

Less than five days after his ordination, he commenced the purge by ordering the demolition of an Arian church. The congregation, much diminished by previous persecutions and seeing they would lose their place of worship anyway, decided to set it ablaze. The result was that nearby buildings were also reduced to ashes.

Undeterred, Nestorius followed this with an attack on the Novatians, but the emperor restrained him. So, he turned his attentions to the Quartodecimans, who stubbornly celebrated Easter on a different date from Orthodox Christians. When Nestorius's agents began persecuting them in the provinces of Asia Minor, they revolted and paid dearly for it. Those who could not endure his tyranny became unwilling converts.

His actions made new patriarch rather unpopular. Many clerics in Constantinople had been hostile to him from the start. This outsider from Antioch was sitting on the episcopal throne that rightly belonged to one of them. Previous aspirants to the vacant see who had schemed against each other were now united against Nestorius. They held their fire and waited patiently for an opportunity.

One of the presbyters, Anastasius, who had accompanied Nestorius from Antioch, unwittingly provided the opportunity. During a sermon, the young cleric announced that no one should refer to Mary, the mother of Jesus, as *Theotokos*. This Greek word meant "God-bearer." Elaborating, he explained that Mary was a mortal woman, and it was impossible for God to be born of a woman. His sermon caused outrage, especially among those who had waited patiently to be outraged.

Nestorius's attempts to clarify the sermon seemed to indicate that he also supported this viewpoint. From his perspective, since the Trinity is one divine being, if Jesus becomes man, then so too must the Father and the Holy Spirit. This made it necessary to distinguish between the divine and human nature of Jesus, both joined together but separate.

Up went the cry, "Heretic!" Nestorius responded with excommunications. Surely anyone who challenged his teaching must be a heretic themselves? The commotion soon reached the ears of Cyril, who immediately seized the chance to undermine the rival patriarchy and enhance the status of Alexandria.

CLASH OF THE PATRIARCHS

A correspondence ensued between the two with hair-splitting disputations using respectful language to disguise mutual revulsion. The conniving Cyril wrote to the pope, enclosing the letters that Nestorius had sent to him. Aware he was being set up, Nestorius sought permission from the emperor to convene a council. The request was seconded by the monks of Constantinople. Nestorius had excommunicated them en masse, and they saw the opportunity to retaliate.

Before the council commenced, Nestorius was dismayed to hear that the pope had already reached a decision. He had even conveyed it to the Patriarch of Alexandria, instructing Cyril to act on his authority. Nestorius was thus thrown to the mercy of his arch-enemy. The pope's communication was delivered to him by a party of four bishops sent by Cyril. Their orders were that Nestorius recant within 10 days or face excommunication.

By way of recantation, he was obliged to submit to a series of definitions (12 anathemas) drawn up by Cyril. But the bishop of Alexandria was a doubtful theologian, and the anathemas were tainted by the Apollinarian heresy, which carried some influence in Alexandria.

Nestorius, who considered that he had been defamed, ignored the ultimatum and continued his preparations for the convention that he hoped would clear his name. In fact he was walking into a trap.

THE COUNCIL OF EPHESUS

The venue for the council was Ephesus in southern Asia Minor, which was not a good omen for Nestorius. The people of the region and their bishop, Memnon, had a special reverence for Mary, who had replaced their former patron, the goddess Artemis.

Nestorius, with 16 bishops and a troop of armed supporters, arrived at Ephesus sometime before Pentecost in 431. Cyril outnumbered him with 50 bishops, numerous mariners, a division of feral monks, and a liberal supply of funds.

When Nestorius cordially proposed that all should join in vespers, Bishop Memnon refused. The latter had allied with Cyril, and his own company of 30 bishops was reinforced by agitated peasants from the neighbourhood. These locals, with the encouragement of Memnon, loudly threatened the enemies of the "Mother of God."

Before the bishop of Antioch and other supporters of Nestorius could arrive, Cyril hastily announced the commencement of the council.

On the first morning of the synod, 160 bishops were present, and by evening, this number had risen to 198. A summons was sent to Nestorius to attend, but he remained in his lodgings, protected by an armed guard.

He regarded the opening of the council before the arrival of his supporters and the papal delegation as prejudicial to his case. Only when the full complement of bishops was present would he agree to attend.

This suited Cyril who proceeded without him. In a hectic first day, letters from Nestorius, Cyril, and the pope were all read and debated. Various bishops gave testimony concerning the writings and pronouncements of the accused. Among the statements attributed to him was, "A baby of two or three months old ought not to be called God."[454] Nestorius would later declare that he actually said, "We must not say that God is two or three months old."[455] Such were the fine lines of disparity.

By evening, the council pronounced its verdict in a language that bore the unmistakable imprint of Cyril: "Our Lord Jesus Christ who has been blasphemed by him, has defined by this holy synod that the same Nestorius is excluded from all episcopal dignity and from every assembly of bishops."[456]

Nestorius was formally condemned. The transcript of his sentence had 198 signatures; more would be added later. A brief notification addressed to "the new Judas" was issued. He refused to receive it, so the messengers affixed the document to his door.

Five days after this victory, Cyril was disturbed by the news that John, bishop of Antioch, and his delegation had arrived. Cyril had excommunicated him and 35 of his supporters in an earlier session. After taking the wise precaution of an armed retinue, the bishop of Antioch joined a separate convention called the Holy Synod, which instantly declared Cyril an enemy of the church and ordered that he and Memnon be deposed.

So now two synods were running concurrently. From their respective assemblies, the holy bishops fired anathemas and excommunications at each other. Meanwhile, their rival supporters sought to resolve matters with stones and clubs in the streets.

Amid this bloody turmoil, the papal legates eventually arrived with a letter from Pope Celestine. It urged the delegates to carry out his previous instructions: to give Nestorius a hearing and condemn him if he failed to recant after 10 days. Since 10 days had already passed with Nestorius failing to attend, Cyril and his supporters considered this a vindication of their decision and celebrated in triumph.

Nestorius penned a letter to the emperor bitterly denouncing the premature commencement of the council. He criticised the violent locals, egged on by Bishop Memnon, who had denied him entry to their churches and threatened him with death.

Not to be outdone, Cyril also wrote to the emperor, complaining about the behaviour of the imperial troops. They had blockaded the assembly in an attempt to restore order and force a settlement. Some of the older bishops had expired due to hardship.

Theodosius II, overwhelmed by the contradictory reports from Ephesus, decided to punish the lot of them. He had Cyril of Alexandria, Memnon of Ephesus, and John of Antioch deposed and issued an arrest warrant for Cyril and Memnon. However, this only provoked the local monks to make a torchlight procession through the streets of Constantinople. Their protest animated the citizens and forced the emperor to back down. He subsequently ratified the council's decision—that is, the council headed by Cyril, rather than the "Holy Synod" of his rivals.

HERETIC PERSECUTOR BECOMES PERSECUTED HERETIC

Nestorius had been outmanoeuvred. He retired to his former monastery in Antioch, stubbornly refusing to recant or appeal to the pope against what he felt was a conspiracy. One by one, his powerful friends deserted him, including even John of Antioch. In the ensuing purge, bishops merely suspected of concurring with his views were deposed. His continued agitation only provoked further punishment. Eventually he was banished to a monastery in the African Oasis of Hibis (modern al-Kharga, Egypt) within the diocese of Cyril, leaving him vulnerable to the mercy of his nemesis.

Local nomads frequently attacked and robbed the community at Hibis. In one such raid, Nestorius was injured, and he later died from his wounds. Yet his soul was not permitted to rest. Myth would attend his memory. His tongue, the instrument of his heresy, was eaten by worms before he died, so went the legend, and his grave was never watered by rain. The persecutor of heretics would be forever remembered as a heretic himself.

A NEW CREED EMERGES

An unexpected consequence of the synod and subsequent persecution by the Orthodox church was that Nestorius's influence outlived him.

Inspired by their western brethren, Christians in Persia had been attacking heathen temples—the heathen, in this case, being Zoroastrians. The Sassanian rulers of Persia, who were Zoroastrians themselves, retaliated against the Christians.

Rising to their protection, Theodosius declared war on Persia in 421. One outcome of this short and inconclusive conflict was the migration of several thousand Persian Christian fugitives into Roman territory. These exiles set up a school in Edessa where they could study in peace and safety. The school practised a theology broadly sympathetic to Nestorius's teachings. In the virulent purge that followed the Council of Ephesus, they were persecuted again, this time by fellow Christians.

Fleeing Edessa, they carried their philosophy and resentment back with them to Persia. Here, their new status as enemies of Rome made them friends of the Sassanid rulers.

Patronised by various Sassanid kings, Nestorians grew to become the dominant Christian sect beyond the eastern boundaries of the Roman Empire. Their doctrine spread as far afield as India, China, the steppes of central Asia, and Mongolia. It would also find its way to the desert sands of Arabia. There, it reinforced the concept of Jesus as a mortal prophet rather than the son of God already introduced by Ebionite migrants. This would have unforeseen consequences in the centuries to come.

With faith as his weapon, Cyril had successfully destroyed Nestorius for personal gain and challenged the authority of Constantinople. It mattered not that he was devoid of moral principles. What populist needs principals? Through him, Alexandria remained a persistent nuisance that could not easily be placated.

The simmering conflict would create more casualties and entangle the Western church in its disputes.

24

DIVIDE WITH THE SWORD THOSE WHO WOULD DIVIDE CHRIST

IF **THE RELIGIOUS** conflict that plagued the eastern empire needed further complication, the pope soon provided it.

In their struggle with the troublesome Egyptians, the emperors tried to bring the Bishop of Rome onside. However, their efforts to "seek peace and pursue it"[457] had quite the opposite effect. Papal interference only complicated the debate, intensified division, and had a further unexpected outcome.

A SIMPLE MONK

Despite Theodosius's censure, Cyril was eventually allowed to return home after bribing various courtiers. Following a triumphal entry to Alexandria, he continued as patriarch until he died in 444, after an episcopacy of nearly 32 years. The feast day of this doubtful saint is celebrated annually by the

Western church on January 28 and by the Greek Orthodox on June 9.

In their anxiety to oppose the Nestorian separation of Christ's divine and human nature, the followers of Cyril championed an opposite extreme, that the human nature of Christ was practically immersed by the divine. This had hints of Apollinarianism and was popular with the faction that opposed Nestorius, especially in Egypt.

It seemed inevitable that such a minor deviation might lead to yet another inter-Christian quarrel. And indeed it did. The spark that ignited the flame of discord was lit in Constantinople, and the unlikely catalyst was a monk called Eutyches.

This old man had spent 70 years, 30 of them as abbot, isolated in a monastery beyond the capital's walls. His proximity to the city and his influence on the emperor through a court eunuch made him a valuable ally to Cyril. The death of Cyril removed whatever theological restraint the old recluse might have had. Having rejected humanity by his chosen isolation, he proposed to reject the humanity of Jesus by an obsessive belief that Christ had but one nature: the divine.

His pronouncements reached the ear of Flavian, Patriarch of Constantinople. After interviewing Eutyches, Flavian considered his ideas the product of an unsophisticated mind rather than a serious theological proposition. However, instead of ignoring him, he heeded the advice of his bishops and called another synod. Here, Eutyches was condemned, deposed, and excommunicated by the patriarch. The verdict was ratified by Pope Leo I.

Flavian ought to have followed his initial instincts. The proceedings highlighted the doctrine of an ignorant monk who would otherwise have remained in the relative obscurity of his monastic isolation.

Dioscorus, who had succeeded Cyril as Patriarch of Alexandria, refused to accept the judgement. This was partly because it challenged the prevailing theology of Egypt. More importantly, it provided another opportunity to reassert the primacy of Alexandria over Constantinople. Dioscorus fostered the suspicion that the victory at Ephesus was about to be reversed and that

Nestorianism might enter by the back door. Even a tome from Pope Leo entitled *Epistola Dogmatica*, defining the two natures of Christ, did nothing to dispel the rising disquiet of the Eastern church.

THE ROBBER COUNCIL

To resolve the issue, Emperor Theodosius convoked another general synod with the pope's approval, and again, the venue was Ephesus. It began in August AD 449, too hastily for western bishops to attend. Dioscorus of Alexandria presided over the synod by command of the emperor. This ensured he, like his predecessor Cyril, would dominate the proceedings.

The question before the council was whether Flavian had justly deposed and excommunicated Eutyches at the local Council of Constantinople. Flavian and the six other bishops who had presided at that council were, therefore, not allowed to sit in judgement, as they had now become the accused.

The assembly summoned the grey-bearded monk, who affirmed his adherence to the Nicene Creed and the previous Council of Ephesus. Eutyches protested that he had been misquoted and feared for his life. However, he avoided stating that Jesus had two natures.

Despite the protests of Flavian, further debate was effectively quashed by Dioscorus. He proceeded to read the judgement of the earlier council against Eutyches without affording those who had passed that judgement an opportunity to explain their case. He also refused to read a letter from the pope delivered by the papal legate.

As Dioscorus recited the acts of the Council of Constantinople, he incited monks and sympathetic bishops to proclaim the innocence of their persecuted brother. With loud yells, they demanded his accusers be burned: "May those who divide Christ be divided with the sword, may they be hewn in pieces, may they be burned alive!"[458]

The atmosphere was turning decidedly nasty for the Flavian party. Dioscorus, having absolved Eutyches, announced that those who had condemned him should be deposed. Preferring forceful action to a tiresome discussion, his supporters launched an assault on their rivals. They were supported by an armed posse of Egyptian monks who invaded the assembly. Together they brutally beat Flavian. Any bishops who begged for their lives were themselves threatened and forced to sign a blank piece of paper.

After uttering the word *"contradicitur"* (annulling the sentence of the synod), the papal legate bade a hasty retreat. He was lucky to escape with his life. Not so fortunate was the Patriarch of Constantinople, who died three days later from his wounds. He obtained the unprofitable reward of sainthood for his misfortune, and thus St. Flavian is numbered among the martyrs.

The blank sheet of paper afforded Dioscorus a rich canvas for his tyranny. He no longer needed the bishops. He had their signatures, 135 in all. Some had signed out of genuine support for the verdict. Others had signed out of genuine belief that they would become martyrs if they didn't. Backed by the Alexandrian faction, Dioscorus condemned, deposed, and excommunicated an assortment of bishops and clergy. The dubious charges ranged from bigamy and blasphemy to Nestorianism. The latter included bishops who had vehemently opposed Nestorius.

Having concluded the synod, the Alexandrian patriarch proceeded to Constantinople to present its ruling to the emperor. He even appointed his secretary, Anatolius, to the now-vacant patriarchy of Constantinople. En route, he fired one final holy missile by pronouncing the sentence of excommunication on no less a personage than the pope himself. When he reached the imperial capital, Theodosius II weakly approved the council's decision.

Pope Leo was not amused. The pontiff who would later confront Attila the Hun and Gaiseric the Vandal was not to be outdone by a primate of Alexandria. He invalidated the acts of the council and excommunicated those who compiled them. He then pardoned all, bar one, whom they had condemned. Finally, he dubbed the second council of Ephesus *Latrocinium*, or Robber Council, the name by which it is forever remembered.

PULCHERIA TAKES CONTROL

It was now incumbent upon those who desired peace in eastern Christendom to settle the dispute. Leo, with the approval of the western emperor Valentinian, demanded a new council to resolve the matter. Emperor Theodosius refused, but his sudden death in a riding accident ended the standoff. He left no heir, so Pulcheria reasserted her power. She married a relatively obscure general called Marcian, who became the new emperor. It was a purely functional arrangement: she would retain her virginity, and he would rule by her sanction.

The re-emergence of Pulcheria signalled a change in religious policy. Under her influence, a new council was convened.

The location was Chalcedon; the year was 451. It would be the fourth ecumenical council of the church, the previous having been Nicaea (325), Constantinople (381), and Ephesus (431). It would also be the largest hitherto assembled, with an estimated 630 bishops plus their entourages.

With Attila and his Huns once again ravaging the empire and its subjects, the bishops began their deliberations. Dioscorus was now the accused rather than the accuser, and the charges were numerous. The Alexandrine patriarch had excommunicated the pope, supported the heretic Eutyches, squandered the church funds on lavish entertainment, shared his bath with prostitutes, and publicly entertained a notorious concubine, allegedly. It was his turn to endure the ferocity of bigotry, at least according to the partisan accounts of his supporters.

Defiantly, he refused to appear before an assembly that would certainly condemn him. So, instead of a throng of bishops, he faced the solitary figure of Pulcheria in all her imperial might.

"In my father's time, there was a man who was stubborn [referring to St. John Chrysostom], and you are aware of what was made of him," she threatened.

"And you may recall," replied the patriarch, "that your mother prayed at his tomb as she was bleeding of sickness."[459] He was referring to the fact that Eudoxia died of an infection shortly after the banishment of Chrysostom.

Some attributed this to divine retribution. However, she could not have prayed at his tomb since he outlived her. But these are mere details.

For this impertinent response, the empress slapped the patriarch in his face with enough ferocity to dislodge a couple of teeth. He was then manhandled roughly by her bodyguards, who pulled some hairs off his bloodstained white beard. He later gathered these bodily relics—teeth and hair—in a box and sent them to his supporters as evidence of his ordeal.

Eutyches and his followers were singled out for retribution, along with the monks of his monastery. They, together with sympathetic clerics, were expelled from the empire. Books supporting his doctrine were burned, and their authors punished. Dioscorus was deposed and joined them in exile. He would never see Alexandria again.

A TENUOUS COMPROMISE

The council then had to deal with the matter of the true nature of Christ and sought to forge a path between the conflicting parties. The good bishops groped for language sufficiently obscure to allow compromise while teetering on the edge of what either party considered heresy. The majority agreed upon the final wording: "We teach, one and the same Christ, Son, Lord, Only begotten, known in two natures, without confusion, without change, without division, without separation."[460]

There was enough ambiguity to allow generous interpretation of "known in two natures ... without division." It was a reconciliation of opposites. "An invisible line was drawn between the heresy of Apollinarius and the faith of St. Cyril; and the road to paradise, a bridge as sharp as a razor, was suspended over the abyss by the master hand of the theological artist."[461]

The great matter having been decided, the council proceeded to debate and approve a further 28 canons. Among them was one prohibiting the reception of a slave into a monastery without his master's permission. Another stipulated that complaints against a bishop or cleric could not be entertained without an investigation into the character of the accuser. All this ensured that the church hierarchy and the ruling elite would be answerable only to each other (or to the occasional lawless mob).

In a double blow to Alexandria, Canon 28 granted the See of Constantinople (New Rome) patriarchal status with equal privileges to the See of Rome, although second in rank and with precedence over the others.[462] This cemented the primacy of the imperial capital over its Egyptian rival, a decision that did not sit well with the hierarchy of Alexandria. It also led to future conflict with Rome.

Adherents of the Monophysite doctrine (that Jesus had a divine nature only), mainly Egyptian, were persuaded to endorse the articles of the council by the proximity of Constantinople and the watchful eye of its heavily armed Orthodox rulers. Well, not quite all were persuaded. Thirteen of the most zealous among them made their feelings known with the cry, "The heretics are now discovered! Anathema to the Nestorians!"[463]

The Council of Chalcedon was a watershed in the early church. It was a culmination of the various synods from Nicaea onward. Together, they defined the Orthodox position on the nature of Jesus and the Trinity. The majority accepted the wording, and a superficial peace was kept in the Eastern church for a short time—a very short time!

Beneath the surface, the rivalry between Alexandria and Constantinople was delineated between Chalcedonians and Monophysites. The Chalcedonians were essentially the Roman establishment that supported its doctrinal definition. The Monophysites were mainly Egyptians who opposed it.

THE FALLOUT FROM CHALCEDON

The Holy City of Jerusalem witnessed the first confrontation between the two. Some disgruntled monks who had been at Chalcedon, but had not accepted the outcome, travelled to Palestine. They urged the local bishop to renounce its acts. When he refused, they went berserk and embarked on a frenzy of "destruction and bloodshed"[464] in the name of Jesus. The imperial guard eventually restored order.

In Alexandria, the arrival of the new patriarch, Proterius, to replace their beloved Dioscorus also provoked a riot. When the garrison intervened, they were attacked with stones and forced to take refuge in a nearby temple. Here, they were pursued by the enraged mob, who set the building aflame and burned it to the ground, together with its occupants.

Within days of receiving the news, the emperor dispatched reinforcements. This time, the Alexandrians were on the receiving end of rough Roman justice.[465] When he deemed that enough blood had been spilled, Governor Floris "heeded their pleas of mercy" and, by threats and persuasion, regained a semblance of order.

In the subdued atmosphere, the new patriarch administered the pro-Chalcedon orthodoxy to a reluctant congregation. When news reached the city of the death of Emperor Marcian, Proterius became the first victim of the backlash. A monk with the charming name of Timothy the Cat incited the rabble—not a difficult thing to do in Alexandria.

The patriarch fled to the cathedral, where he was pursued and murdered in the baptistery. His lifeless body was dragged through the city before being torn apart and consigned to the flames. Monophysite accounts of the event blamed the local garrison, which seems unlikely. In any case, Timothy the Cat, "having bribed a throng of disorderly men,"[466] assumed the title of patriarch for himself.

Alexandria and the rest of Egypt became engulfed in vicious civil strife as the opposing religious factions fought each other with the passion of the righteous. Bishop Victor of Tunnuna described it thus: "The people of Alexandria, and all Egypt, were seized with a strange and diabolical frenzy: great and small, slaves and freedmen, monks and clergy, the natives of the land, who opposed the synod of Chalcedon, lost their speech and reason, barked like dogs, and tore, with their own teeth the flesh from their hands and arms."[467]

The bloody strife continued for more than 30 years. Monophysites dominated the church in Alexandria, Ethiopia, Armenia, and Syria. The patriarchies of Antioch and Jerusalem remained faithful to pro-Chalcedon orthodoxy despite considerable local opposition. Alexandria had two rival patriarchs of each sect. While the Greek-speaking establishment was pro-Chalcedon, most Copts remained defiantly Monophysite. ("Copt" was initially used to describe pre-Islamic Egyptians but would later mean Christian Egyptians.)

Today, the Egyptian Coptic, Armenian, Abyssinian (Ethiopian), and Jacobite Church of Syria still hold fast to this doctrine. However, they dislike the term "Monophysite," meaning Jesus has a single divine nature. They prefer the less radical term "Miaphysite," which means two natures, divine and human, mystically united in one composite being.

How does this differ from the Orthodox position of one being having two natures, one may ask? In truth, very little. Quite simply, the Egyptians and Syrians did not like to be pushed around by the Greeks, so it was different, and that was it. Political divisions amplified the doctrinal rift, and the doctrinal rift amplified the political ones.

The intensity of the split posed a threat to the stability of the church and the eastern empire itself. This threat prompted Emperor Zeno to intervene in 482. He issued the *Henotikon* ("instrument of union"), a document formulated by the Patriarch of Constantinople, Acacius. This sought to restore order by ignoring Chalcedon and reverting to the Nicene Creed as the benchmark for orthodoxy. Controversies over the incarnation were tackled by evasion. The Catholic formula of one Christ with two natures was omitted and replaced with the neutral phrase, "One of the Trinity was incarnate."

The intervention of the emperor promoted some semblance of peace among the more reasonable on either side. On pain of punishment, the *Henotikon* was enforced. Bishops—whether Orthodox, Miaphysite, or Monophysite—who refused to sign were deposed and replaced by those who would. After the death of Zeno, his elderly successor Anastasius continued the policy.

Like any attempt at conciliation, it had no chance against those who would not be reconciled. Since no assertions of the document could be deemed heretical, they became offended by its omissions.

Radicals resented the interference of a layman in a matter of faith. They wailed against a ruler who forced them to be reasonable, and they disputed his authority to persecute their fellow Christians. That was a privilege they reserved for themselves. Deposed clerics on either side lurked in the wings, ready to shatter the peace of compromise and steer their straying flocks to the true path. For these purists, any contrary route was a gateway to hell.

SCHISM WITH ROME

Enter Pope Felix III. The pontiff challenged Patriarch Acacius for his endorsement of the *Henotikon*. Felix then dispatched two priests to Constantinople with a summons for Acacius to appear in Rome on the charge of deposing pro-Chalcedon bishops. Acacius, instead of complying, arrested the envoys and coerced them into publicly receiving Holy Communion with him. Humiliated, they returned to Rome, where an enraged pope excommunicated the patriarch for his defiance and his own two priests for submitting to him.

Acacius responded by striking the name of Pope Felix from the ivory tablets called *diptychs* that commemorated senior government and ecclesiastical officials. The break between the Eastern and Western churches, which had smouldered since the Council of Serdica in 343, finally became official. Thus began the Acacian schism, which lasted 35 years (484–519).

The Great Church of Constantinople witnessed the next step in the conflict. It happened during a service as the choir sang the trisagion: "Holy, Holy, Holy, Lord God of Hosts!" Or rather, one choir sang it, for there were two. A rival choir in the same basilica sang a slightly different version: "Holy, Holy, Holy, Lord God of Hosts, *who was crucified for us* [emphasis added]."

This trifling addition highlighted a theological uncertainty. That Jesus was crucified on the cross, no one disputed. The Orthodox position was that God had become a man who ended his life on the cross. That Christ, the second person of the Trinity, possessed only a divine form implied a blasphemous concept. It suggested that it was a divinity, or God, and not a human being that was nailed to the cross. By such minutiae were the faithful provoked.

Each choir shouted at the top of their voices, anxious to drown out the rival chorus. When words no longer sufficed, they settled for blows. The service disintegrated into turmoil as battling choristers and congregation spilled into the streets. Within a short time, bystanders, shopkeepers, courtiers, slaves, and the inevitable monks joined the melee. Soon, the fight descended into a deadly rampage.

The patriarch Macedonius had succeeded Acacius but did not share his views. He supported the Chalcedonian faction, while the Emperor Anastasius supported the other. The emperor had contributed to tensions by appointing a Miaphysite bishop to the vacant see in Chalcedon. In Constantinople, Macedonius had the advantage of numbers. His supporters forcefully entered the house of a monk called Marinus the Syrian, whom they blamed for adding the offensive coda to the trisagion, and cut off his head. Then, having fixed his head upon a pole, they jeeringly exclaimed, "See the plotter against the Trinity!"[468]

Beyond the city walls, the bloodshed escalated. Thrace was laid bare, and Constantinople was besieged by a general sympathetic to the Chalcedonian cause. In desperation, the ailing emperor appeared in the Hippodrome in a pitiful state. Without his crown and in humble attire, Anastasius offered his resignation to the assembled crowd. This self-abasement had a calming effect and led to peace negotiations. The *Henotikon* was abandoned, the Council of Chalcedon reimposed, and exiled bishops restored, while an estimated 65,000 lay dead in the city and its hinterland.

However, the rift with Rome was not healed, as the emperor refused to accept the excommunication of the deceased Acacius. Anastasius did not live long after his ordeal, and having no male successor, the purple passed on to the commander of the imperial guard.

Justin was an illiterate peasant from Dardania (modern Kosovo) who joined the army as a youth, distinguished himself in the Persian wars, and ascended the ranks. He had reached a position of wealth and power that enabled him to assume the succession following the demise of Anastasius. He faced the daunting challenge of uniting a deeply divided realm with no resolution in sight.

Having involved Rome in its disputes, the empire had provoked a serious split with the Western church. This diminished the emperor's claim to be the leader of all Christendom and further undermined attempts to achieve peace and harmony with the warring Christian factions.

Justin had to address these vexing issues. It helped that he had the support of the troops, but like his predecessor, he had no son. His choice of heir would determine the final chapter in the story of early Christianity and significantly transform the course of European history.

25

FAITH BY FORCE OF ARMS

LOVE THY NEIGHBOUR, save his soul, and if he resists, kill him.

In a period afflicted by war, pestilence, and famine, the regime in Constantinople aimed to impose its version of orthodoxy on believers and non-believers alike. Amid the "visible decrease in the human species,"[469] Christianity would triumph.

By the time he became emperor, Justin was advanced in years but enjoyed the support of his energetic nephew Justinian. The short, curly-haired youth had left the backwater that was Tauresium (near modern Skopje, North Macedonia) and was adopted by Justin's sister. She ensured he received a good education in history, theology, and the law. When the older man ascended the throne, Justinian was promoted to the rank of *magister militum* of the army. As the elderly uncle descended into senility, his ambitious nephew stealthily grasped the reins of power. This left Justin as emperor in name only.

Justinian was a devout Christian of Chalcedonian persuasion. He retained the superstition of a peasant and a reverence for the clergy. The welfare of the church preoccupied him above all else. His nights were spent studying theological tomes or conversing with learned clerics. In the first years of his uncle's reign, he sought to end the Acacian schism and achieve a reconciliation with Rome. A temperate and affable man, his tastes were simple, his disposition holy, and considering all that, his choice of wife surprising.

BLUES, GREENS, AND A FUTURE EMPRESS

Constantinople, like most Roman cities, was regularly entertained by the spectacle of chariot races. Since the Republic, teams had been divided into four groups—Reds, Greens, Whites, and Blues—each attracting fanatical supporters who donned the colours of their champions. By the time of the eastern empire, these factions were reduced to two: Blues and Greens. Their intense rivalry frequently descended into pitched battles as youths on either side clashed in the streets like modern-day football hooligans. Some fashioned their hair "in the manner of the Huns"[470] and provoked respectable citizens with their petty crimes and intimidating behaviour.

In Constantinople, the two groups had developed into sizeable organisations that controlled the circus, various forms of entertainment, and the welfare of those who made a living from them. This gave them a degree of power that no legislator, bishop, or even emperor could ignore. Ambitious nobles and officials found it profitable to align with one or another of the factions. In the recent religious conflicts, the Greens had favoured the Miaphysites, while the Blues had sided with the establishment Orthodox party.

When a bear-keeper of the Green faction died, his distraught widow hastily remarried in the hope that her new husband would inherit the position and provide for her family. But the dancing master of the Greens, whose duty it was to make such appointments, gave the job to another in return for a bribe. In desperation, the wretched woman headed for the Hippodrome, followed by her three young daughters, the eldest of whom was younger than seven.

As the crowds gathered for the games, the widow approached the Greens and threw herself at their mercy. She begged them to take her and her orphans under their protection. The indifferent Greens ignored her pleas, but the

Blues, whose bear-keeper had also passed away, came to her rescue. The incident was forever imprinted in the memory of her second daughter, Theodora.

As her children reached a suitable age, the mother, herself a performer, put them on the stage. Comito, the eldest, had already become a "leading *hetaerae* [prostitute] of the day." Theodora, "dressed in a little tunic with sleeves, like a slave girl, waited on Comito and followed her around ... while still too young to know the normal relation of man with maid ... but consented to the unnatural violence of villainous slaves. And for some time in a brothel, she suffered such misuse."[471]

When she was older, Theodora joined a troop of players who acted out bawdy comedy plays for entertainment at the theatre. She practised a stage show, a striptease that excited interest and drew the city's crowds. In private, she reserved her charms for those who could pay the price. Those who feared scandal studiously avoided her company, according to the writer Procopius, who despised her.

Through her contacts in the Blue faction, she managed to meet, attract, and enchant Justinian, who was now firmly in control of his uncle's affairs. For a while, she became his concubine. However, his religious scruples were averse to a relationship of that kind, so he eventually proposed marriage.

It was a scandalous proposition. From the time of Constantine, the law prohibited marriage between a man of senatorial rank and a slave or actress. Since the church denied the sacraments to actresses, who were equated in the Christian mind with prostitution, matrimony was impossible anyway. To make matters worse, Theodora was a Miaphysite.

These were minor obstacles to a man of Justinian's determination. His aunt's pleas were ignored, the law was changed, and the church willingly forgave a future empress of her past misdeeds. The marriage went ahead, oblivious to the disapproving whispers of the social elite. When the ailing emperor passed the purple to his nephew, thus granting official legitimacy to what was already in play, Justinian and Theodora sat as equals on the throne. The patriarch placed the diadem on their heads, and before them, in respectful supplication, the assembly of magistrates, ministers, bishops, and foreign monarchs paid their respects. From humble origins, the two would become, for a time, the most powerful couple on Earth. Together, they would write the last bloody chapter of early Christianity.

Procopius of Caesarea, who served as secretary to his general, Belisarius, undertook the task of chronicling the emperor's reign. In five volumes, he recounted the magnificent achievements of Justinian, reserving lavish praise for his general and only vaguely hinting at darker deeds. In a separate book, *Secret History*, he revealed his hatred for the emperor, empress, and their entourage. The latter tome never saw the light of day during the monarch's reign.

RUTHLESS PERSECUTOR

Justinian viewed his domain and the lands beyond with some disquiet. The provinces of Europe and North Africa that once made up the Western Roman Empire were overrun by Arian barbarians. However, the former senatorial class that constituted the hierarchy was still predominantly Catholic. The eastern realm was split between Miaphysites and Chalcedonians. Numerous other heresies thrived, even in Constantinople itself. Pagan idolaters still lurked in the countryside, the Jews prospered, and fanatical monks held sway in the provinces of Syria and Egypt.

Justinian planned a ruthless extermination to impose the Chalcedonian creed on those who already were and would soon become his subjects, notwithstanding the Miaphysite empress who shared his bed. He believed orthodoxy was essential for public order, and public order would be maintained by force of arms.

He commenced his reign as he would continue it, with a series of edicts against non-believers and heretics. The decrees of the four principal councils, Nicaea, Constantinople, Ephesus, and Chalcedon, were written into law. Death was the punishment for apostasy. Heathen books were burned.

Like Constantine I, Justinian saw religious dissent as a threat to imperial cohesion. However, compelling his subjects to unite under one Orthodox creed would prove more elusive to him than it did to Constantine. It would prove calamitous for many of his subjects as he launched a brutal campaign against heresy.

Remnants of the Montanist sect that lived in Phrygia on the southern coast of the Sea of Marmara welcomed the death of martyrdom, as was their custom. Arians who still inhabited Constantinople were stripped of their wealth. Manichaeans were tortured and executed by burning or drowning, some apparently in the emperor's presence. Other Christian sects who ignored the canons of the four councils were given three months to remedy their errors or face imperial justice.

For polytheists who had survived the destruction of their temples but continued to practise their secretive practices, Justinian's reign was a watershed. He appointed an inquisitor bishop to root out the remnants of this ancient religion. The adherents, no longer a threat to Christian supremacy, had been neutral witnesses to their fratricidal conflicts. Like unwelcome guests at a household quarrel, they now had to either leave or join the family. Forced baptism would cure their "insane beliefs."

Employing the methods of John Chrysostom from a century earlier, the faithful were encouraged to spy on their neighbours. They were asked to expose those who performed forbidden rites or read improper texts. The zealous prelate soon discovered idolaters in their tens of thousands scattered among the towns and countryside of the provinces and even in the imperial Senate itself.

Faced with the threat of persecution, most accepted the forced baptism and dutifully attended one of the 96 new churches commissioned by the emperor for their benefit. They practised the rituals and adhered to Orthodox doctrines in an outward show of faith. They gratefully accepted gifts of Bibles and holy paraphernalia. Many risked severe punishment by secretly observing their ancient traditions. Some nobles chose to end their lives by the self-inflicted thrust of the dagger. Others, including one senator, suffered execution. Most pagans received a lesser punishment. However, once baptism was administered, any reversion to polytheism equated to apostasy. And apostasy merited the death sentence.

Persecution of the Jews was intensified with an edict commanding them not to observe the Passover whenever it fell before Easter. Instead, they should wait until afterward. The absurdity of this law is underlined by the fact that the Christians themselves could not agree on a date for the former pagan festival. Even among the Orthodox, there was disagreement. This resulted in the Passover being celebrated at different times in Alexandria, Constantinople, and Rome. To this day, there is a disparity between the Eastern and Western churches on the timing of Easter. Regardless of when it occurred, the Passover would have to wait.

In practice, Justinian was more tolerant towards the chosen people than his edicts might imply. His ambitious projects demanded robust finances, and the emperor granted exemptions in return for their support.

Not so for the Samaritans. On the ladder of discrimination, they occupied the bottom rung. Although the Orthodox and Miaphysites despised each other, they united in mutual loathing of Arians. For their part, the Arians scorned the lesser brethren who had been condemned with them at Nicaea. No Christian, whether heretic or otherwise, would give a second glance to a Nestorian if they could find one. The Nestorians shared the contempt of their fellow Christians for the Jews. The Jews positively reviled the Samaritans.

This unfortunate race possessed neither the pure blood nor the pure creed of the chosen people. For that reason, they had been disbarred from the temple and city of Jerusalem during the time of Jesus. Yet, in the eyes of Christians, this absence did not absolve them from the guilt of the crucifixion, which they shared by virtue of their faith. The prospect of salvation, as exemplified by the evangelists,[472] was offered by Justinian in the form of a threat: accept baptism or accept the consequences. They accepted neither and revolted.

The conflict engulfed Palestine, where the Samaritans carried out reprisals against local Christians who had abused them. This only further provoked the emperor. The Roman army, backed by Arab auxiliaries, crushed the rebels, leaving the province a smoking ruin. Thousands were massacred. Survivors were given as slaves to the Arabs as payment for their military support. Today, their descendants reside in Israel, divided between Kiryat Luza on Mount Gerizim and Holon near Tel Aviv.

WAR, PEACE, AND PESTILENCE

In the meantime, war with the old enemy Persia reached a stalemate. In 530, a treaty optimistically dubbed the Endless Peace fixed the border between the two empires. Justinian's ambitions lay elsewhere, and in his anxiety for peace, he granted a generous sum to the shah.

However, several years into Justinian's reign, the planet was hit by several calamities. In 536, a mini–Ice Age began, which endured into the next century. Crops failed, and famines raged for several years.[473]

The low temperatures indirectly led to a further catastrophe in 541. The bubonic plague, which was called the Black Death in later centuries, made its first recorded visit to Europe. The Plague of Justinian, as contemporaries called it, wiped out between one-third and one-half of the inhabitants in the affected areas.

These calamities were further exacerbated by a profligate emperor. The healthy treasury that Emperor Anastasius had accumulated was exhausted by Justinian on his massive church-building programme, persecutions, and wars. Heavy taxes were placed on merchants, discouraging trade, reducing commodities, and increasing inflation. The poor, as always, felt the brunt of these measures, as the price of food and essentials increased.

THE NIKA RIOTS

In Constantinople, many wealthy merchants disproportionately affected by Justinian's taxes were members of the Green faction. This was unsurprising since Justinian favoured the Blues, and Theodora still nurtured her childhood hatred for the Greens. Reforms of the civil service reduced their numbers and impacted the aristocracy. Hostility intensified against the low-born imperial couple.

Constantinople experienced a rise in crimes by armed youths allied to both factions. As the streets became unsafe to walk at night, Justinian took steps to bring matters under control.

When a particularly vicious confrontation erupted after a chariot race, seven men were sentenced to execution for murder. As the final two were about to be hanged, the poorly constructed scaffold collapsed beneath their feet. The pair managed to escape to a nearby monastery. By coincidence, one was a Green, the other a Blue. An angry mob surrounded the building and demanded that the emperor grant mercy to the convicts. When Justinian reduced the sentence to imprisonment, it failed to appease either faction. Suddenly, these implacable enemies found a common cause.

At the next chariot race, the usual cries of "Blue" or "Green" changed to "*Nika*" ("victory") as the angry spectators openly taunted Justinian while he watched the games from the imperial box. As the crowd egged each other on, their protests reached a crescendo and developed into a riot that spread throughout the city.

With Constantinople in turmoil and the army unable to contain the rampaging mobs, the wealthy inhabitants fled by boat to the Asiatic coast. Anarchy prevailed as homes were looted and set aflame. Even the pleas of monks and clergy who tried to exercise a restraining influence were ineffective. Soon, the Great Church, *Magna Ecclesia*, was engulfed in the inferno.

For five days, the emperor remained under siege in his fortified palace, surrounded by the imperial guard and his faithful general Belisarius. Justinian's position seemed hopeless. Outside on the waterfront, galleys were ready to escort him with his wife and their possessions to the doubtful safety of exile. In the moment of despair, Theodora showed her mettle. "Even if escape will bring us safety," she said, "I will not flee. May I never be separated from the purple[474] nor live to see the day when I cease to be addressed by the title of empress."[475] Inspired by her courage and embarrassed by their fears, the men around her decided on a bold plan of attack.

Allegiance was secured with the Blue faction by the promise of reward and the reminder of old rivalries with the Greens. Troops were dispatched undercover to the Hippodrome, where the assembled crowd had proclaimed a new emperor. A bloody massacre followed as the soldiers, with support from the Blues, fell upon the Greens. They scythed through the massed spectators, spilling their blood onto the terraces. By the time they were finished, 30,000 corpses filled the arena.

The *Nika* riots were over. The games ceased for many years while the Hippodrome became a memorial for the families of the slain. The victory gave Justinian and Theodora a degree of absolute control that would never again be seriously challenged. Privately, the empress could reflect that she had settled an old score and avenged a transgression against her childhood.

HOLY WISDOM

The ruins of the burned-out cathedral were removed. Nearby properties were purchased for a generous sum. Soon, a new edifice emerged from the waste and was dedicated to the glory of Justinian and God.

The Hagia Sophia cathedral became a marvel of the medieval world. Consecrated in 537, its massive dome rose 56 metres above ground, appearing to rest on a circle of light from windows at its base. Christianity had its greatest shrine. Round-domed churches became Justinian's signature, inspiring future Byzantine and Muslim architecture.

After a turbulent start to their reign, the emperor and empress had prevailed. Justinian had presided over a merciless crackdown on non-believers, Jews, and heretics, instilling fear and death on those who challenged the Chalcedon creed. Hagia Sophia would stand as a monument to his triumph. Only the Miaphysites, thanks to their political strength and the protection of the empress, escaped unscathed. Meanwhile, the ranks of orthodoxy were increased by the addition of reluctant and insincere converts.

Justinian's administration did not regard freedom of conscience as a private matter but rather a potential menace to public order, safety, and morals. This was not a new concept, nor would it become obsolete. Cancellation of hateful thoughts, speech, and text became synonymous with salvation of the soul, the community, and the state. The faithful enjoyed a safe place free of disturbing ideas, under the shadow of a benevolent ruler.

This was just the beginning. Heretics still controlled the former provinces of Africa and Europe. Justinian mobilised his resources to eradicate these dissenters and prepared to enforce the true faith by military might.

26

WAR IN GOD'S NAME

THOU SHALT NOT kill—unless, of course, God wills it.

Having contributed to its downfall, Christians longed to retake the western empire and unite it with the east. Rome would then be restored to its former glory. Not the Rome of the polytheist era with its classical scholarship and traditions—the scriptures had rendered such concepts superfluous—but rather the era of Constantine and Theodosius. One emperor, one true faith. This could only be achieved by bloody war and conquest in the name of God.

AFRICAN EXPEDITION

The construction of Hagia Sophia had just begun when the emperor set in motion the first of his conquests. The ongoing conflict between the dominant Vandal Arians of North Africa and their Trinitarian subjects was the stimulus. Following the death of Gaiseric, his son Huneric proved an even more enthusiastic persecutor of Catholics than his father. He seized their churches and gave the congregations the choice of conversion or exile and confiscation of their goods. North Africa's current king, Gelimer, continued the persecution, prompting African Catholics to petition Constantinople to intervene.

John of Cappadocia, the cautious finance minister, warned Justinian against the expense and danger of sending an army on a long sea voyage to an uncertain outcome in a distant war. If victorious, he would have to secure his conquest by attacking and occupying Sicily and Italy to neutralise the Ostrogoths, who now controlled that region. The exhausted empire would be vulnerable to barbarian and Persian conquest if he failed.

The emperor received conflicting advice of a less rational nature from his patriarch Epiphanius: "I have seen a vision; it is the will of Heaven, O Emperor! That you should not abandon your holy enterprise for the deliverance of the African church. The God of Battles will march before your standard and disperse your enemies who are the enemies of his Son."[476]

Command of the enterprise was given to Belisarius, a veteran of the Persian Wars who had demonstrated his loyalty during the *Nika* revolt. Under his shrewd direction, a Roman army went forth to battle with Carthage, as Scipio had done more than seven centuries earlier during the Punic wars.

After a relatively safe voyage, the fleet cast anchor at the promontory of Caput Vada (in modern Tunisia), where the troops disembarked. This was about five days' journey to the south of Carthage. With their veteran troops deployed in Sardinia, the Vandals were unprepared for the assault. Belisarius easily defeated the force they assembled to confront him. Carthage was taken, and eventually, the remainder of the Vandals' North African territory, together with the islands of Sardinia, Corsica, Majorca, and Minorca, were brought under Roman control.

The victorious Catholics reasserted their authority, regained their wealth, and enjoyed their former immunities. Arian worship was suppressed, and Donatist meetings were once again prohibited. A synod was held at Carthage, where edicts of retribution were sealed with the stamp of imperial approval.

Belisarius received a triumphal welcome on his return. Among the trophies of war displayed to an appreciative public were the golden ornaments plundered from the temple of Jerusalem by the Romans following the Jewish revolt in AD 66. Gaiseric had seized these during his raid on Rome and they would now adorn the palace of Constantinople. They would be plundered yet again in the distant future.

NEXT STOP, ITALY

Justinian had meanwhile formed a secret alliance with Amalasuintha, daughter of Theodoric, queen regent of the Ostrogoths and de facto queen regent of Italy. Following the death of Amalasuintha's son and heir, she became embroiled in a struggle for succession and turned to Justinian for assistance. This suited the emperor, who had designs on Italy. Amalasuintha lost the contest. She was imprisoned and later murdered. Procopius hinted that agents of a jealous Theodora committed the act. Theodahad, her rival, was the more likely suspect. In any case, Justinian had his justification for war.

In 535, Belisarius again sailed for Sicily with an army under his command. He swiftly secured the island before advancing to the mainland. After taking Rhegium (modern Reggio Calabria, Italy) and Naples, he advanced to Rome. The Catholic bishops and their flock opened the gates to his triumphant forces. Rome was again united with the empire. Belisarius would be among the final witnesses to its old imperial grandeur.

Belatedly, the Ostrogoth army, distracted by an invasion of Franks to the north, marched south to begin the siege. Under Belisarius's stern leadership, the Roman citizens, so useless against previous barbarian assaults, now resisted bravely. As the standoff dragged on and weeks became months, food scarcity, hunger, and hardship put their new-found courage to the test. The famished citizens wondered if it mattered whether their overlords were Gothic or Greek, Arian or Catholic.

Aware of the growing discontent, Belisarius feared that his troops, spread thinly along the city's walls, could easily be overcome if one of the many gates were opened to the enemy. The treachery he feared came from the highest quarter.

Pope Silverius was a mere subdeacon when elected to the papacy. Theodahad had instigated this sudden elevation. He needed a pontiff sympathetic to the Ostrogoth cause to prevent Constantinople from placing their own man, Vigilius, on the throne.

Silverius was brought before Belisarius and accused of treacherous correspondence with the Ostrogoths. A letter he had written offering them entry via a secret passage was produced as evidence. Silverius protested his innocence, claiming the letter was a forgery. He might have been telling the truth; the scheme was not beyond Theodora. She had arranged for Vigilius, who was sympathetic towards the Miaphysite cause, to accompany the Roman army.

Silverius was stripped of his papal attire, clothed in the rough garment of a monk, and dispatched to an uninhabited island, where he starved to death, apparently on the orders of Vigilius. With the papal throne empty, Vigilius, armed with a generous purse, soon won the esteem and love of the local clergy and was consecrated pope in March 537.

The siege dragged on for a year. After plundering the hostile countryside of its resources, the besiegers suffered the same deprivation as the city's inhabitants. When supplies and reinforcements arrived by sea from Constantinople, the Goths were forced to sue for peace. They retreated northward to protect their capital, Ravenna, from attack.

With the Roman army in hot pursuit, the Catholic Italians revolted against their barbarian overlords. In Milan, the Arian clergy were massacred, while in Rimini, a second Roman army landed under the command of the eunuch Narses. Caught in a pincer movement, the Ostrogoths found themselves besieged in the impregnable city of Ravenna. The country was lost to them, and although they were still strong in numbers, they opted for a capitulation that allowed them to retain their property and estates under the jurisdiction of Constantinople.

Belisarius triumphantly entered the last barbarian stronghold of Italy at the head of a Roman force composed of Greeks, Isuranians, Illyrians, and Italians. The warlike Gothic women watching in dismay spat in the faces of their sons and husbands who had surrendered their kingdom to this scrawny army, small in number and diminutive in physique. All of Italy and North Africa were once again under Catholic hegemony.

Civil war among the Visigoths gave the Romans a pretext to invade Spain. Soon, they controlled the south-eastern provinces of the peninsula. In roughly six years, Justinian had recaptured the better half of the former western empire. Holding on to it proved to be a challenge.

Belisarius was recalled to Constantinople by a jealous emperor amid suspicion that he had conspired with the Ostrogoths to retain for himself what he had conquered for the empire. An exarch was appointed in his place.

THE PRICE OF VICTORY

The vacuum left by the general's departure and the absence of a strong Gothic army soon tempted the barbarians of the north. Armed bands of Franks, Burgundians, and Lombards were soon crossing the Alps to plunder Italy. This prompted the Ostrogoths to revolt. The citizens were deprived of their wealth by taxation, while Roman soldiers frequently went unpaid. Justinian had sown the seeds of anarchy without sufficiently arming those who might prevent it. Corruption, allied with an avaricious church and grasping monks, absorbed the empire's wealth.

Justinian reluctantly dispatched Belisarius to quell the unrest. However, the suspicious monarch never fully trusted his able commander. Eventually, he recalled him, this time for good. At the urging of Pope Vigilius, another force was sent in AD 552 under the command of Narses. After a successful campaign, order was restored, Italy lay in ruins, and Rome was depopulated. It was the peace of desolation described by Tacitus centuries earlier: "To ravage and slaughter they call empire, and when they make a desert they call it peace."[477]

The transformation of the old imperial capital into a medieval city of priests, monks, and robbers was now underway. Their emperor resided in a distant land. Their Pontifex Maximus was the pope. Bishops replaced senators, and a college of cardinals eventually replaced the Senate. A theocracy slowly emerged from the ancient ruins of the Forum and Pantheon.

APPEASING THE MIAPHYSITES, CONFRONTING THE POPE

Religious controversy continued despite the persecution. In the latter years of his rule, the emperor shifted his focus from war to theology. He probed the dusty tomes of learned clerics late into the night. The Miaphysites remained numerically greater in the east and continued to challenge the Chalcedonians. Theodora's devotion to the sect and the need to secure harmony with the eastern provinces drove Justinian to seek a compromise.

In a convoluted way, he sought to achieve this by endorsing a controversy over the writings of Origen. The Church Father, dead for two centuries, was resurrected (in a metaphysical sense), tried, denounced, and condemned to the flames of the hell whose eternal existence he had denied. To deflect attention, the Origenists highlighted some unfinished business from the Council of Chalcedon. How this aided the reconciliation of the Miaphysite and Orthodox churches would require a tiresome explanation that, without boring the reader and at the risk of slight imprecision, can be summed up as follows.

The Miaphysites felt that the Council of Chalcedon had been too hard on them and too lenient towards those they believed had lapsed into Nestorianism. The Origenists, supported by Theodora, encouraged Justinian to redress the balance and thus achieve rapprochement with the Miaphysites by attacking selected writings of three theologians: Theodore of Mopsuestia, Theodoret of Cyrus, and Ibas of Edessa. Known as the Three Chapters, these long-dead clerics were accused of having Nestorian tendencies. Whereas Chalcedon had merely condemned excerpts from their texts and at the same time absolved them of heresy, Justinian went further and pronounced anathema against the writings and especially against the person of Theodore.

When Pope Vigilius refused to endorse the anathema, the emperor summoned him to Constantinople, much to the annoyance of the people of Rome, who pelted stones and sticks at the parting entourage. They had good reason to be angry. The city was again under siege by the Goths, and it seemed the emperor deemed a theological dispute more pressing than their rescue.

In Constantinople, Vigilius was warmly greeted by Justinian with an embrace and a kiss. It went downhill from there. The pope was detained in the city for several years while the emperor and his agents tried to bend him to their wishes. Contrary to expectations, he refused. Theodora was not surprised. Despite indications to the contrary, he had also failed to support her pro-Miaphysite policies since assuming the papacy.

Caught between the terror of God, terror of the emperor, and terror of the western bishops, who threatened excommunication if he relented, Vigilius vacillated between opposing camps while remaining steadfast to the letter of Chalcedon.

His behaviour provoked the anger of the imperial court. Faced with accusations that he was guilty of grievous misdeeds, including the death of his predecessor, Pope Silverius, he fled to the sanctuary of St. Peter's Church and refused to budge. Exasperated, Justinian sent his imperial guard to remove the stubborn pontiff by force.

This led to the unseemly spectacle of the pope desperately clinging to the altar while the sturdy officers pulled him by his beard, hair, and legs, attempting to prise him away. When the altar itself finally collapsed, the guards abandoned the effort. Shaken by the ordeal, Vigilius gave himself up and was imprisoned for a while. Perhaps this was divine punishment for his earlier treatment of Silverius, or so the dejected pontiff speculated in his letters.

Justinian called the Second Council of Constantinople to ratify his condemnation of the Three Chapters. In June 553, the 165, mainly eastern, bishops who were present duly complied. Pope Vigilius remained in his lodgings and refused to attend, fearing further violence against his person.

Finally, after eight turbulent years, the pope, in poor health and no doubt eager to return to Rome, agreed to endorse the anathema on the condition that the canons of Chalcedon remained in force. For this concession, many western clerics ceased communication with him. The African bishops went further and issued the dreaded excommunication order. God it seems, did not smile on compromisers.

Justinian permitted him to leave, but Vigilius died during the voyage back to Rome with nothing to show for all his years of obstinacy. His deacon and successor, Pope Pelagius I, was left to face the wrath of the Latin Church and the suspicion that he secretly supported the Miaphysite cause.

CHRISTIAN DISHARMONY

In his attempt to satisfy opposing dogmatists of east and west by condemning the Three Chapters while upholding the Chalcedon Creed, Justinian managed only to alienate both. Most Miaphysites still retained a sullen opposition to orthodoxy. His rough treatment of Pope Vigilius, coupled with his wife's prior manipulation of the papacy, caused a rift with the Latin Church that endured for nearly a century.

In his final years, the champion of orthodoxy himself lapsed into a semi-Miaphysite heresy, declaring that the body of Jesus was incorruptible. The bishop of Trier, in the Rhineland and therefore safely beyond reprisal, sent a letter warning the emperor to realign with orthodoxy and seek repentance lest he join Nestorius and others in eternal flames.

Despite these differences, Justinian's reign represents the ultimate triumph of Christian ideology in the western world. It also gave rise to an independent Miaphysite church that had not existed before in Syria and Egypt. This was partly thanks to his wife's influence. His conquests had weakened the other major heresies so that they no longer played a significant role in the church west of Constantinople.

The theological controversies that characterised Justinian's reign were intertwined with politics. The religious element made them intractable, highlighted differences, and hindered the search for moderation or concession. Pragmatism gave way to emotive metaphysical debate; compromise equated to surrender. It set the tone for political-religious conflicts to come.

JUSTINIAN CODE

Perhaps Justinian's most outstanding achievement, and, along with Hagia Sophia, the most enduring monument to his reign, was the Justinian Code (*Corpus Juris Civilis*).

Hitherto the laws of the Roman Empire had evolved over time, without cross-references and often with manifest contradictions. They were recorded on countless manuscripts—impossible for any law student to purchase, let alone remember.

Justinian handed the task of codifying these laws to a committee of 12 jurists, headed by his chief legal minister, Tribonian. Working diligently, the team trawled through the old manuscripts of Roman jurisprudence, starting from the earliest "Twelve Tables," written in 450 BC, right up to the most recent, removing inconsistencies and defunct laws.

They compiled a final anthology comprising 12 volumes covering private contracts and criminal and administrative law. This digest of juristic literature and consensus ended with the *Novellae*, a summary of edicts issued by Justinian himself. The *Corpus Juris Civilis*, also known as the Code of Justinian, formed the basis of future laws of the Roman Empire and eventually the basis of the legal system in Europe and its later colonies.

The laws contain the elements of religious compulsion that had permeated Roman legislation since the time of Constantine. For example, "Let no place be afforded to heretics for the conduct of their ceremonies, and let no occasion be offered for them to display the insanity of their obstinate minds."[478] Or this law from the time of Emperor Marcion restricting freedom of discussion: "No one ... shall ... attempt to discuss the Christian religion publicly ... for the violators of this law shall not go unpunished, because they not only oppose the true faith, but they also profane its venerated mysteries by engaging in contests of this kind with Jews and pagans."[479]

Novella LXVIII forbade private gatherings for worship. Only state-sponsored worship would be allowed—and only in approved non-heretical churches.

Some of the most draconian measures were reserved for diviners and faith healers—that is, those who made a living by performing miracle cures. Seen by Christian rulers as parasites exploiting the poor and gullible, perpetrators were subject to the most brutal punishment due to their association with sedition—the Code stipulated torture by hooks tied to the flesh. Had Jesus been alive, he might have fallen foul of these laws.

Compiling the Code remains one of the most significant milestones in the history of legislation. It encapsulated Justinian's vision: one empire, one law, one religion.

NO LONGER NECESSARY TO THINK

The edicts of book 1, section X proved fatal to what remained of classical teaching. These included decrees issued in the name of Gratian, Valentinian, and Theodosius: "We order all those who follow this law to assume the name of Catholic Christians and considering others as demented and insane."[480]

According to the chronicler John Malalas, who lived during that time, this led to the closing of the Academy in Athens in 529, thus restraining whatever philosophical challenge remained to Christian dogma.

In practice, Justinian might merely have withheld public funding for this and other similar institutions within his realm. The schools seem to have functioned for a while after that date. The radically divergent philosophies of the Stoics, Platonists, Epicureans, and Peripatetics that had managed to coexist peacefully in opposition were censured by his dogmatic hand, though not entirely extinguished.

The suppression of dissenting creeds ratified the first commandment, "Thou shalt not have strange gods before me." The Hellenistic religions and all non-Christian forms of worship were destroyed by apathy combined with boycotts, assaults, lynchings, and executions. Some executions were commissioned by imperial decree, others by local mobs of fanatics led by monks, clergy, or pious saints. Every non-Christian tradition was either absorbed or abolished. Non-religious events, such as the Olympic Games, outlawed during Theodosius's reign, and other sporting and theatrical events were not immune.

The outcome was the suspension of free thought. Church doctrine could not withstand investigation. Its power was based on faith, and its survival depended on maintaining its congregations in subservient devotion.

"It is certain because it is absurd,"[481] said Tertullian, referring to the Resurrection. With some degree of hyperbole, he signalled the intention of the new religion towards learning in general and the Academy in particular with the comment, "What has Jerusalem to do with Athens? What concord is there between the Academy and the Church? Our instructions come from the porch of Solomon. We want no curious disputation after possessing Jesus Christ, no enquiry after enjoying the Gospel. With our faith, we desire no other belief. For this is our palmary faith, there is nothing which we ought to believe besides."[482]

St. Augustine followed suit: "Since God has spoken to us, it is no longer necessary for us to think." He went on, "Restrain yourselves from … the false name of knowledge … for the poison of curiosity is the motion of the dead soul,"[483] and "for so you would become like those silly women of whom the apostle says that they are 'always learning, and never able to come to the knowledge of the truth.' "[484]

St. John Chrysostom urged his followers to "put into you sufficient religious knowledge and to cast out all secular reasoning."[485]

And finally, that persecutor of pagans and heretics, real and imagined, in Cyprus, St. Epiphanius: "We can tell the solution of any question not through our own reasonings but from what follows from the Scriptures."[486]

Tertullian and Augustine, both learned classicists, might have exaggerated a point for effect. However, all believed that knowledge was determined by the authority of the apostolic rule of faith and Scripture, rendering further inquiries superfluous. Under the Christian government, opposition to science and learning was sustained wherever it challenged that authority. As with other proscriptions, these were occasionally sanctioned by decree; at other times, by the actions of local zealots.

Ancient manuscripts were destroyed or left to decay, though not always with the consent of learned Christians. When Emperor Jovian burned the library of Antioch in 364, thinking the destruction of heathen books would impress the local Christians, he was dismayed when they joined their pagan townsmen in condemning it as an act of barbarity. Christian scholars continued to study the ancient writings, but others succumbed to the fear that their collections might contain some forbidden work, leaving them open to accusations of heresy. Such fears alone could condemn a private library to the flames.

LAST OF THE SCHOLARS

Regardless of whether Justinian closed the Academy of Athens or merely withdrew its funding, his Code created the conditions that made the Academy's survival impossible. The philosopher Damascius, dubbed the Last of the Neoplatonists, abandoned this hallowed school with his fellow academics.

This was not the first time the old philosopher had felt compelled to flee. As a youth in Alexandria, he had witnessed the violence meted out to academics that continued long after the murder of Hypatia. His brother was severely tortured, and others were executed either by order of Roman officials or by axe-wielding monks. Together with his tutor, he escaped one night by ship and arrived in the more amenable atmosphere of Athens.

In this last outpost of ancient learning, he had thrived, deliberated, and lectured on the classics, careful not to offend his Christian neighbours and ever aware of the dark clouds closing in. Finally, in 632, in his sixties, with the threat of forced baptism or confiscation of property hanging over all non-believers, he and the remaining lecturers abandoned their precious school and began the long trek to Persia.

Here they were welcomed by Shah Khosrow IV, whose reputation for liberality and learning attracted scholars from Rome to India. Schools founded by the shah contributed to a new age of learning that would long outlive his reign.

END OF ENDLESS PEACE

Khosrow, keenly aware that Justinian was distracted by lingering wars in the Mediterranean, was well briefed on the empire's state. He knew Roman soldiers often went unpaid, and supplies were delayed due to state finances being directed to the massive church-building programme. The shah needed little persuasion when envoys from the Ostrogoths asked him to open a second front on the east.

Emboldened, the Persians broke the Endless Peace, attacked Roman possessions in Mesopotamia and Syria, and even took Antioch, where the shah bathed in the sea and organised chariot races between local Blues and Greens, making sure Justinian's favoured Blues were trounced.

After a protracted and costly war that favoured the Persians, a new and less ambitiously titled Fifty Years Peace was signed. One condition of the treaty was that Damascius and his fellow philosophers be allowed to return without fear of reprisal or persecution. However, their time had passed, and they henceforth disappear from the pages of history.

These distractions also facilitated a Bulgar incursion on the European region, where they would pose a military challenge to the empire in the coming centuries. In 559, during a bitter winter, the tribesmen crossed the frozen Danube, followed by a host of Slavs. Fighting and plundering their way southward, the horde managed to reach the forts of Thrace and threatened Constantinople itself.

Trembling in his palace, the emperor looked to the old warrior Belisarius for deliverance. Under his inspired leadership, a hastily gathered militia of citizens and refugees that hardly deserved the name of army managed to put the barbarians to flight. The aged Justinian, relieved but even more envious, greeted the hero's triumphal return with a cold embrace.

The great general passed the remainder of his years under the shadow of a suspicious and ungrateful emperor. His death in 565 was followed eight months later by the death of Justinian, who, at 83, left no heir. Theodora, his devoted wife and companion, had died many years earlier, in 548, probably from cancer.

LEGACY

Justinian's attempt to reverse history by reconquering the west proved temporary and ultimately disastrous. By 600, only the lower half of Italy remained in Roman hands, and Spain was lost completely. In removing the relatively stable Vandal and Goth regimes from Africa and Italy, he worsened rather than helped the plight of those regions. Both became vulnerable to further invasions and distracted Romans from the greater danger in the Balkans and the Persian borders.

From his perspective, the destruction of heresy in Europe and North Africa justified a bloody conquest. The empire had been restored under one Christian emperor and one Orthodox creed. For the inhabitants of these regions, it came at a terrible cost. They could only grieve at the pointless loss of life.

Even in Syria and Egypt, Justinian's policies had the opposite effect to what he intended. Christians could not "live in harmony with one another" (Romans 12:6) and were further alienated from Constantinople. Forced to pay high taxes for wars they never wanted, they grew resentful of their imperial overlords.

His successors bore the consequences of his policies and were tasked with handling the repercussions that arose from them.

27

MUTUAL DESTRUCTION

SHORTLY AFTER THE emperor's death, the realm reaped his bitter harvest.

Justinian was a hard act to follow. His mixed legacy, epic reputation, extended borders, strained resources, divided empire, emboldened enemies, and empty treasury presented massive problems for his successors.

The first of those, his nephew Justin II, tried to cope with Bulgar incursions across the Danube, loss of territory in Italy, and attacks from Persia. Not surprisingly, he had a nervous breakdown.

His successors attempted to balance these military challenges while addressing the financial burden inherited from the Justinian reign. Dissatisfaction in the overburdened military and impoverished population led to a revolt.

In the midst of this anarchy, the Persians grasped the opportunity to launch their most devastating attack on the Roman Empire. They recaptured Antioch and Palestine (including the city of Jerusalem), and even Egypt. Disaffected elements in the east, especially the Jews, contributed to the Persian victories.

Among the spoils of war was the True Cross, so beloved of St. Helena.

Sweeping across Asia Minor, the Persians were soon outside the walls of Constantinople itself. With Persians attacking from the east and Bulgars and Slavs from the west, the empire seemed ready to follow the western part into oblivion.

The empire was saved by the genius of a general called Heraclius. In a series of spectacular victories, he repulsed the Persians and forced them to sue for peace.

The wars between Persia and Rome, a recurring feature of the previous 400 years, finally ended. In the process, both empires were gravely weakened and vulnerable. During their invasion, the Persians had wrought terrible destruction on the conquered lands. The Romans had responded in equal measure when they entered Persia. Misery and devastation triumphed in a pointless struggle that merely restored both empires to their pre-war borders. Only the rough Arabian tribesmen who served as paid auxiliaries in the opposing armies had profited from the conflict.

The victorious emperor adopted a doctrine called Monothelitism to reconcile Chalcedonians, Miaphysites, and Nestorians, who were now strong in Persia and beyond. As one might expect, it was rejected by all sides and only succeeded in highlighting existing divisions.

Exhausted by war and fraught with religious dissent, the Persian and Roman empires were ill prepared for the coming storm. Its source would be the dusty settlement of Mecca, where a boy, soon to be an orphan, was born five years after the death of Justinian.

By the time Heraclius had defeated the Persians and replanted the True Cross in Jerusalem, the boy had grown, become a prophet, and run the course of his life. But his legacy and the desert tribesmen who carried it with them were ready to enter the stage from the sands of Arabia. No longer mercenaries, they would arrive as adversaries against their former paymasters.

Christianity in general, and the policies of Justinian in particular, had failed to unite the eastern empire. In fact, they had weakened it by alienating whole populations that might otherwise have been loyal subjects. The Jews had good reason to support the Persian invaders, while Syrians and Egyptians had no good reason to oppose them.

Had the state permitted its people to freely exercise their own conscience and beliefs, they might have been united. Instead, all attempts to impose one God, one creed in the interests of state solidarity had the opposite effect. Ironically, it divided and destabilised the state.

The Christian empire had somehow survived, as had its nemesis across the Euphrates. Neither was equipped to face the new followers of the god of war.

CONCLUSION

AND SO YAHWEH, god of war, chosen among the other deities for His military powers, became the ultimate and only true god. At least, so it was for the inhabitants of the Roman Empire and the regions within its influence.

He had indeed vanquished His enemies and watched as His faithful adherents fought among themselves. He had led them to victory and despair, exile and persecution. He had seen His people conquered by the barbarian and seen the barbarian, in turn, bow to His great power. Adored by slave and king alike, He had grown in dominion and influence.

His strength lay not just in the arms of his warriors and the authority of the state, but in the hearts of His believers and the cohesion of their communities. The faithful found meaning, identity, and guidance in their Scriptures. These writings transmitted by prophets and clerics evolved and adapted to resonate with people of diverse backgrounds and beliefs. They created a strong community structure that fostered a sense of belonging and solidarity.

For the faithful, the greatest enemies were no longer the polytheists. They had been vanquished; their ideas were trodden underfoot. The literary treasures of Greece and Rome were consigned to the flames, while statues and artworks were mercilessly shattered. Free thought was suppressed by a dogmatic doctrine that feared any challenge to its ideas. Dissenters were brutally suppressed. Ironically, this would include the chosen people of Yahweh, the Jews who had formulated its basic tenets.

Paradoxically, the religion that united communities had become a source of political division. Internal dissension tore the empire apart and hindered the resolution of geopolitical conflicts. The burning strength of faith acted as a counterfoil to rational discussion and compromise. Ultimately, this weakened the empire.

The most fervent believers, those who had been exiled, had already imprinted their version of Yahweh's religion on the desert nomads. These hardy warriors found employment as mercenaries in the armies of Persia and Rome. They knew how to fight; soon, they would learn how to pray.

Under their banners, the god of war would revisit His flock in an unexpected and more virulent form. The faithful would become the infidel. This will be the next chapter in our story (*The God of War Volume II*).

ACKNOWLEDGEMENTS

Thanks to all the staff at Book Launchers for their helpful assistance and advice in preparing this book for publication.

ENDNOTES

1. Genesis 22:7 (paraphrase).
2. "Religions," The World Factbook, CIA.gov, accessed November 24, 2023, https://www.cia.gov/the-world-factbook/field/religions/.
3. The name change to Abraham would come later.
4. Genesis 12:7 (NIV).
5. Genesis 20:12.
6. Genesis 13:2 (Alter).
7. Genesis 14:14–16.
8. Genesis 19:8 (GWT).
9. Genesis 19:32–36.
10. Genesis 16:6 (NLT).
11. Genesis 16:12 (NRSV).
12. Qur'an 2:127.
13. Genesis 18:1–2.
14. Genesis 15:7 (NIV).
15. Genesis 12:7 (NIV).
16. Genesis 15:18 (LSV).
17. Genesis 17:21.
18. Unless one considers an aversion to Sodomy as ethical.
19. Genesis 12:3 (DRB).
20. Genesis 12:17.
21. Genesis 20.
22. Genesis 22:17.
23. Genesis 21:9.
24. Genesis 27.
25. "How Old Was Isaac When Abraham Almost Sacrificed Him?," Got Questions, accessed December 4, 2023, https://www.gotquestions.org/how-old-was-Isaac.html.

26 Genesis 23.
27 Genesis 22:12 (NIV).
28 Jeff Diamant, "Anti-Jewish Harassment Occurred in 94 countries in 2020, Up from Earlier Years," Pew Research Center, March 17, 2023, https://www.pewresearch.org/short-reads/2023/03/17/anti-jewish-harassment-occurred-in-94-countries-in-2020-up-from-earlier-years/.
29 Rosalie David, *Handbook to Life in Ancient Egypt* (New York: Facts on File, Inc., 1998).
30 "Hebrew," *Encyclopedia Britannica*, September 22, 2023, https://www.britannica.com/topic/Hebrew.
31 Deuteronomy 7:3 (NIV).
32 Numbers 25.
33 Deuteronomy 7:6 (NIV).
34 Deuteronomy 3:22 (NIV).
35 Exodus 15:3 (NIV).
36 Exodus 25:8 (NIV).
37 Deuteronomy 9:3 (NIV).
38 Exodus 20:5 (NIV).
39 Deuteronomy 12:3 (NIV).
40 Leviticus 26:7 (NIV).
41 Numbers 31:7–10 (NIV).
42 Numbers 31:15 (NIV).
43 Numbers 31:17–18 (NIV).
44 Deuteronomy 2:33–34 (NIV).
45 Judges 18:27 (NRSV).
46 Deuteronomy 7:16 (NIV).
47 Joshua 10:40 (NIV).
48 Joshua 6:21 (NIV).
49 Numbers 33:50–52 (NIV).
50 Deuteronomy 7:2 (NIV).
51 Numbers 33:55–56 (NIV).
52 Joshua 10:28 (NIV).
53 Joshua 24:13 (NIV).
54 Exodus, Leviticus, and Deuteronomy.
55 Genesis makes several references Canaanite behaviour as immoral or evil.
56 Judges 21:25 (NIV).
57 E.g., 12 annual lunar cycles, 12 Greek Olympian gods, 12 signs of the Western and Chinese zodiacs.
58 Judges 21:11 (NIV).
59 Judges 21:12 (NLT).
60 Judges 21:15–21.
61 1 Samuel 15:2–3 (NIV).
62 1 Samuel 15:35.
63 A counter-argument holds that pork consumption was reserved for the non-Hebrew inhabitants of the region. Scholars continue to debate the issue.
64 1 Kings 18.
65 2 Kings 2:23–24 (NIV).

ENDNOTES

66 2 Kings 2:9 (NIV).
67 2 Kings 17:24 (NIV).
68 Flavius Josephus, *Antiquities of the Jews*.
69 Isaiah 37:33–37; 2 Chronicles 32:21.
70 Simon Schama, *The Story of the Jews: Finding the Words, 1000BCE–1492CE*, vol. 1(The Bodley Head, 2013).
71 *The Annals of Sennacherib*, trans. Daniel David Luckenbill (Chicago: University of Chicago Press, 1924).
72 Jeremiah 8:8 (NIV).
73 Jeremiah 42:14 (NIV).
74 Jeremiah 42:22 (NIV).
75 Ezekiel 20:30 (NIV).
76 "Mrs. Meir Says Moses Made Israel Oil-Poor," *New York Times*, June 11, 1973, https://www.nytimes.com/1973/06/11/archives/mrs-meir-says-moses-made-israel-oilpoor.html.
77 The power to change the future by reinventing the past is neatly summarised in George Orwell's *1984*: "Who controls the past controls the future; who controls the present controls the past." George Orwell, *1984* (Secker & Warburg, 1949).
78 Book of Daniel.
79 Psalm 137:1 (NIV).
80 Psalm 137:8–9 (NIV).
81 Isaiah 45:1 (NLT).
82 Isaiah 45:5 (HCSB).
83 Nehemiah 2:20.
84 Nehemiah 6:15.
85 Numbers 12:1.
86 Deuteronomy 23:3.
87 Malachi 2:11 (NRSV).
88 Nehemiah 13:25 (ESV).
89 Nehemiah 13:30 (NIV).
90 Ezra 9:2 (HCSB).
91 Ezra 7:26 (NIV).
92 Ezra 9:2 (NIV).
93 Ezra 10.
94 Genesis 3:9 (NIV).
95 Israel Finkelstein and Neil Asher Silbermann, *The Bible Unearthed: Archaeology's New Vision of Ancient Israel and the Origin of its Sacred Texts* (New York: Simon & Schuster, 2002).
96 First highlighted by Raphael Patai in 1967, then Francesca Stavrakopoulou in 2010. See for example *Mercer Dictionary of the Bible*, ed. Watson E. Mills (December 31, 1999, revised January 10, 2022).
97 1 Kings 15:13.
98 Bible Hub, s.v. "842. Asherah," accessed October 10, 2023, https://biblehub.com/hebrew/842.htm.
99 Irving Finkel, *The Ark before Noah: Decoding the Story of the Flood* (London: Hodder Paperback, 2014).
100 Genesis 24:11.

[101] Lidar Sapir-Hen and Erez Ben-Yosef, "The Introduction of Domestic Camels to the Southern Levant: Evidence from the Aravah Valley," *Tel Aviv* 40, no. 2 (November 2013): 277–85, https://doi.org/10.1179/033443513X13753505864089.
[102] Israel Finkelstein, "The Wilderness Narrative and Itineraries and the Evolution of the Exodus Tradition" in *Israel's Exodus in Transdisciplinary Perspective: Text, Archaeology, Culture, and Geoscience*, eds. Thomas E. Levy, Thomas Schneider, and William H.C. Propp (Springer: New York, 2015), 39–54, https://doi.org/10.1007/978-3-319-04768-3.
[103] Genesis 6:20, 7:8–9.
[104] Genesis 7:2–3.
[105] Genesis 7:17.
[106] Genesis 7:24.
[107] Genesis 7:11, 8:1.
[108] Genesis 7:16.
[109] Exodus 12:37–38 (NRSV).
[110] Carol A. Redmount, "Bitter Lives: Israel In and Out of Egypt," in *The Oxford History of the Biblical World*, ed. Michael David Coogan (Oxford University Press, 2001).
[111] Robert Hetzron, ed., *The Semitic Languages* (New York: Routledge, 1997).
[112] Leviticus 1:11 (NIV).
[113] Exodus 29:14 (NIV).
[114] Deuteronomy 23:1–2 (NIV).
[115] Deuteronomy 27:21 (NIV).
[116] Deuteronomy 27:23 (NIV).
[117] Leviticus 19:20 (NAB).
[118] Deuteronomy 22:1 (NIV).
[119] Deuteronomy 25:4 (NIV).
[120] Deuteronomy 22:10 (HCSB).
[121] Deuteronomy 22:11 (HCSB).
[122] Deuteronomy 28:25–31 (NIV).
[123] Exodus 34:10–26.
[124] Exodus 20:2–3 (NIV).
[125] Exodus 20:4 (NIV).
[126] Exodus 20:7 (NIV).
[127] Exodus 20:10 (NIV).
[128] Exodus 22:20.
[129] Leviticus 24:16 (NIV).
[130] 1 Kings 10:23 (NIV).
[131] Exodus 23:31 (NIV).
[132] Leviticus 26:6 (NIV).
[133] Daniel 9:27 (HCSB).
[134] Exodus 23:32 (NIV).
[135] Exodus 20:5 (NIV).
[136] Ezra 9:1 (NIV).
[137] Isaiah 14:2 (NIV).
[138] Isaiah 65:15 (NIV).
[139] Isaiah 66:16 (NIV).
[140] Isaiah 66:17 (NIV).

ENDNOTES

141. Isaiah 34:3 (NIV).
142. Isaiah 11:6 (NIV).
143. Isaiah 61:6 (NIV).
144. Isaiah 60:16 (DRB).
145. Isaiah 49:23 (NIV).
146. Isaiah 61:5 (NIV).
147. Isaiah 7:14 (NIV).
148. Jeremiah 23:5 (NIV).
149. Joel 3:17 (NIV).
150. Micah 5:8 (NIV).
151. Micah 5:15 (NIV).
152. Micah 7:17 (NIV).
153. Zechariah 14:17 (NIV).
154. Malachi 4:5 (NIV).
155. Micah 4:13 (NIV).
156. Ezekiel 34:23 (NIV).
157. Ezekiel 34:28 (AMP).
158. R.A. Horsley, "Ancient Jewish Banditry and the Revolt Against Rome, AD 66–70," *The Catholic Biblical Quarterly* 43, no. 3 (July 1981): 409–32.
159. Josephus, *Antiquities of the Jews*.
160. Luke 13:32.
161. Flavius Josephus, *The Jewish War*, 3.3.2.
162. Josephus, *Antiquities of the Jews*.
163. Reza Aslan, *Zealot: The Life and Times of Jesus of Nazareth* (Random House, New York. 2013).
164. Mark 3:31–33.
165. Mark 6:18–19.
166. Maurice Casey, *Jesus of Nazareth: An Independent Historian's Account of His Life and Teaching* (London: T&T Clark, 2010).
167. Luke 9:60 (NIV).
168. Matthew 5:39 (paraphrase).
169. Mark 1:15 (GWT).
170. Mark 2:16–18.
171. Matthew 11:2.
172. Mark 2:19.
173. Mark 3:21.
174. Mark 6:3 (NIV).
175. Mark 6:4 (NIV).
176. Mark 6:29–32.
177. Mark 4:9 (NIV).
178. Mark 4:12 (NIV).
179. Luke 8:3 (NRSV).
180. Luke 8:2.
181. Mark 1:15; 13:30; Luke 9:27.
182. Mark 9:1 (BSB).
183. Mark 7:27 (NIV).

184 Mark 7:2–5.
185 Mark 11:12–14.
186 Mark 11:27–33.
187 Mark 12:17 (NIV).
188 Aslan, *Zealot*.
189 Mark 14:63–64.
190 Leviticus 24:16.
191 Matthew 27:11 (HCSB).
192 Mark 16:9.
193 Mark 15:40.
194 Joe Zias, "Crucifixion in Antiquity: The Evidence," CenturyOne Foundation, 1998, https://mercaba.org/FICHAS/upsa/crucifixion.htm.
195 Mark 15:43 (LSV).
196 Isaiah 53:9 (NIV). The "he" referred to is a servant. Christians assume this to be Jesus. Jews have various interpretations, including a metaphor for righteous Jews.
197 Mark 16:7.
198 Acts 4:13 (NIV).
199 James 5:4–5 (NIV).
200 Josephus, *Antiquities of the Jews*.
201 Acts 7:51–53.
202 Marcus J. Borg and John Dominic Crossan, *The First Christmas: What the Gospels Really Teach About Jesus's Birth* (New York: HarperCollins, 2009), 95.
203 Malachi 4:5 (NIV).
204 Micah 5:2 (NIV).
205 "Did Jesus Actually Come from Nazareth?" *The Bart Ehrman Blog*, December 21, 2022, https://ehrmanblog.org/did-jesus-come-from-nazareth/.
206 Isaiah 7:14 (NIV).
207 Josephus, *The Jewish War*, 6.5.3.
208 Josephus, *The Jewish War*, 2.13.4.
209 Malachi 4:5 (NIV).
210 Josephus, *The Jewish War*, 6.4.6.
211 Josephus, *The Jewish War*, 6.1.1.
212 *Codex Sinaiticus* and *Codex Vaticanus*, as confirmed by statements from the early Church Fathers Eusebius and Jerome.
213 Mark 6:3.
214 Mark 10:18.
215 Mark 14:61–62 (ESV).
216 Mark 7:27.
217 Mark 15:14 (ESV).
218 Philo of Alexandria, *Legatio ad Gaium*.
219 Matthew 28:6–8.
220 Matthew 27:46 (NIV), inspired by Psalm 22.
221 Matthew 10:5–8.
222 Matthew 24:34.
223 Nicholas F. Gier, *God, Reason, and the Evangelicals* (Lanham, MD: University Press of America, 1987).

ENDNOTES

Bart D. Ehrman, *Jesus: Apocalyptic Prophet of the New Millennium* (Oxford University Press, 2001).

224 Ehrman, *Jesus*.
225 Luke 4:16–17.
226 "For the Very First Time: A Residential Building from the Time of Jesus Was Exposed in the Heart of Nazareth," Israel Antiques Authority, December 21, 2009, https://www.antiquities.org.il/article_eng.aspx?sec_id=25&subj_id=240&id=1638.
227 Matthew 26:65.
228 Matthew 19:8 (NIV).
229 E.g., Isaiah 14:15; Daniel 12:2; Matthew 5:17–18, 23:1–3; John 10:35; Acts 7:1–53, 24:14.
230 Confucius, *Analects* XV.24.
231 *Mahābhārata* 5; Thales, Sextus the Pythagorean, and Isocrates; *Shayast-na-Shayast* 13:29.
232 Celsus, *The True Word*, quoted in Origen, *Contra Celsum*, 1.28.
233 Nicholas P. L. Allen, *Christian Forgeries in Jewish Antiquities: Josephus Interrupted* (Newcastle upon Tyne, UK: Cambridge Scholars Publishing, 2020).
234 Josephus, *Antiquities of the Jews*.
235 Matthew 26:47–50; Mark 14:43–45.
236 Luke 2:32 (NIV).
237 Acts 21:37.
238 Acts 26:14.
239 Bart D. Ehrman, *Lost Christianities: The Battles for Scripture and the Faiths We Never Knew* (Oxford University Press, 2005).

Jewish Encyclopedia, s.v. "Ebionites," by Kaufmann Kohler, accessed October 22, 2023, https://www.jewishencyclopedia.com/articles/5411-ebionites.

Hyam Maccoby, *The Mythmaker: Paul and the Invention of Christianity* (HarperCollins, 1987).

240 Acts 18:3.
241 Acts of Paul and 2 Corinthians 10:10.
242 Acts 20:7, 20:9.
243 Acts 9:4 (NIV).
244 Merkabah mysticism, a school of early Jewish mysticism that sometimes involved visionary experiences.
245 Acts 15:7–11, 19–20.
246 Galatians 2:11 (NIV).
247 Galatians 2:11–14.
248 2 Peter 3:15 (NLT).
249 Bart D. Ehrman, *Forged: Writing in the Name of God—Why the Bible's Authors Are Not Who We Think They Are* (HarperOne, 2011).

Stephen L. Harris, *Understanding the Bible* (Palo Alto: Mayfield, 1985).

D.A. Carson and Douglas J. Moo, *An Introduction to the New Testament* (Zondervan Academic, 2009).

250 Philippians 3:2 (NIV).
251 2 Corinthians 11:13–15 (NIV).
252 Romans 2:17–29, 3:9–28, 5:1–11; 1 Corinthians 7:17–21, 9:20–23; Titus 1:10–16.
253 1 Corinthians 10:25–26 (NIV).
254 Galatians 2:6 (NIV).

255 Justin Martyr, *Dialogue with Trypho*.
256 Acts 20:22 (NIV).
257 Acts 21:17 (NIV).
258 Acts 21:24 (NIV).
259 Acts 21:39, 22:24.
260 Acts 24:5 (NIV).
261 Philemon 1:22 (NIV).
262 Romans 15:28 (NIV).
263 Clement of Rome, *First Epistle*, 5.8.
264 Romans 2:13.
265 Galatians 3:13 (NIV).
266 2 Corinthians 3:7 (NIV).
267 1 Corinthians 9:20–21 (NIV).
268 1 Corinthians 9:20 (NIV).
269 Matthew 3:2, 4:17.
270 Matthew 2:1–2; Luke 1:32–33; Zechariah 14:9.
271 John 14:6.
272 Romans 14:17.
273 Acts 2:22–36, 3:12–26.
274 1 Corinthians 1:18.
275 Acts 20:24; Romans 16:25; Galatians 1:11–12; 1 Timothy 1:11.
276 Luke 19:10 (NIV).
277 1 Corinthians 1:22–23.
278 Romans 7:25 (NRSV).
279 James 1:22 (HCSB).
280 James 2:14 (NIV).
281 James 2:17 (NIV).
282 James 2:19–20 (NIV).
283 Zechariah 8:20–23.
284 Moses Maimonides, "Hilkhot M'lakhim (Laws of Kings and Wars)" in *Mishneh Torah*, trans. Reuven Brauner, 8.14, https://www.sefaria.org/Mishneh_Torah%2C_Kings_and_Wars.8?lang=bi.
285 Acts 4:13.
286 John 1:1 (NIV).
287 John 1:14 (NIV).
288 John 20:2 (NIV).
289 John 20:15.
290 John 8:44 (NIV).
291 John 14:6 (NIV).
292 John 8:1–11.
293 John 11.
294 Edward Gibbon, *The History of the Decline and Fall of the Roman Empire*, vol. 1 (London: Strahan & Cadell, 1776–89).
295 Gibbon, *Decline and Fall*.
296 Suetonius, *Lives of the Twelve Caesars*.
297 Acts 18:14–16 (NIV).

ENDNOTES

298 Tacitus, *The Annals of Imperial Rome*, 15.44.
299 Romans 13:1 (NIV).
300 Revelation 17:1 (LSV).
301 Revelation 13:1, 17:3 (LSV).
   L. Michael White, "Understanding the Book of Revelation," Frontline, PBS, accessed December 5, 2023, https://www.pbs.org/wgbh/pages/frontline/shows/apocalypse/revelation/white.html.
302 Revelation 1:1 (NIV).
303 Peter 2:13–14 (NIV).
304 Tacitus, *The Annals of Imperial Rome*, 15.47.
305 Lucian, *The Passing of Peregrinus*, 13.
306 Pliny, *Epistles*, 10.96.
307 Pliny, *Epistles*, 10.96.
308 Trajan to Pliny (letter 97) in *Pliny the Younger, Letters*, vol. 2, books 8–10, trans. Betty Radice (Cambridge, MA: Harvard University Press, 1969).
309 Matthew 10:35–37 (NIV).
310 Matthew 23:9 (NIV).
311 Tertullian, *De Idolatria*.
312 Celsus, *The True Word*, quoted in Origen, *Contra Celsum*.
313 Celsus, *The True Word*, 6.78.
314 Origen, *Contra Celsum*, 3.44.
315 Origen, *Contra Celsum*, 8.68.
316 Tertullian, *Apologeticum*.
317 St. Ignatius of Antioch, Epistle to the Romans.
318 *Martyrdom of Polycarp*. Attributed to the "Church Fathers."
319 Marcus Aurelius, *Meditations*.
320 *The Acts of the Christian Martyrs*, quoted in Catherine Nixey, *The Darkening Age: The Christian Destruction of the Classical World* (Macmillan Publishers, 2017).
321 Eusebius, *Historia Ecclesiastica*, quoted in Nixey, *The Darkening Age*.
322 Arthur J. Droge and James D. Tabor, *A Noble Death: Suicide and Martyrdom Among Christians and Jews in Antiquity* (HarperCollins, 1992).
323 Vibia Perpetua, *Passio sanctarum Perpetuae et Felicitatis*.
324 Perpetua, *Passio sanctarum Perpetuae et Felicitatis*.
325 Perpetua, *Passio sanctarum Perpetuae et Felicitatis*.
326 Perpetua, *Passio sanctarum Perpetuae et Felicitatis*.
327 Sabine Baring-Gould, *The Lives of the Saints* (John Hodges, 1914).
328 Tertullian, *Apologeticum*, 49.
329 Tertullian, *De Fuga in Persecutione*.
330 Origen, *Contra Celsum*, 3.8.
331 Geoffrey Blainey, *A Short History of Christianity* (Lanham, MD: Rowman & Littlefield, 2014).
332 Tertullian, *Apologeticum*.
333 For a historical analysis of this, see Dennis J. Preato, "Junia, A Female Apostle: An Examination of the Historical Record," *Priscilla Papers: Bible Translation* 33, no. 2 (Spring 2019), https://www.cbeinternational.org/resource/junia-female-apostle-examination-historical-record.

[334] Celsus, *The True Word*, quoted in Origen, *Contra Celsum*, 2.16.
[335] Cyprian, Epistle 14.
[336] Cyprian, Letter to Donatus, chapter 10.
[337] Mud brick in Egypt and Syria.
[338] Tertullian, *De praescriptione haereticorum* 40:3–4.
[339] Justin Martyr, *Apology 1*.
[340] Lactantius, Letter to Donatus, https://www.newadvent.org/fathers/0705.htm.
[341] *Collatio Legum Mosaicarum et Romanarum*, 15.3.4.
[342] Lactantius, *De Mortibus Persecutorum*.
[343] Gibbon, *Decline and Fall*.
[344] Matthew 22:14 (NLT).
[345] Timothy D. Barnes, *Constantine and Eusebius* (Harvard University Press, 1984).
[346] Henry Palmer Chapman, *Catholic Encyclopedia*.
[347] E.g., Matthew 7:14.
[348] Augustine, *Letter 88:8*.
[349] Pseudo Jerome, *Indiculus de Haeresibus*, quoted in Nixey, *The Darkening Age*.
[350] Ammianus Marcellinus, *Res Gestae*, XXII:5.
[351] Lactantius, *De Mortibus Persecutorum*.
[352] E.g., *Historia Ecclesiastica*.
[353] Lactantius, *De Mortibus Persecutorum*.
[354] Rodney Stark, *The Rise of Christianity: A Sociologist Reconsiders History*, (Princeton: Princeton University Press, 1996).
  Benjamin Harnett, "The Diffusion of the Codex," *Classical Antiquity* 36, no. 2 (2017): 183–235, https://doi.org/10.1525/ca.2017.36.2.183.
[355] Ibid.
[356] Ibid.
[357] Eusebius, *Oration XVI*.
[358] Eusebius, *Oration I*.
[359] Eusebius, *Oration XVI*.
[360] Epiphanius, *Panarion*; Philastrius, *Diversarum Hereseon Liber*.
[361] Eusebius, *Vita Constantini*, 3.12.
[362] Eusebius, *Vita Constantini*, 3.63.
[363] Cyprian, *De Catholicae Ecclesiae Unitate*.
[364] Eusebius, *Vita Constantini*, 3.64.
[365] Eusebius, *Vita Constantini*, 2.68.
[366] Eusebius, *Vita Constantini*, 3.18.
[367] Eusebius, *Vita Constantini*, 3.65.
[368] Eusebius, *Vita Constantini*, 3.65.
[369] Socrates Scholasticus, *Historia Ecclesiastica*.
[370] Socrates Scholasticus, *Historia Ecclesiastica*.
[371] Athanasius, *The Life of Saint Anthony*.
[372] Gibbon, *Decline and Fall*.
[373] Officially known as Simeon Stylites the Elder to distinguish him from a later Stylites who shared the same name.
[374] Tertullian, *Contra Marcion*.
[375] Candida Moss, *The Myth of Persecution: How Early Christians Invented a Story of*

ENDNOTES

Martyrdom (HarperCollins, 2013)
  Tom Bissell, *Apostle: Travels Among the Tombs of the Twelve* (Pantheon Books, 2016).
376 Gibbon, *Decline and Fall*.
377 Socrates Scholasticus, *Historia Ecclesiastica*.
378 Socrates Scholasticus, *Historia Ecclesiastica*.
379 Sozomen, *Historia Ecclesiastica*.
380 1 John 5:17 (DRB).
381 Julian Epistles.
382 Julian Epistles.
383 Socrates Scholasticus, *Historia Ecclesiastica*.
384 Ammianus, *Res Gestae*, XXI.
385 Socrates Scholasticus, *Historia Ecclesiastica*.
386 Gibbon, *Decline and Fall*.
387 Eusebius, quoting Constantine, *Vita Constantini*, 3.18.
388 Gibbon, *Decline and Fall*.
389 Ammianus, *Res Gestae*, XXV.
390 2 Corinthians 6:14 (BSB).
391 Socrates Scholasticus, *Historia Ecclesiastica*.
392 Rulers were sensitive to "seers" and "diviners" who professed to tell the future, often predicting events unfavourable to the empire or emperor.
393 Gibbon, *Decline and Fall*.
394 Ammianus, *Res Gestae*, Battle of Adrianople.
395 Athanasius, Letter to Epictetus.
396 Sozomen, *Historia Ecclesiastica*.
397 Matthew 5:9.
398 Valentinian was the younger half-brother of Gratian. Their mother was the Arian Justina.
399 Gregory, *De Vita Sua* vv. 439–46, in *Patrologia Graeca* 37.1059–60.
400 Gregory to Nectarius in *Letters*, 1.202.
401 Gregory to Theodore in *Letters*, 7.77.
402 *Codex Theodosianus*, 16.1.2.
403 Oswald Hunter-Blair, "St. Gregory of Nazianzus," *The Catholic Encyclopedia* (New York: Robert Appleton Company, 1910), https://www.newadvent.org/cathen/07010b.htm.
404 Ambrose, Epistle XX, https://orthodoxchurchfathers.com/fathers/npnf210/npnf2147.htm.
405 Gibbon, *Decline and Fall*.
406 Ambrose, Epistle XXII, https://www.newadvent.org/fathers/340922.htm.
407 Gibbon, *Decline and Fall*.
408 Sulpicius Severus, *On the Life of St. Martin*.
409 Libanius, Oration 30 (Addressed to the Emperor Theodosius) in *Libanius: Autobiography and Selected Letters: Autobiography, Letters 1-50*, vol. I, trans. A. F. Norman (Harvard University Press, 1992).
410 St. Epiphanius, *Panarion*.
411 Gibbon, *Decline and Fall*.
412 H. A. Drake, *Constantine and the Bishops: The Politics of Intolerance* (Johns Hopkins University Press, 2002).
413 Basil of Caesarea, "Address to Young Men on the Right Use of Greek Literature," 4.105.
414 Matthew 24:15 (NIV).

[415] Basil of Caesarea, "Address to Young Men on the Right Use of Greek Literature."
[416] Ammianus, *Res Gestae*.
[417] Theodoret, *Therapeutike*.
  Read Catherine Nixey, *The Darkening Age* (Macmillan Publishers, 2017) for an excellent account of the destruction of classical literature and art during this period.
[418] Ambrose, Epistle XL.
[419] Augustine, *Confessions*.
[420] Augustine, *Confessions*, trans. and ed. Albert C. Outler, 3.13, Internet Medieval Sourcebook, Fordham University, https://sourcebooks.fordham.edu/source/aug-conv.asp.
[421] Augustine, *City of God*, 20.2, quoting Romans 11:33.
[422] Augustine, *De Gestis Pelagii*.
[423] Augustine to Vincentius, Letter XCIII, 1.2.
[424] Augustine to Vincentius, Letter XCIII, 5.17.
[425] Augustine, *City of God*.
[426] Augustine, *Confessions*.
[427] Zosimus, *Historia Nova*.
[428] Council of Carthage 419, Canon 129.
[429] John Chrysostom, *De Virginitate*.
[430] Ammianus, *History*, XIV.16.
[431] William Jones, *Ecclesiastical History*, vol. 1 (G. Wightman and G.J. McCombie, 1838).
[432] Orosius, *Historium Adversum Paganos Libri VII*.
[433] Sozomen, *Historia Ecclesiastica*.
[434] Augustine, *City of God*.
[435] Procopius, *The Vandalic Wars*.
[436] Possidius, *Life of St. Augustine*.
[437] Leo I, Letter IV to the Bishops.
[438] Chris Wickham, *The Inheritance of Rome: A History of Europe from 400 to 1000* (London: Allen Lane, 2009).
[439] Salvian, *The Governance of God*.
[440] John Chrysostom, "Homily IV on Romans."
[441] John Chrysostom, "Homily XXIV on Romans."
[442] John Chrysostom, *Adversus Judaeos*.
[443] Nixey, *The Darkening Age*.
[444] Socrates Scholasticus, *Historia Ecclesiastica*.
[445] John Chrysostom, "Homily Against Publishing the Errors of the Brethren."
[446] Socrates Scholasticus, *Historia Ecclesiastica*.
[447] Theophilus had destroyed the Serapeum and other pagan temples in Egypt. See chapter 17.
[448] Socrates Scholasticus, *Historia Ecclesiastica*.
[449] Palladius, *Dialogues*.
[450] Socrates Scholasticus, *Historia Ecclesiastica*.
[451] Socrates Scholasticus, *Historia Ecclesiastica*.
[452] John Chrysostom to Pope Innocent in *Nicene and Post-Nicene Fathers, First Series*, vol. 9, trans. W. R. W. Stephens, ed. Philip Schaff (Buffalo, NY: Christian Literature Publishing Co., 1889), http://www.newadvent.org/fathers/1918.htm.
[453] Socrates Scholasticus, *Historia Ecclesiastica*.

ENDNOTES

454 Socrates Scholasticus, *Historia Ecclesiastica*.
455 Nestorius, *Apologia pro vita sua*.
456 Extract from Decree of the Council of Ephesus.
457 Psalm 34:14 (NIV).
458 Gibbon, *Decline and Fall*.
459 Father Menassa Yuhanna, *History of the Coptic Church*.
460 *Catholic Encyclopedia* (1913).
461 Gibbon, *Decline and Fall*.
462 *Catholic Encyclopedia* (1913).
463 Gibbon, *Decline and Fall*.
464 Evagrius Scholasticus, *Historia Ecclesiastica*.
465 Evagrius Scholasticus, *Historia Ecclesiastica*.
466 Theophanes, *Chronicle*.
467 Gibbon, *Decline and Fall*.
468 Evagrius Scholasticus, *Historia Ecclesiastica*.
469 Gibbon, *Decline and Fall*.
470 Procopius, *Secret History*.
471 Procopius, *Secret History*.
472 Luke 10:30–37; John 4:5–42.
473 The cause was a volcanic eruption in Iceland, Indonesia, or Central America (possibly more than one). This eruption had left a plume of smoke over the atmosphere.
474 Clothes in the colour purple were reserved for the imperial class.
475 Procopius, *History of the Wars*.
476 Procopius, *History of the Wars*.
477 Tacitus, *Agricola*.
478 Justinian Code, 1.3.
479 Justinian Code, 1.3.
480 Justinian Code, 1.1.
481 Tertullian, *De Carne Christi*.
482 Tertullian, *De Praescriptionibus adversus Haereticos*.
483 Augustine, *Confessions*.
484 Augustine, *City of God*, quoting 2 Timothy 3:7.
485 Chrysostom, "Homily Against Publishing Errors."
486 Epiphanius, *Panarion* 65, as quoted by Martin Chemnitz, *Examination of the Council of Trent* (Concordia Printing House, 1971–86).

www.ingramcontent.com/pod-product-compliance
Lightning Source LLC
Chambersburg PA
CBHW072147070526
44585CB00015B/1033